A DAO FOR THE THIRD MILLENNIUM

First published by Oz Canon 2023

Copyright © 2023 by Jack Parkinson

ISBN: 9780987446015 - eBook

ISBN: 9780987446046 - Print

All rights reserved. No part of this publication may be reproduced, stored or transmitted in any form or by any means, electronic, mechanical, photocopying, recording, scanning, or otherwise without written permission from the publisher. It is illegal to copy this book, post it to a website, or distribute it by any other means without permission.

Jack Parkinson asserts the moral right to be identified as the author of this work.

A Dao for the Third Millennium

The politics, psychology, philosophy, and practice of the common good.

JACK PARKINSON

Oz Canon

REVIEWS

Praise for: 'A Dao for the Third Millennium: The politics, psychology, philosophy, and practice of the common good.

"Without a doubt, the most captivating aspect of the book lies in the multitude of life lessons it imparts. (the author) excels at simplifying the intricate concepts within the 'Dao De Jing,' making them accessible to readers from all walks of life. Reading this book, one can't help but feel as though they are being gently guided by a venerable sage whose words are nothing short of profound wisdom... (the) rating for this book is a resounding **five out of five stars**. It stands as a masterful work that bridges the ancient wisdom of the Dao De Jing with the complexities of our contemporary world, offering invaluable guidance and wisdom.
OnlineBookClub.org

"Cogent, often inspiring essays emphasize both the pragmatic advice of Laozi, and... also societal and cosmic concerns... Clear, crisp, engaging prose that boils the teachings down to essences... (an) inviting celebration and in-depth explication of the collection of ancient wisdom known as the Dao De Jing"
BookLife.

"I enjoyed your turn of phrase and could almost visualize the quiet effort that brought your intuitions and wisdom onto the page... A lot of people would get a kick out of seeing how you have realized other translations... (Of the Dao De Jing) ... into a more holistic contemplation of self... this is a book that many readers will appreciate and keep going back to..."

Dr Mark Stevenson, (Dept. of Asian Studies, Victoria University, Australia.

CONTENTS

Reviews   v
Dedication   xvi
Acknowledgements   xvii

Foreword   1

Preface   2

Groundwork – Understanding is a personal thing.   7

Verse the first: Beginnings - In at the deep end.   25

Verse the second: On making ends meet – The union of opposites.   39

Verse the third: On the perils of mere 'cleverness' – Life is not stasis.   44

Verse the fourth: Emptiness and plenty - Echoes of all the dead Gods.   53

VIII - CONTENTS

Verse the fifth: The breath of the universe – The cycle of opposites.   60

Verse the sixth: The Mother lode – The primal one.   65

Verse the seventh: Signposts along the way - Personal virtue.   67

Verse the eighth: On honest acceptance - Going with the flow.   69

Verse the ninth: The middle ground of work-on-the-self - Simplicity of action.   73

Verse the tenth: Moderation and acceptance are key - The dangers of intolerance.   75

Verse the eleventh: Something from nothing – The germ of change.   81

Verse the twelfth: A world of desire - On avoiding distraction.   85

Verse the thirteenth: From decency to dishonor - Keeping to the way.   87

Verse the fourteenth: Isolation, self-denial - And connection.   92

Verse the fifteenth: Glory days - A glimpse of transcendence.   97

Verse the sixteenth: The evolutionary great cycle – Tranquility of mind.	101
Verse the seventeenth: Strength in weakness - Power in the unseen.	104
Verse the eighteenth: Regression - Weakness, pretension, and turmoil.	107
Verse the nineteenth: On the frontiers of knowledge – Dilemma.	110
Verse the twentieth: On overthinking – The virtue of simplicity.	113
Verse the twenty-first: On searching in the obvious places first – Work and play.	117
Verse the twenty-second: Bend before you break – The advantages of humility and acceptance.	120
Verse the twenty-third: A place in the cosmos – The ebb and flow of nature.	123
Verse the twenty-fourth: On inner vision – A question of balance.	126

Verse the twenty-fifth: Into the wellspring of the unknown - Chaos and creativity - heaven and hell. 128

Verse the twenty-sixth: On the small matters – Inner stillness and equilibrium. 134

Verse the twenty-seventh: On the path of greater good – Finding solid ground. 137

Verse the twenty-eighth: On the uncarved block - The multitude of forms. 141

Verse the twenty-ninth: The world is out of our control – Accepting transience. 146

Verse the thirtieth: Snatching defeat from the jaws of victory – War and ruination. 148

Verse the thirty first: On weeping at the death of an enemy – False purpose. 153

Verse the thirty-second: Something hidden, something found – The one within. 156

Verse the thirty-third: On knowing yourself – A kind of immortality. 159

Verse the thirty fourth: On orientation – Being content with what we have.   161

Verse the thirty-fifth: Illumination - A unity of heaven and earth.   166

Verse the thirty-sixth: The pulse of the universe – Alternating lows and highs.   168

Verse the thirty-seventh: On transformation and equilibrium – Natural law.   171

Verse the thirty-eighth: Inner passion – Impressions of high virtue.   175

Verse the thirty-ninth: On fragmentation in the group - Integrity in the one.   183

Verses the fortieth and forty-first: On the power of the positive – Progress is a force.   192

Verses the forty-second: On violence and opposition – The softly-spoken warrior.   196

Verse the forty third: On quiet achievement – And a meditation on faith.   198

Verse the forty-fourth: On self-sufficiency – When enough is enough. 204

Verse the forty-fifth: On the middle path - In praise of the average. 208

Verse the forty-sixth: On confrontation – The misfortunes of war. 211

Verse the forty-seventh: On feeling the sun on your face - Live, work, play, laugh, love. 215

Verse the forty-eighth: On letting go – Clarity of vision. 219

Verse the forty-ninth: On the hallmarks of wisdom - Doing what is good for others, is also good for you. 221

Verses the fiftieth and fifty-first: A tantalizing vision – Of imperfect reality… 225

Verse the fifty-second: On the light of understanding – Holding back when appropriate. 229

Verse the fifty-third: On predatory leadership – Subjugation and servitude. 232

Verse the fifty-fourth: On proper action - To know others, first know yourself. 236

Verse the fifty-fifth: On vitality - The potential in simplicity.   239

Verse the fifty-sixth: On lucidity and integrity – Trust and respect.   241

Verse the fifty-seventh and fifty eighth: On wisdom and leadership – Justice and law.   245

Verses the fifty-ninth to sixty first: On tactical inaction - Conquest, defeat, and restraint.   252

Verse the sixty-second: On sanctuary and self-delusion – Stages of being.   257

Verse the sixty-third: On correct modes of being - Abandoning the baggage.   261

Verse the sixty-fourth: On maintaining participation – Contexts of action.   264

Verse the sixty-fifth: On knowing enough to realize you know little – A clash of half-measures.   268

Verse the sixty-sixth: On apex and bedrock – The path follows the watercourse in the valley.   272

Verse the sixty-seventh: On the three great strengths - Compassion, frugality, and humility.   275

Verse the sixty eighth and sixty-ninth: On war, failure, and waste – The momentum of disaster.	279
Verse the seventieth and seventy-first: On the way things fall apart – Fragmented reality.	284
Verse the seventy-second: On minimal control - The wise and distant leader.	289
Verses the seventy-third: On arbitrary misfortune – Taking the valley road.	291
Verses the seventy-fourth and seventy-fifth: On oppression, fear, and liberation.	295
Verse the seventy-sixth: On life-force and identity – The world always turns.	299
Verse the seventy-seventh: On correct balance and fine tuning.	302
Verse the seventy-eighth: On effortless action – The water of life.	305
Verse the seventy-ninth: On being yourself, looking within – and letting it go.	309
Verse the eightieth: On the ideal life – the bare necessities.	314

Verse the Eighty-First: Transcendence. 318

About The Author 323
Works Cited 325

For Annie - and also for Morgan, Emily, Alissa, and Leila.
Time is the most valuable thing we spend.
So I write this now while the clock still ticks.
Use your time well.
And remember that the best time to plant a tree was twenty years ago...
...And the second-best time to do it is now.

There is no coming to consciousness without pain...
C. G. Jung.

Life has no meaning a priori... It is up to you to give it a meaning, and value is nothing but the meaning that you choose.
Jean-Paul Sartre.

The unexamined life is not worth living.
Socrates.

ACKNOWLEDGEMENTS

Thanks to those former colleagues in the Language Center at Xi'an Jiaotong – Liverpool University in Suzhou, People's Republic of China, who offered help and support, suggestions, criticisms, comments, better translations, and encouragement. It was all a big help.

Since considerable liberties have been taken with Daoist ideas in this work, further thanks and acknowledgment is due to Dr Mark Stevenson, of the Department of Asian Studies at Victoria University, Australia. He was kind enough to be the first to review the early and incomplete work, provide some reassurance and to make the first encouraging comments.

Foreword

A brief note on the transliteration of Chinese - Why 'Dao' and not 'Tao?'

At this beginning, a brief aside on language and Chinese translation is probably in order. So, is it 'Dao' or is it the 'Tao'? This is primarily, a matter of courtesy and the observation of modern convention. Rendering the nuances of Chinese into clear English is undeniably as difficult as you might imagine and rendering 2,300-year-old Chinese text is exponentially worse.

Over the years several different methods for the transliteration of Chinese characters into our alphabet have been used, and most recently the Wade-Giles system was predominant in much of Western publishing, which is why we are mostly familiar with the form 'Tao.' This usage is outdated however, and since 1982, the 'Pinyin' system of transliteration has emerged as both the officially sanctioned Chinese government system and the UN endorsed and internationally agreed standard in rendering Chinese characters into our script.

It is from that point of adoption that in this book, 'Dao' replaces 'Tao,' similarly, 'Beijing' using the same system, takes the place of the old 'Peking,' 'Fuzhou' is the updated 'Foochow,' and so on. Although the old ways and spellings still linger on in southern enclaves such as Hong Kong and the old Cantonese regions around Guangzhou as well as in Taiwan, these days, the average Chinese restaurant menu, public notice, hotel sign, and road and shop signs will generally reflect the newer convention as you wander further afield through China.

Preface

The world's most powerful meme - And the tests of time.

This book is about the classic work known as the 'Dao De Jing,' an instructive philosophical text and guide to living that predates the Bible. It is not however, about investigating antiquated poetic insights, or indeed the history and cultural context of good conduct in ancient China, it is much more about untangling the vital essence of what the author, the ancient sage known as 'Laozi' actually meant by the word 'Dao' and a consideration of its timeless and universal relevance to life here and now.

Scholarly analysis of the text is likewise not the real priority here. Although there are some academic references to guide and inform, the focus here is on what Laozi has to tell us, at this moment in time, about the process of living a better more harmonious life. This contemporary rendition of an ancient, but timelessly universal set of basic principles is meant, as was the original when first outlined more than two thousand years ago, to offer practical advice and to assist ordinary people in living their ordinary everyday lives.

What this work is then, is not just a new interpretation of the text, but a series of reflections on the real meaning of the eighty-one short verses of the Dao De Jing which tell us, from that historical perspective of over two thousand years, how anyone of us might benefit by following just a handful of simple guidelines that have stood the test of time.

There are no sermons here and no requirement to have (or not have) a particular faith or philosophy. All that is required is the willingness to listen for a while with an uncluttered mind to some early wisdom couched as reasonable advice on how any one of us might proceed when searching for a more personally satisfying life of fulfilled potential.

This practical guidance is offered by Laozi as something to be gained without too much hard work, although as will be seen – this is up to us. A little soul-searching and reflection will certainly be needed in developing a healthy and growing appreciation of what really constitutes the ideal of 'better living' along the way...

The Dao explored here is all about the practicalities of attitude, behavior, and self-realization that make a life more harmonious. It is about our contemporary understanding and application of an ancient set of ideas, embracing what might appear at first encounter seem hopelessly self-contradictory, and even occasionally wildly irrational, totally obtuse, and perhaps even laughable sentiments.

And yet, if there was ever a set of ideas which has stood the test of time - this is it.

The antiquity of the Dao and the timelessness of the message - a brief history.

The concept of the Dao has been around for about two and a half millennia, during which time it has been the mother lode of inspiration for at least three distinct world religions. The most basic precepts of the 'Dao De Jing' are also to be found at the moral and ethical cores of all the other religions and in much of philosophy and contemporary psychology too – but more on that later.

The ideas espoused here are undeniably old, and given the misty origins of the concept of the Dao in ancient China, one might fairly ask what possible relevance could there be for us in revisiting these antiquated ideas here today, in an age of high technology and at the dawn of the third millennium? Is it not true to say that for most ordinary folk in both the contemporary East and the West, an idea such as this, literally going back to the beginning of history (prehistory for much of the world) can be safely dismissed as a quaint classical hangover possessing perhaps only some residual value as a chronicle of historical literature - and nothing much more?

In this work, this viewpoint is firmly rejected.

Some notions and conceptualizations are ageless, they permeate societies and infuse entire cultures with the power of their message. Way back in 1976, evolutionary biologist Richard Dawkins coined the term 'meme,' to describe this phenomenon (Dawkins, 1989). The 'meme' is a sort of cultural equivalent to the gene in biology, and, just as genetics is concerned with the propagation of physical and mental characteristics in biology, memetics is concerned with the transmission and reproduction of information and ideas across and between cultures.

Both genes and memes spread in a way that can be best be described as 'viral,' and both can be anywhere on a spectrum between wholly beneficial to actively harmful to the viral host. It is long recognized that while some genes are favorable in nature and may pass on an advantage, others may cause a crippling defect. Similarly, memes may spread useful knowledge or vital information, or conversely, disinformation leading towards harmful action - in the fostering for example, of destructive political or religious extremism. When ideas are considered as 'viral' memes, those people who have not been 'infected' are considered susceptible, those who are 'infected' have been exposed to the idea and can now pass on the meme, and those who have 'recovered' have been exposed but now do not pass it on.

This book traces the relevance of one very old and effective meme, and its significance from the distant past up to our current times.

So, aside from its venerable age, why should this meme in particular be considered in any way out of the ordinary? Sometimes, a short but diverse assortment of famous names can serve to illustrate the power and reach of an idea better than any collection of maps, references and tables could.

What is it for instance, that could possibly be the connecting link between these well-known identities; D.T. Suzuki: Zen master and professor of philosophy; Carl Gustav Jung: pioneering psychologist, humanitarian and contemporary philosophical thinker; Bruce Lee: martial artist and screen idol; Alan Watts: academic, philosopher and writer; A. A. Milne: author of 'Winnie-the-Pooh,' the 'Bear of Little Brain' and beloved children's character; Confucius (Kongzi): great philosopher sage; Jack Kerouac: author and voice of the 'beat' generation - to name but a few.

The answer is that along with billions of other people worldwide over the last two and a half millennia, this unlikely fellowship is linked in sharing a debt to this compact, but highly influential set of teachings commonly attributed to a single ancient master.

In addition to being the inspiration for any number of individuals around the world, this body of knowledge has shaped the direction of major religions providing guidance for billions of people. The Buddhist, Hindu and Confucian creeds all owe something vital in their development to these teachings, and without them, there would be no enlightenment through Zen, and no Samurai tradition of Bushido.

According to legend, all of this began when a white-haired, bushy-bearded old man with a reputation for extraordinary wisdom and scholarship, decided to leave city life in ancient China, and spend his declining years in the serenity of the countryside. Legend has it, that just before his disappearance into final obscurity, he was recognized as a famous academic teacher-philosopher and persuaded by a lowly city gatekeeper to write down the essence of his teaching for the world before departing. Agreeing to this request, he penned the essential nature of life's meaning, and his entire set of guidelines for personal fulfillment, in a scant five thousand words, all completed in just over two days.

This short tract was to become one of the most important texts in world history, exerting considerable influence not only on the world's great religions, but also on the world's great thinkers, inspiring academics, and philosophers for century after century. Over time, this simple set of guidelines became a major force in the intellectual and spiritual history of all of humanity. In short, this is one of the pre-eminent, epoch-making texts of its era, and has influenced every other era since.

Of course, no matter how compelling the idea, nothing that is recorded and discussed, analyzed, and criticized ad infinitum, can remain in vogue forever; and much later, as the tide of history ebbed and flowed, there were periods of time when this seminal work eventually ceased to be so widely regarded (except among a very few) as having anything more than an archaic significance. It is true to say that, in Western cultures, even in relatively recent times, and even despite the fact that there has been something of a resurgence of interest in this field of personal development and optimal lifestyle since the mid to late twentieth century, the work is still hardly commonly known and consulted, is certainly widely misunderstood - or at least only partially understood - and is not generally considered to be that genuinely relevant to the modern world.

The old man who authored this colossus of humanitarian ideas was Laozi, and the work in question is of course the 'Dao De Jing' - and this current work is built on the premise that, if Laozi had something to say that was genuinely so important that he could sway the whole world back in the sixth century BCE and for centuries later...

Then perhaps we could all still benefit by listening now.

Groundwork – Understanding is a personal thing.

At this starting point, it should be said that my interpretation of Laozi is necessarily based on my own understanding of Laozi and his message and therefore may not please everyone. As previously stated, the focus here is on the meaning originally intended, and not on the direct translation of the actual words used, a practice which often only succeeds in baffling the reader who is grappling with the probable context of antiquated usage. This is my own rendition - for better or for worse. It is garnered from a lifetime of conjecture, meditation, and research on this topic, including thirteen years living and working in China, where I was fortunate enough, in teaching on Chinese university campuses and international schools, to have lots of opportunities for topical discussion with academics and ordinary people there, and even to access ready assistance and suggestions from professional academic translators when needed.

While the aim here is to make these ancient ideas accessible and relevant to people today, some liberties have been taken, both with the poetic text itself and with the probable attitude of the old boy towards some familiar contemporary dilemmas. These are therefore, my own perhaps sometimes idiosyncratic thoughts, essays, meditations and inferences taken from directly translating the characters in several 'original' Chinese texts, and after studying dozens of the different historical and contemporary variations of the translation over the years. Since there are any number of versions vying to be considered as a candidate for best approximation of the 'original' text, it is a minefield out there...

This is my own best effort at a (hopefully) more accessible and comprehensive version and commentary - and interested readers will find a more detailed rationale for this quite personal and more contemporary approach to the text below.

Any mistakes found are of course mine.

Prologue: Some context - And the conundrum of the philosophers of yore.

The question "How shall we live our lives?" is one that has kept generations of philosophers busy and at odds with each other. The accumulation of all their labor is an immense legacy of enormous libraries packed full of research, deduction, intuition, and conjecture. With that huge body of knowledge available for anyone to dip into, it is tempting to believe that the answers to life's dilemmas may already be all available in philosophic literature - if only we knew just where to look...

Then again, since the library is now so vast, and the wisdom still accumulating at what seem to be exponential rates, perhaps this task should be delegated to those with experience in the field. Maybe it is something best left to the experts...

There is, however, a crucial factor that weighs against allowing, or even seriously considering the idea of allowing, such fundamentally crucial elements of our own individual being to become the exclusive domain of a small and highly educated elite. This crucial factor is the recognition of our own independent reality. We all have our lives to lead, and we are all stuck with moral choices and life decisions that are ours alone to take. The answers to life's dilemmas are of little use if they are known to a privileged handful, and yet remain inaccessible to the majority of those that need them.

Martial artist, film icon, and sometime philosopher Bruce Lee had this to say:

"All types of knowledge ultimately mean self-knowledge."

And:

"Remember, success is a journey, not a destination. Have faith in your ability. You will do just fine." (Lee, 2009)

These are sentiments Laozi would be entirely in agreement with. Learning is a life-long process, and in our daily lives we want practical information and direction to keep us on the right track of making progress towards fulfilling our true potential and of navigating the inevitable difficulties to be encountered along the way. In this endeavor, occasional access to an 'expert' simply will not do. The facility to research and evaluate our mistakes in hindsight is interesting, but hardly the best use of the available information on how to live a fulfilled and happy life - if indeed such information is available at all...

Anyone seeking a kind of personal 'spiritual compass' for guidance in day-to-day living and thinking of entering the rarefied world of the great philosophers and academics with a view to appraising all that has been said there - is facing a seriously daunting challenge. The range of opinion on offer is immense, the intellectual challenges potentially overwhelming. Whole lifetimes and the prodigious output of a good many extraordinary minds have gone into even relatively limited areas of this quest, and distilling this down to a single set of the crucial conditions for a happy life appears to be a lost cause.

A person seeking to swallow the sum of all philosophy and extract from this body of knowledge, insight, opinion, and dogma some vision of a personal 'way of living,' is in the same position as the person seeking to absorb every specialty in the field of medicine or to learn every language in the world. Life is too short. And, if it takes many lifetimes to establish the meaning of a single lifetime, why would anyone bother?

Beyond these considerations, there is yet another nagging problem to consider. All those great philosophers who devoted their lives to the problems of existence undoubtedly had at least some of the answers. They knew a thing or two about life and how to live it. So, they should have been, by and large, happy, contented and fulfilled people; or at least one might so assume. After all, they spent years researching and refining the key questions, did they not? But the nagging question remains, were they really any better off than the rest of us?

This is a question worth asking.

Although some of the great thinkers in history undoubtedly lived lives of quiet satisfaction, the available evidence suggests that this was most emphatically not always the case. In fact, a close examination across a range of the personal histories of the great thinkers of history reveals eccentricities galore: pessimists and depressives, neurotics, megalomaniacs, and obsessives. Many of the people we think of as the great philosophers, scholars and savants of their times were socially dysfunctional. Some were marginalized or outcast, culturally inept, lonely, and even outright suicidal in a few instances. Quite frequently, their contemporaries regarded them with anything from incomprehension, ranging through mild derision to outright contempt.

For a good many philosophers, the innate complexities of their studies and their absorption in the intellectual task ensured that any semblance of 'normal' family or social life came a distant second to their musings and theorizing. They often lacked a solid presence in our real world. Hegel and Kant certainly do not appear as particularly warm figures, Schopenhauer and Sartre shared a penchant for the bleakest pessimism if little else. Nietzsche became insane and was institutionalized after his writings deteriorated to rantings.

The grandiose militaristic uniformed pomp and pseudo-scientific allure of Nazism seduced Heidegger. Plato, Husserl, William James, Kierkegaard, Merleau-Ponty and many others lived cloistered lives in academe far away from everyday reality. For Diogenes, a barrel was allegedly enough and for Thoreau, a hideaway (albeit briefly) from the world in the form of a hut in the woods. Marx lived in poverty, Freud was brilliant, but narrowly fixated on matters sexual and on trying to foist his own eccentric and biased traits into the psyches of the rest of the world. And of the ancient masters Kongzi (Confucius) and Laozi, little is known but legend...

Essentially, what you get when approaching the great philosophers for guidance on living an ordinary life is mostly endless complexity. Days spent grappling with Kant's 'Critique of Pure Reason' can leave you dizzy, and perhaps even awestruck by the author's impeccable mastery of topic, and yet no wiser in any kind of practical sense when it comes to applying what you have learned to *your* life.

The great philosophers are, as often as not, impenetrable, or their thoughts far removed from the daily trials and tribulations of our own lives. Similarly, a sound knowledge of the beings en-soi and pour-soi and the nature of freedom may help you understand what drove Jean Paul Sartre to some of his bleaker conclusions on human nature, but as a lesson in living, his work is as likely to be more depressing than uplifting and is certainly not guaranteed to better your situation.

There can be any number of dead ends and meandering diversions for the person seeking enlightenment from the traditional gurus of philosophy and theology. You may not be impressed or inspired by the ecstasies of the religious visionaries. You may be disinclined to follow the übermensch as portrayed in Nietzsche's 'Thus Spake Zarathustra' and you may quickly weary of the various schools of received wisdom, the technical arguments, the syllogisms, the formality of proposition and refutation.

Sometimes, it is best to get back to the absolute basics, and the good news is that there is an alternative. When one is worn down by the semantics and the theoretical constructs, when practical, simple advice untainted by any pretense or sophistry is all that is needed, there is still a resource available. For those who really want to get down to essentials, there is still the 'Dao De Jing' - a concise introduction to the ultimate profundities that has been around for about two and half millennia.

The Laozi text can be considered as a kind of universal primer to enlightenment for anyone with an interest in their own spiritual development. For those with the capacity, and the inclination to accept the advice tendered, it is of little import what their religious inclination may be, or even if they reject all brands of theism and the personified deity altogether. Laozi is not about faith, except insofar as one might need to have at least some belief in one's own abilities.

The old boy: A brief history and background to the text of the 'Dao De Jing' and its variations.

The history of the 'Dao De Jing' is more a matter of legend than recorded fact. 'Laozi' translates sometimes as the 'old man,' or more pleasingly - the 'old boy' - as he shall be referred to from here on in. Some authorities mention that he was born with white hair. According to popular legend and at least some of the scholarship, the old boy was the librarian-academic who authored the 'Dao De Jing' around 500 BC. Scholarly opinions on precise dating can differ by several hundred years or so, and it also becomes periodically fashionable in academic circles to attribute the work to a group rather than a single individual, which means that even the very existence of the old boy as an individual is contentious from time to time.

The original text of the 'Dao De Jing' has presented generations of scholars with huge problems in translation, or more accurately, in transliteration, since the subtleties of Chinese characters rarely translate in any direct and easy manner into English words. The complicating use of historic metaphor and allusion, not to mention the contextual cultural gap, the immense antiquity of the text and the very real possibility that the work has been amended, edited, and otherwise 'improved' by later scholars are all factors that might, and in some cases have, conspired to obscure essential meaning.

Yet for all that, when given adequate reflection, the Laozi text has rare qualities of clarity of insight. And, but for the obscurity of context and the accumulation of errata over the years, perhaps it might even now be widely recognized as one of the most straightforward and uncomplicated guides to the age-old question posed by social scientists, philosophers, theologians and more importantly, by ordinary people everywhere. The question: 'How should we live our lives?'

My own first experience with the 'Dao De Jing' was as a teenager, discovering the text in the Penguin Classics translation by DC Lau (Lau, 1963). At first encounter, some of the grammatical intricacies and the odd word usage, together with the vagueness of many of the references lost me almost immediately, but despite the problematical elements, elsewhere in the book the message was clear enough to compel a succession of revisits. It was also forceful enough to make a lasting impression.

To help place it within a cultural context, the 'Dao De Jing' has something in common with what may reasonably be considered companion (if not quite contemporary) texts, works such as 'The Secret of the Golden Flower (Wilhelm, The Secret of the Golden Flower, 1979) and the 'I Ching - The Book of Changes.' These are all seminal works in the development of Eastern thought, although the 'Dao De Jing' remains (arguably perhaps) the earliest, simplest, and most succinct text.

The other books each have their areas of specialization: 'The Secret of the Golden Flower' is generally of greater interest to those wishing to develop meditative techniques, and is also for those interested in the Dao of longevity and personal power. The 'I Ching,' despite its many centuries as the object of serious scholarly philosophic study, is often regarded today as primarily a fortune-telling oracle in the West. It should be said here that, although it is regularly given the same dismissive treatment any fairground pretender in clairvoyance might attract, the 'I Ching' nevertheless remains an unparalleled resource for the genuine student of philosophic ideas as they are applied in a practical context; and especially when it is read in the justly renowned Richard Wilhelm translation with an introduction by C.G. Jung (Wilhelm, The I Ching or Book of Changes, 1977).

Eastern thought has an exceptionally long tradition of convergence in which Daoist and Confucian texts have both been shaped by, and become infused with, Buddhist and other influences. The old boy's work, along with its various commentaries, is no exception. The 'Dao

De Jing', a little over 5,000 words of simple, yet compelling elegance, has occupied scholars and philosophers for more than two millennia. As well as providing the inspiration for the entire Confucian school, this work is the source of much of later Buddhist thought, and famously inspired the philosophic school of enlightenment through revelation that is known to us as Zen.

The Laozi teachings I first encountered had a compelling power, and even in the series of sometimes clumsy translations generally then available, appeared to hold out the promise of some tantalizing insights. This despite the obvious accretion of linguistic errors and doubtful annotations. Even in some of the more obviously inept commentaries and translations, the old boy appeared to be offering a fleeting glimpse of some enormous revelation, something of cosmic significance - but perceived at the faint margins of everyday comprehension. It was also a glimpse too often lost at some misconstrued or partly understood referent.

Unfortunately, the 'Dao De Jing' as it is commonly available, is a work frequently replete with arcane references whose essential meaning is often shrouded in extraneous information. Many readers may, quite rightly, feel confused by the apparent necessity of having their attention drawn to consideration of the range of factors that might logically explain the text, for example, its cultural and historical setting, its history of scholarly revision, etc.

Over time though, my own growing suspicion was that in actual practice, these ever-growing interpretive and compensatory frameworks might only serve to overlay a quite unnecessary series of layers of complexity on something that was meant to stand alone and uncluttered in its simplicity. But of course, by the time this realization was reached, most of those areas of linguistic and cultural complication had also been thoroughly examined - and a lot of time had passed...

All this is not to say that the old boy's thought can, right now, be made instantly comprehensible to all. Laozi's brand of unifying philosophy was, and is, only ever going to be accessible to those with the will to tackle the broader conceptual framework of living and meaning; to tackle the job the Daoists style, 'work-on-the-self.'

As we shall see, the old boy himself insists that this willingness to embrace personal growth is the essential prerequisite of wisdom, harmony and working towards the greater good of the Dao. Given that this commitment from the reader is forthcoming, he then puts the words on the page to further our understanding - and most definitely not to baffle and bemuse us with a display of his superior and soaring intellect.

As I returned to the original, and some favored variations of the text in later years, what struck me repeatedly, even as I began to get my own personal feel for the underlying composition, were some of the glaring inconsistencies of the 'Dao De Jing.' There were without doubt, some basic distortions, and misplacement of lines. There were also some less than generous summations by subsequent critics and the misinterpretations of those historians who clearly either did not care about or did not grasp the real philosophical import of the text to any significant extent.

The final obscuring factors were the interpretations of those literalists and fundamentalists interested only in the semantic associations of the words on the page and their historical contexts in ancient Chinese culture. These authors seemed often unconcerned with the import of the message and quite blindly focused on the medium of communication.

The old boy is certainly a lot more than words on a page, my initial summation was that he is communicating what he would consider to be a vital and coherent creed on how to live a life of fullness and integrity. It is not his failure that the conceptual framework of his thinking does not always suit our contemporary understanding, or even perhaps in some instances, the contemporary understanding of his peers.

When for instance, Laozi emphasizes the virtue of inaction or no action, he leaves plenty of scope for misinterpretation. However, he is not, as some might say, advocating a life of aimless drifting, and he is most assuredly not turning his back on anything that should or must be done. That the old boy might ever promote passive resignation is a viewpoint quite untenable to anyone who has considered the deeper import of the text, and this remains true regardless of how scholarly and intimidating the authority proposing it. The old boy is never cowed into submission, but he refuses to let ego-driven confrontation rule the day. He has the patience and humility to embrace a strategic retreat and bide his time when necessary.

By any reasoned evaluation, the old boy was also no advocate of laziness and self-delusion; Laozi is generally counseling a disciplined restraint, and a harmonious understanding of reality, a very different proposition to passive acceptance. Yet historically, some authorities have accepted the 'inaction principle' in the 'Dao De Jing' as a literal truth, failing to see that the old boy demonstrates the capacity for action often enough when the occasion warrants.

In reality, 'No action' Laozi style is best equated with the martial arts principle whereby a smaller, weaker person gets the better of a heavier, stronger opponent by using the opponent's own strength to defeat an attack. 'No action' in this sense is 'going with the universal flow' and taking the line of minimal effort. It is having the patience to await the right moment and, whatever else it may be; it is strength applied at the critical moment rather than weakness expressed as submissive acquiescence.

Among other material points the old boy is trying to make with his 'principle of inaction' is the idea that 'action' is a means to an end, and not generally an end in itself. This simply means that when the goal is achieved, no more action is necessary, and tranquility and harmony are now made possible.

To take this a step further, for Laozi, the very essence of 'proper action,' is that it leads to inaction via completion. The old boy would equate this process to the honest self-reflection he calls the necessary 'work-on-the-self.' Completion represents a step towards satisfaction, or lack of desire, and through that, to peace, harmony, and ultimately towards that nebulous happy wholeness or unity we call 'Dao.'

The real 'virtue' here is economy of action. Laozi has no time for the ill-considered deed, or the pointless 'busywork' by which individuals lacking any real purpose or guidance fritter away their lives. In this respect, he would have some sympathy for the corporate drone, compelled by financial necessity to profess a 'passion' for a poorly-paid employment opportunity pretending to be a fulfilling vocation – and simultaneously demanding a level of engaged commitment and loyalty which will never be reciprocated.

Although much of the advice offered by Laozi is proffered as correct conduct for leaders, that is, those people most likely to be in positions of power and influence, the sentiments are always universal and scalable, and this is very much suitable advice for any ordinary person. The old boy addresses himself to those with the most freedom and authority to act, simply because this was the place his message would mostly likely be received and would have the best social impact.

To take the old boy's concept of 'inaction' as example once more, in the context of leadership of the state rather than the individual, his advice, is that 'inaction' means more restraint, less rigorous management, and less intervention by authority. Laozi is very much a proponent of government with a light hand. He sees a heavy-handed administration as a form of over-steering, in which the vehicle of state continually oscillates between opposing and unduly immoderate policy positions like an overloaded truck veering uncontrollably from one side of the road to the other.

To put this idea in a more contemporary context, consider for a moment the history of Western governments since World War II. Except perhaps in times of war, governments are almost invariably judged by their citizens to be more heavy-handed than they need to be, and since WWII, Western-style governments have vacillated between polarized extremes in their social engineering - on the one hand by implementing communal ownership policies such as the socializing (nationalizing) of key institutions such as telecommunications, education, health and medicine, banking, transportation, and industries such as steel and mining.

In stark contrast on the other hand, privatization policies of a quite opposing nature were also put in place during the same period, these included; divestiture of public assets and control of resources and governmental functions to corporate interests, treating aged care, health, education, as business opportunities to be monetized, and even outsourcing the drafting of legislation, and ceding the operation of prisons and detention centers to private enterprise rather than considering them the responsibility of government authorities via elected officials.

In the last few generations, this rather crude and heavy-handed oscillation between opposing policy positions has been manifest in what seems to be increasingly radical extremes of governmental action at both the left and right sides of the political spectrum - and these trends are evident in many different countries.

Laozi is relevant here, and indeed, the old boy's message is as pertinent now as it was two millennia ago. He advocates that by avoiding over governance, and simply loosening the reins a little, these 'over-steer' forays into the kind of radical extremism that periodically grip some proportion of the populace, or even entire societies, can be avoided, or at least minimized, thereby enabling a straighter and easier course. Moderation in all things is the key. This in essence, is a further example of his principle of least effort for the greatest good.

One additional vital reason why governments should rule with the lightest of hands, is that only by allowing a high level of individual freedom and personal choice can a government ensure that the ordinary people retain the possibility of being allowed to develop to their full natural potential of creativity and self-determination.

In this way, with just a little untangling of the textual web, Laozi presents a simple but powerful message on how to foster the common good and offers a succinct and impeccably common-sense case for moderation of word and deed - all while maintaining harmony at the levels of both individual and state. Nothing is hidden, nothing left unsaid. The whole of the work is a model of poetic economy; and as germane now as it was in 500 BCE. That such a brief and simply written tract could have such timelessly profound personal and political implications is a powerful tribute to its economy of thought and expression.

The old boy: Focusing on the meaning of the whole, and not the parts.

Extracting essential meaning from the extant texts is not all plain sailing however, the conceptualization of inaction is not the only problematical area in the 'Dao De Jing.' If the whole work is really an attempt at self-evident simplicity, there is no place at all for any baffling passages of mystic rumination. There must be a relatively distinct and simple meaning to be grasped everywhere.

This presents some major, challenges to the would-be analyst given the antiquated language and metaphor of the original text. What, for example, is 'the gateway of manifold secrets?' What did the old boy have in mind when he said, 'When the gates of heaven open and shut, are you capable of keeping to the role of the female?' and what is this apparently vague 'nothing' from which even the highest good comes?

Leaving aside those seemingly inscrutable passages for a moment, let us make our first reasonable assumption about this text here and now. This assumption is that the text of the 'Dao De Jing' was *meant* to be a readily comprehensible lesson for an ordinary educated contemporary of the old boy's era. The second assumption, and one that seems equally reasonable, is that Laozi was genuinely trying to communicate the 'meaning of life' as he saw it.

One logical first step in unraveling a puzzle such this is to consult a selection of the numerous other translations and commentaries of the work. In doing this, over an extended period, I concluded that the difficulties are in two principal areas. These are linguistic difficulties, firstly, there is the problem of literal versus actual or intended meaning in the many translated texts, and secondly, there is the frequently encountered problem of the actual meaning imputed to a passage being obscured by ancient metaphor and allusion, tainted with commentary and re-writes, and masked by the cultural and other prejudices of previous translators and scholars.

Many of the translations and commentaries on the 'Dao De Jing' are surprisingly poor, some are incomplete, and in many instances, the authors and commentators seem content to simply highlight the problematical passages and point out that they are probably corrupt or misplaced without offering much in the way of an explanation of what was intended. It also seemed to me at least, that elsewhere in the work, discussion of possible viable alternative meanings of the words on the page was frequently taking precedence over accurate discernment of the meaning of the whole. In other words, the main message of the text was lost or at least obscured in examination of the minutiae.

Thinking about these problems, I could almost imagine hearing the old boy chuckling to himself. After all, if a work has genuine contemporary as well as historic value it must lend itself to interpretation into a contemporary framework of meaning. Indeed, the instant this becomes impossible is the precise instant that the text exchanges any genuine contemporary relevance for a lesser existence as a document of old-world historic interest.

Furthermore, it seems reasonable to assume that in any attempt to express a profundity within a conceptual framework, the ultimate meaning is beyond any doubt, always more important than the scaffolding of the language used to express it. So, in order that we do not to get bogged down in the definitions of individual words, we are justified in being a little more ruthless in seeking more vital and holistic meanings.

Despite this apparent necessity to tear through the scholarly obfuscations, there is always a reluctance to engage in a radical dissection of a very old and respected work. Since no one wants to be accused of despoiling a masterpiece by frivolous revision, there is a tendency to sanctify the literal text of ancient documents at the expense of real meaning. By way of illustration, consider the various translations of the Bible. The King James Version for example, is known to have copious amounts of translation errors long acknowledged by scholars and yet perpetuated for generations in successive reprints and tolerated by long habituation.

As a document of comparable antiquity to the 'Dao De Jing,' the Bible is also a work argued over by those who would literally accept the sanctity of the 'word' on the page and might blithely disregard the fact that the text has already seen centuries of additions, revisions, and commentaries from those scholars and philosophers seeking analogies that render the text more accessible and more meaningful to their own contemporary readers.

After following this train of thought for a while, I felt much more comfortable with introducing my own 'cultural and other prejudices' to the work of Laozi, but even more impatient with translations that appeared bogged down in the literal meanings of individual words. Whatever else the old boy was doing, he was not deliberately trying to be obscure. There are no fancy semantics. He wanted to communicate some profound ideas and to make them as accessible as he knew how. The fact that he was stuck with the word-usage forms, and the conventions of allusion, allegory and metaphor of his day is unfortunate for us in attempting to bridge the gap, but ultimately the descriptive limitations and changeable nature of language and conventional reason are our problem to deal with, and not his lack of accountability in framing his meaning more precisely.

The antiquity of the syntax and the unfamiliar descriptive imagery are the factors, which, more than anything else, tend to make the 'Dao De Jing' text less accessible to the broad range of ordinary educated people it was originally meant for. These difficulties have often conspired, regrettably, to relegate the work to a narrower group of readers than it deserves, specialists and individuals with a 'suitably informed viewpoint' have become the target audience, although there is no doubt that the work does have lay value and appeal and was never meant for an exclusive audience.

The old boy speaks to all who will listen.

With these considerations in mind, my concern that I was in some way performing an act of desecration in mangling or distorting the original text with my overlay of interpretation lessened. In fact, I now felt much freer to engage in a hunt for underlying meaning, even one that might ultimately be at the expense of the poetic form that has survived for twenty-six centuries. What this means of course is that this interpretive work may not be agreeable to everyone. How one person relates to this ancient classic is hardly likely to hold true for all.

It does not really matter. There is something for everyone.

The final justification, for what may be seen by some as a cavalier treatment of an old and venerable text is that nothing is lost in the process and nothing is hidden - and anyone who wishes to do so is still free to consult, and reinterpret for themselves, any of the original ancient texts at any time. The truth is that the outward form is always more a lot more accessible than any deeper meaning that can be ascribed to it.

This pragmatic prioritizing of the fundamentals of meaning over the superficialities of expression was something the old boy would surely have thought reasonable, even if he himself disagreed with some of the interpretations. The Laozi I was getting to know is essentially practical and a realist. He aims unerringly towards the heart of the matter and has no patience with idle intellectualizing, point scoring or prevarication. In fact, his every sentence seeks to cut to the very core of the topic under discussion. In this respect, the 'Dao De Jing' may be considered as an exercise in restrained lucidity.

One further point to make is this, to succeed in his quest to get his readers to comprehend his meaning through what he terms 'work-on-the-self,' Laozi also needs to sometimes force them to leave the comfort zones of their familiar modes of being and thinking. The old boy appreciates that a proper grasp of his teaching (i.e., 'the approach to the mysterious Dao') generally involves a new, or at least unfamiliar, mental orientation. Understanding of the abstractions he is communicating may not come easily to minds laser focused on the trivia of everyday affairs. The old boy requires the broadly inclusive mental parameters of 'the big picture' way of thinking, together with an ability to engage in some profound and honest reflection on the self.

The 'big picture,' this is what the old boy is all about. To seek inclusive solutions to the questions of life is to get ever closer to the all-embracing realization of self that is the path of the Dao. Much of the scholarly commentary on the 'Dao De Jing' is closely focused on breaking down perceptions of the text to a series of discrete analyses - but not this one. This rendering of the text is unashamedly prioritizing overall meaning beyond all other considerations.

Though the Dao is often visualized as a kind of universal exegesis, or a template for higher consciousness, it is more accurate to think of it as more a process than a thing, and more of a journey than a goal. The old boy frequently refers to the Dao as 'the path' or the 'great way' to signify it is more about the steps we take in getting there than any anticipation of some remote arrival.

Most of all, it is the understanding and acceptance of a few simple and quite basic truths. Far from being an intellectual edifice resting on a whole series of rationalizations, it is much more like a direct apprehension of the way in which all things interrelate. It is the pursuit of the common good in every aspect of living. It could even be thought of as a feeling of intrinsic rightness in surrendering the self to the natural order.

The old boy is a minimalist, but when Laozi advocates the application of minimal effort to every problem in life, this is not because he is unaware of occasions where real exertion is required, or is innately indifferent to the actual needs of individuals and to the important crises in the physical world. The context of his advice is given in terms of the universal ebb and flow of events and the reciprocally connected poles of experience. In doing this, he lives with the comprehension that much of human energy is wasted on actions that go against nature and, since humanity is part of nature, are therefore ultimately futile and self-defeating.

The old boy thinks globally and acts locally in the most literal, natural, common sense, and yet self-effacing way he can. He wants neither personal power nor personal riches; his sole intent is the pursuit of the harmony that comes from appropriate action at the proper time.

From the very beginning he accepts the difficulty of the task he has set himself.

In the Penguin Classic translation by DC Lau, he opens with these famous lines:

> *"The way that can be spoken of, is not the constant way;*
> *The name that can be named, is not the constant name." (Lau, 1963).*

Lau goes on to speak of "manifestations" of the "nameless," "manifold secrets," and the "myriad creatures." Here, at the beginning of the third millennium, a first glance at this ancient passage might easily result in a dismissive judgment. Perhaps it appears a little too transcendent and esoteric to be truly relevant to the nitty-gritty of contemporary affairs.

But in fact, the old boy is no woolly mystic, he is issuing a serious warning and within a few words, he is already cutting direct to the core of the mysterious Dao essence. Only the linguistic and cultural detritus of the intervening centuries obscures the essential meaning.

So at this point, if the need for meaning really does conquer the urge to respect the form, we are free to re-translate, rephrase, and re-make the text until we have a new interpretive rendition in whatever form makes sense to us. A first step is necessary.

And, this is what made sense…

Verse the first: Beginnings - In at the deep end.

What we are taught of being is not all there is to know.
The knowledge that would define our reality is not all there is to learn.

In the unknown is the beginning of things - before heaven or earth.
The known is the place where we experience our reality in the world.
When we cease longing – we gain insight into what is unknown,
To embrace wanting - gives insight into the known.
The known and the unknown begin in each other,

In this way, darkness is born,
And a gateway to the light opens in the shadows.

With this introduction, we start to get a glimpse of exactly where the old boy is coming from. These initial lines require a more extended exploration than subsequent verses as we investigate some of the ideas introduced and some of the methods and sources that might be used to further an understanding of them.

Here, Laozi is setting the ground rules and pointing out that some of the supposedly stable bedrock underpinning our comprehension of reality may not be quite as solid as we supposed it to be. This unaffected opening is full of meaning. In fact, the multi-layered strands of significance are so extensive in these few simple lines that several levels of 'unpacking' are needed to extract anything like an overall picture.

Typically, Laozi makes no attempt whatsoever to ease us into his thought patterns, his very first lines aim straight at the innermost heart of the mysterious Dao - he simply tells it the way he sees it without preface. Consider these interpretations and implications for instance – and these are just a part of what may be extrapolated from the density of information in this opening message:

Among other things, Laozi is telling us here that no amount of factual knowledge guarantees wisdom, and that reason alone is insufficient for total understanding. He points out that we are fixed in a 'now' we may pretend to understand, but we must also realize that there is a fuzzy margin to our understanding and neither a proper beginning nor a proper end to it. He wants us to accept that uncertainty permeates our discernment and open our minds to the possibility that all that is unknown, may cast doubt on all that we think we may know.

Here too, in these opening lines, is the first mention of the being/non-being divide. In common with the philosophers of many schools and religions, Laozi insists that there is more to life than facts quantifiable and capable of being categorized in rational inquiry. So, it should perhaps come as no surprise that the predominantly scientific and rational orientation of much of Western thought runs into some early difficulties with Laozi - unless it is also accompanied by a flexible appreciation of the intractable human dilemmas against which rationality often struggles to no avail.

This first conflict arises in our culturally influenced, but generally overly simplistic acceptance of the rationalist principle at the very foundations of our Western modes of thought. Science seeks closure by limiting and defining, it rejects anything that cannot be conclusively described. In its probing and microscopically detailed examination of the nature of reality, serious science is innately the province of specialists in narrow areas and their conclusions are all expected to be tried, tested, and proven. By contrast, the old boy is an unabashed universalist, and despite the simplicity of the language, he searches for the all-inclusive and seeks to incorporate the indefinable, and even the irrational, on the grandest of macrocosmic scales.

The micro and macro of the respective juggernauts of empirical science and human intuition, emotion, and religious or spiritual unification appear irreconcilable. But perhaps there is not as much distance between them as superficial consideration might indicate. Indeed, if Laozi is right, there must be a way of reconciling and integrating these contradictory conceptualizations of our world. And in fact, if we consider some of the advances made over the last one or two generations, some progress is being made.

There are now researchers in fields as diverse as physics, mathematics, statistics, and the social sciences who are prepared to admit that our 'natural laws' are all capable of being subsumed into a more comprehensive and universally collective 'bigger picture.' We live in a world of contradiction and paradox, and as science proliferates, so does faith, with the two being uneasy partners at best and sworn enemies at worst.

The metaphysics of spiritual unity and the empirical realms of science seem worlds apart, yet Laozi insists that the 'the whole' is just that; these apparent opposites must - and can - be reconciled. It was Karl Popper (Popper, 2002) who showed the world that no scientific theory is ever conclusively proven as true. However, the bad news is that any theory can be conclusively proven as false - if even a single contrary fact is admitted as valid.

The point here is that even a theory that has stood the test of time for generations is not immune to the sudden revelation of some contrary fact that will disprove it. Our view of the way the world works is never fully explained by science, it is simply our best practical current modeling of the reality we experience. The old boy is never anti-science, far from it, he just asks us to recognize that the rational model is incomplete, and not the be all and end all – there are instinctive and intuitive ways of understanding and connecting with the world.

This is a major line of cleavage in our relationship to the world around us. The fact is that anyone of us may live our lives by choosing between a spiritual, or by a scientific paradigm of existence, each choice being a rejection of the other. Neither of these however, represents the true way of the Dao, and the old boy would immediately say we are well advised to find our ultimate realization of self in the reconciliation of both these life pathways.

Right now, across the range of Western cultures and beyond, in the rising nations of the global south, it is generally science and rationalism that hold sway, and as knowledge and insight expands, our model of the cosmos grows with it, or is replaced by something more functionally representative of each new perception we have. Sometimes during the evolution of our thinking, there is a scientific or social revolution and the entire world jumps to a new level of comprehension almost overnight; the Earth is *not* flat and *does* orbit the sun. Microbes *can* cause disease; the seat of intelligence *is* in the mind and not in the heart etc.

The principle of all scientific advance is the same as that by which Einstein's physics subsumed Newton's, and some often-postulated 'grand unified theory' of physics may eventually enclose and unite both the micro world of quantum mechanics and the macro world of relativity. Each successive revision provides a bigger picture, although even that picture may be one that still falls well short of the ultimate whole.

What Laozi offers us is an insight into a model of our own internal, rational, spiritual, emotional, and instinct focused universe. But this is a model that does not attempt to rival any paradigm of physical reality advanced by science, but to incorporate it entirely. The old boy is engaged in focusing his and his reader's will and ambition on the biggest picture of them all, something we can at this stage, still only refer to vaguely as the 'whole' or the 'Dao.'

We need to stop at this point for a moment of critical awareness. In proceeding, we must accept that in trying to grasp this Dao totality purely at the level of intellectual reasoning and rationalization, we are undertaking a fundamentally futile task. We are like the tape measure that tries to measure itself, the box that tries to enclose itself, and like Jorge Luis Borge's map that attempts to be so inclusive it becomes indistinguishable from the ground that it is mapping. (Borges, 1999)

In essence, any teaching that looks at ultimate totality (and the old boy is doing just that) is looking at something that incorporates and subsumes all of science, all of nature, all emotion, all spirituality, all of physical existence and possible experience - everything...

When we try to grasp the vastness of that totality, we are in the position of the person attempting to drain the ocean by bailing with a bucket, reason fails us, and we feel we are lost. However, all is not lost. Inability to grasp a thing in its entirety does not imply we should simply abandon any hope of achieving some measure of understanding of the concept at all. If we adopted this attitude of resignation our position in the world would be precarious indeed. After all, we do know a lot about oceans despite our shortcomings with the bucket.

In practice, we work to our capacity, with whatever level of understanding (and misunderstanding) we can muster to the problems of our lives, and this is generally sufficient for most people to get by.

To further illustrate this point, think of the ways in which we 'understand' or have a notion of something. Take an object called 'engine' for example. This is a familiar idea to everyone. We mostly know what it is for, and what it can do, and we are satisfied there is no further knowledge required to utilize it effectively now and for the foreseeable future.

Yet, the reality is that for most people at least, their knowledge has some severe limitations. Faced with a mountain of individual parts, few could lecture with any authority on their specific relation to the whole, much less proceed to build the engine itself. We simply accept, or more likely, are blissfully unconscious of the multitude of the constituent parts and only really see them and recognize them in the context of the whole they will become.

Similarly, Laozi addresses throughout his writing, those individuals mired in the intricacies of the spare parts that make up the world. His focus is on making people look to the totality, the world as the end product of all of history and experience so far. Within that totality is found harmony, the ultimate meaning of existence is in the way the parts fit together to form the whole, and not so much in the particulars of the technical details that underpin that unity.

The temptation of course, is always to limit our perception of the world to that small portion which we know and feel comfortable with, to voluntarily put on the blinkers and choose to ignore or deny everything not directly relevant to our own lives.

Laozi's message is that this is the inferior way. Figuratively at least, the old boy is now all bristling white beard and concern. Although he is very much an advocate of the simple life, he tells us that we court disaster by denying a vital part of life. We are rejecting the whole for something lesser in the comfort zone, and in that possible whole is the greater good - the place of self-actualization he calls the Dao.

And with this we are back to the nature of this mysterious unifying principle just as Laozi will return to it repeatedly and inexorably. We already know we cannot get a direct grip or definition of the whole, certainly language is insufficient. Just occasionally though, we may get a flash of illumination that reveals some facet of this hidden essence and provides a sudden epiphany - that bombshell moment of inspired understanding that comes when some hidden aspect of obscure nature is momentarily revealed and comprehension dawns.

The old boy steadfastly insists that there is a universal meaning hidden in the idea of Dao, which given the right setting, will resonate for almost everyone. We might also note here in passing that this pursuit of 'something hidden' is a ubiquitous principle, something common to all of religion and philosophy, and indeed to all of humanity. There is compelling evidence from any number of sources that at some point in life, almost everyone needs and seeks a mysterious 'other' to achieve completion.

While the names of our Gods change and proliferate as new religions arise and the old beliefs are denied, and while the means of approaching these mystical icons fall into disuse as ever more, and newer representations of the 'absolute' capture the common imagination, the personal quest for individual realization through spirituality, or even the acceptance of dogma – some kind of life-affirming passion - is something that endures down through the centuries and the millennia.

Any observer of the human condition might rightly conclude that humanity generally wants, even needs, this unseen something or other with some fervor. That is even though individual ideas of what 'it' might be may differ in a host of diverse ways: grace, the all, harmony, the Godhead, tranquility, enlightenment, wisdom, Buddha-hood, the divine light, unity, integration, nirvana, understanding, totality, peace, fulfillment, completion, 'getting your head together,' the meaning of life... The Dao.

What is more, based on the historical evidence, humanity is prepared to go to any lengths to obtain this essence - although the journey may not always be one of light and celebration. Those set on a path of personal self-realization include both saints and sinners.

Some have been known to give up family, friends and creature comforts on this quest, some train their minds, even at the expense of their physical bodies, some choose to expiate sin and cleanse their souls by deliberately condemning themselves to lives of poverty and discomfort. Some, moved by a force beyond reason, will radically transform themselves - and not always for the better. Some will slip into madness or despair.

The spiritual search can inspire much more than the realization of the potential of a single human life, it can be bent as a crusade to murder and torture in some God's name – in the past, some have allowed this impulse to lead them to the sacrifice of their own kind on a bloody altar. Motivated by the desire for communion in some realm of the absolute, soul-searchers have been known to embrace mysticism, ingest poisons and mind-bending drugs. Some have performed superhuman feats of endurance, relinquished all comforts of life, and suffered any torment on themselves - or others - which might lead them closer to their ultimate goal.

Looked at in this light, when we consider the concept of Dao, and the urge towards some unrealized unity in general, we are not simply indulging in some frivolous academic exercise. We are looking at a characteristic almost universally acknowledged, though not always consciously or directly - as being central to our humanity.

Somewhere in this all-encompassing whole is, necessarily, as much powerful potential for the debasement of a life as there is for its fulfillment. This shapeless, nameless thing the old boy calls Dao, and which we sometimes endow with the name of a God, has a reality and a strength we cannot deny, and while for most the goal is harmony, self-knowledge, and a contented appreciation of the world, for some, its investigation may be fraught with peril.

For us, in a historical sense, the counterpart of unity with the bright image of our benevolent deity is something deeply rooted in our cultural heritage – the mindset of extreme, alienated isolation, often equated in medieval times as possession by some dark and demonic force, which once found within, can only with difficulty be exorcised.

There is no need to resort to superstition here though, for thanks to the pioneering work of Carl Jung and others, twentieth century psychology has at least a partial key to our understanding of this occurrence. 'Exorcism' and 'demonic possession' are all in a day's work for both the priesthood and for practitioners of psychotherapy. Although the vocabulary of the inner experience may have changed substantially, the reality of the human condition is the same as it ever was. Jung tells us that the demons and dark forces of our ancient mythologies have never left us - but now that we have updated their labels, they are known as 'neuroses', 'complexes' and 'psychological trauma.' (Jung C. G., Civilization in Transition, 1981)

Conflating ancient Chinese philosophy with contemporary psychotherapy may seem incongruous at first glance, but the prefix 'psycho' in the original Greek has the meaning of 'soul' or 'spirit, and the suffix here 'therapy,' which is also from the Greek, and has the original meaning of 'healing' or 'treatment.' So, what is the difference between psychic healing through this modern therapy and the time-honored quest of reaching for completion in the all-encompassing Dao? Or even perhaps surrendering to the mercy of a divine being? The old boy is giving us a metaphorical shrug here and saying, 'Does it really matter?' The Dao is a great journey with a multitude of ways.

We are all free to choose a route or no route at all…

The old boy: Dimensions of understanding and experience in language.

Looking beyond the obvious evidence of what a legion of theologians and philosophers have been telling us for centuries, there is now emerging the beginnings of a scientific acceptance of the hazy realms of paradox and confusion. We now have the uncertainty principle, chaos theory, notions of multiple dimensions in string theory and the inexplicable behavior of quanta as examples to support the notion of things vague at the limits of all scientific knowledge and experience.

No matter which scientific and empirical branch of knowledge any researcher may care to explore, and no matter how certain and conclusive the core of that discipline may be, somewhere at the outer edge is a fuzzy area where things become inexplicit, and theories start to melt into each other. This is the place where physics rubs shoulders with metaphysics with an ease that might upset minds raised on the idea that an irrational conceptualization cannot be held as truly significant.

The 'something' that intimates the beginning of this unknown territory is the first glimpse of the essence that the old boy simply calls the 'Dao.' This idea, as we have already discussed, has a multitude of interpretations and associations; it can be the way, the Godhead, the supreme mystery, and the source. It is the unity of all opposites, the encompassing whole, and the greater good. It is at once the vital inner essence of the soul and the concept of universal being - whether deified or not.

Whatever else it may be, argues the old boy, it is the embodiment of the natural flow of both rational and irrational events, and opposing it is like opposing the wind, the tide, or the onset of darkness at night.

Since we have already confessed to a lack of appropriate language to fully describe the Dao, one way we can attempt to obtain some kind of delineation and further our understanding is to switch perspectives from time to time, in for example, employing the jargon and the unique insights of specialists in other areas. Indeed, this is something we have done already done in equating ancient fears of possession by demons to contemporary mental disturbance requiring psycho-therapeutic intervention.

In this respect, some interesting comparisons with the old boy's 'manifold gateway' and 'crux of all mystery,' can be made by references to contemporary thinkers as diverse as French existential philosopher Jean Paul Sartre, and Carl Jung, the Swiss philosopher and father of analytical psychology.

These two giants of twentieth century ideas may seem odd companions for the old boy when we are attempting a clarification of ancient Daoist values, but Jung especially was keenly interested in, and wrote extensively and with profound empathy on Eastern philosophy. Furthermore, in his psychological work, he parallels and supports a fundamental precept of Laozi's in that he always staunchly maintains that the irrational unknown has just as much right to thoughtful consideration and investigation as the rational known. Essentially, Jung is a humanitarian philosopher who interprets individual experience in terms of an all-inclusive viewpoint; Jung is 'big picture' by nature. He was also a friend and occasional scholarly collaborator of noted Sinologist (and by far the most credible translator of the classic 'I Ching'), Richard Wilhelm.

For Jung, the mysterious ultimate source we characterize here as the Dao, finds its resonance in the unplumbed depths of the collective unconscious within each of us. In addition, for Jung as for Laozi, the greater good is always a product of individual rather than group effort.

This is important. All progress leading to every revolution in thinking is the product of individual effort. It is not that the principles of the Dao do not hold true for organizations, they do. They apply to corporate and community enterprise large and small, and even to the sovereign state itself. But the integration of the whole comes only from personal insight, a kind of unification or reconciliation of the external and internal aspects of the self.

Exactly what this means and how it is to be achieved will become clearer later, for now it is enough to say that both Laozi and Jung view the average person as in some sense incomplete - there is something lacking, something that may nag at our consciousness and be a source of frustration, anxiety, and tension. We live polarized multi-faceted lives, and present our cheerful, our impassive or our stoic facades to the world. We hide our inner selves, we commonly live with tension in strained or failing relationships, and often lack real connections to those around us in the world. We experience our moments of elation perhaps, but also grief, a sense of unease or quiet desperation and not unusually, just a vast indifference and apathy. We are generally partially conscious of missing something vital that might give us strength and purpose – but what can we do?

In this situation, even being part of a community, or cooperating within a group does not help resolve the situation, though it may relieve some feelings of isolation and disaffection and give us some sense of belonging. In short, we are something less than whole, and that is still true when there are several of us together. The important thing is always the individual, and never the group, and in this sense, putting any number of 'disintegrated' individuals together can never make an integrated whole, this would be like trying to form one good bottle from the shattered remnants of several.

In his lectures given in Cologne and Essen in 1933, Carl Jung illustrates the pre-eminent significance of the individual when he proposes that everything that is worthwhile in humanity relies ultimately on the sense of responsibility of each individual person. When considered in totality, any large group of people becomes a nameless, mindless, amoral thing that evades responsibility and is always unaccountable...

In words that echo the thoughts of Laozi with some precision, Jung goes on to say that the problems experienced in the world, reflect the problems experienced by individuals. In other words, the wise do not attempt to fix the world until they have first fixed themselves. The priority therefore is always self-improvement leading to proper action for each person - a process entailing a deeper understanding of one's own innermost being.

This psychological description by Jung of the self-focused intuition the old boy calls 'work-on-the-self' is very strongly reminiscent of Laozi speaking of the Dao:

> "Small and hidden is the door that leads inward, and the entrance is barred by countless prejudices, mistaken assumptions, and fear..." (Jung C. G., Civilization in Transition, 1981)

The work of Jean Paul Sartre is another extraordinarily useful resource in interpreting Laozi, especially when it comes to really getting a feel for what it means to grapple with the concept of a mysterious 'other,' even including the unknown aspects of the 'whole' of the Dao itself. Sartre even uses some of the same terms as the old boy, including the concept of 'that which cannot be named.' Even though the purpose and thrust of his work is to show how consciousness operates for the individual in the world, Sartre's rational insights extend well into the fuzzy area most people would consider esoteric, and right into the mind-bending concept of nothingness itself.

Just as does the old boy, Sartre traverses unfamiliar regions of the soul.

Sartre's 'nothingness' is quite literally 'no thing.' But, think for a moment, how does a concept like 'nothing' even arise in the first place? After all, everything that can be named is a 'something,' even 'the nameless' in being termed 'the nameless' is reified and becomes a 'thing.' The word 'nothing' itself, being a word, apparently defies itself in the naming to become 'something.' By the same token, 'emptiness' is still 'something' and so are 'blank' and 'vacuum'...

The mental gymnastics needed to comprehend these statements are necessary here. A 'nothing' cannot be referred to as an 'itself'; strictly, it cannot be referred to at all, without the 'it' 'being' 'something.' Yet the idea, the concept remains and is familiar to all despite the difficulty in knowing how it might ever arise. How do you detect a 'nothing' when the absence of anything still leaves something?

Since there is nowhere in the world, and logically for that matter, no place in the entire physical universe for a 'nothing' to hide, Sartre concludes that 'nothingness' is hidden deep in the heart of every individual being. It is in our consciousness, and is only, but always, present there. (Sartre, Being and Nothingness, 1993)

Considering Sartre's nothingness is like studying the impossible mechanics of an Escher print, perhaps blinking incredulously at one of those pictures of the kind that trick the eye into first seeing a vase and then two faces staring at each other. The brain is forced into unfamiliar patterns of recognition. Take, for instance, these lines adapted from the writings of R.D. Laing, the noted existential psychologist (Laing, The Politics of Experience & the Bird of Paradise , 1984):

Nothing can keep me from success.
Nothing can prevent me from being happy.
There is nothing to fear.

This seems at first sight a positive message of buoyant affirmation, full of confidence that the individual can overcome all adversity. Now, read the lines again, but this time think of that 'nothing' as the heart of darkness; an 'anti-thing,' a monster, a lurking, vague and hostile impalpable presence with malevolent intent. When that menacing 'nothing' becomes real in the consciousness and is directly experienced, it is as though the world is suddenly turned on its head. Now, you can empathize with the child lying fearfully in the dark. Now, you know there really is 'nothing' there to terrify you... 'Nothing' *can* stop you now... 'Nothing' *can* prevent you from fulfillment...

And suddenly, that buoyant affirmation becomes absolute terror...

There is as much unlimited potential for pure evil in this vision of the unknown as there is for pure good. Yet the old boy insists that embracing all in the Dao means just that. The world is not all sweetness and light, there are perils to be navigated and negative aspects to be confronted. Further yet, the old boy, Jung and Sartre are all agreed that in realization of the possibilities lurking in the shadowy unknown lies the individual's path to freedom and control of their own destiny. Is it that 'nothing' sets you free? Or that you set yourself free? Or are they the same? In any event you have 'nothing' to lose…

Sartre's rather dark and pessimistic vision and the old boy's image of the greater good seem poles apart, and in some respects, they are. There is a sense however in which they might also be considered as the flip sides of the same coin. For Laozi, the fulfillment of life lies in the striving by the individual for the unity of the one, for Sartre the emptiness of life derives from the severance of the individual from the unattainable unity of the one.

In this sense they are the same. Just imagine yourself at any point on the 'Way,' the personal experience of living the Dao as a great journey. From anywhere on the way, it would be possible to empathize with either point of view by simply viewing the goal as drawing either ever-closer or ever-further away…

From the old boy's point of view, Sartre's bleak, and despairing acknowledgment of the impossibility of personal fulfillment is simply that he is seeing the Dao receding in the rear-view mirror.

And yet, one can always turn around…

My glass is half-full, or my glass is half-empty - it is all a matter of attitude.

Verse the second: On making ends meet – The union of opposites.

Humanity can define beauty, only because people also know ugliness,
The world recognizes good, only because there is also evil.

Accordingly, the known and the unknown are natural partners.
The difficult and the easy are complementary.
The long and short are always in contrast, and always together.
The high and the low depend on their relativity for meaning.
Voice and notes can together produce harmony.
Before and after each follow the other in cycle.

The wise know how to accept the contradictory union of opposites,
They do not try or need to capture the indefinable using only words.
Through this acceptance an example of altruism is created.
A tolerance that embraces the vast complexity of the world.
And nothing is lost or left undone.
This is a benefit for all - yet seeks no acclaim.

When important work is done without laying claim to merit,
The merit, though unclaimed, is always there.

Laozi is here establishing the syncretic bona fides of his thought. The Dao is the 'all.' There can be no half-measures here, the ultimate greater good must have room for everything and everyone. Remarkably, considering the simplicity of his expression, the old boy does succeed in framing his thoughts in an all-inclusive way. A measure of this success can be taken in noting that the philosophy he outlines in the text has timeless universal appeal. It is generally equally acceptable to the liberal open-minded among Christians, Muslims, Jews, Buddhists, and followers of other major and minor religions alike.

The old boy illustrates here the rather obvious precondition to any understanding of the Dao; that any connected and truly integrated 'whole' involves a reconciliation or union of antithetical elements, and much of what he has to say revolves around the ways and means of eradicating conflict within the self. Before there is enlightenment, there is the absolute necessity to unite opposites and resolve disharmony. This may be a problem for some as we shall see, since it will involve feeling comfortable with who and what we are. For most people though, this should not require the mental dexterity demanded of poor Alice when confronted by the White Queen:

> Alice laughed: "There's no use trying," she said; "one can't believe impossible things."
>
> "I dare say you haven't had much practice," said the Queen. "When I was younger, I always did it for half an hour a day. Why, sometimes I've believed as many as six impossible things before breakfast." (Carroll, 1984)

Self-realization and the unity of mind and body it implies certainly cannot be accomplished by simply rejecting or ignoring those irksome factors that prove inconvenient or difficult to reconcile. That would be to warp and twist the truth to the required end, as opposed to embracing an honest acceptance of the whole of reality.

The real goal here is to remove the dichotomy in the mind of the individual. There is a potentially major problem here, we live in a polarized world, and much though the old boy might be inclined to deride the strictness of our adherence to rational empiricism, we are all the products of our contemporary cultures. Carl Jung for one, believed that no purely rational process could satisfactorily resolve two diametrically opposed beliefs and yet let them both stand, but notes that in saying this he does not preclude an 'intuitive' (for this read 'non-rational') leap towards integration.

In his writings on the ancient spiritual alchemical text 'The Secret of the Golden Flower,' Jung indicates that possibly, the only answer to this impasse may be to 'grow out' of the limiting mind-set, to literally wait until the middle or later years of life before even attempting this kind of mental synthesis. (Jung C. G., Psychology and Religion: West and East, 1981). In this respect, Jung was wise enough to know that even the most stubbornly concrete mindset might well develop some fluidity in the longer term, though he was perhaps, somewhat pessimistic in estimating both the time required, and the conditions necessary, to achieve this kind of maturity of outlook.

Interestingly, there is anecdotal evidence that the great sage Kongzi (Confucius) was of similar mind to Jung in this regard. According to several of the available English accounts of his life, he did not think himself ready to tackle the intricacies of the 'I Ching' until he had reached the age of seventy and had a lifetime of study to underpin his temerity in attempting this major work.

It appears from these accounts, that a genuine understanding of the deeper meaning of the union of opposites requires a certain mental flexibility and maturity of understanding arising from self-knowledge. Obviously, there is at least some scholarly opinion that this depth of intuitive understanding and resolution of personal internal conflict is not something we might expect to fall into our laps, at least not without heeding the old boy's warning that some diligent prior 'work-on-the-self' is a prerequisite and then taking the appropriate steps.

However, in reaching this apparent dead-end to our quest, we are once again at risk of over-complicating the old boy. The metaphorical scowl on his expressive, white-bearded face is now accompanied by an impatient tapping of fingers on tabletop as he once again implores us, 'Listen to the message!' The old boy has information we would do well to absorb, and while a certain humility concerning our own lack of maturity is necessary and appropriate, we should not become so self-deprecating as to underestimate our own potential for fulfillment.

Laozi will steadfastly tell you that the essence of the Dao remains eternally available to all.

In heeding this message, we should never let any perceived difficulty - including our own self-doubt, or our perceived need for some preparatory personal change, stand in the way of the approach to the ultimate mysteries of the Dao. Benjamin Hoff wrote a beautiful little book, 'The Tao of Pooh' which perfectly illustrates this point. In the book he convincingly makes the case that Winnie the Pooh is in essence a Daoist master... And if the 'Bear of Little Brain' can do it, there is hope yet for us all... (Hoff, 1983)

This may seem somewhat implausible, but the old boy would certainly approve of the way Pooh never opposes the natural order. Pooh embodies uncomplicated simplicity, he enjoys sunshine, rain, and wind, all the while serenely coping with whatever occurs. He experiences pleasure and harmony in the flow of the days and seasons and the company of his friends. This total unquestioning acceptance of the world and delight in one's place in it clearly characterizes one who has reconciled all the disparate elements of the self.

Some further meditation is probably necessary here on the old boy's lines in the second verse which highlight for the first time, the paradoxical nature of the Dao essence, but at this early juncture, it is sufficient for now if we can accept that the old boy is communicating an important truth in good faith. Concepts such as 'good,' 'evil,' 'beauty,' and 'ugliness' are not absolutes, they are points along a spectrum, and also quite relative and arbitrary labels with shifting meanings and interpretations. The old boy will advise later that every one of these (apparently) irreconcilable pairs contains the germ of its opposite. Beauty and ugliness for example, are a matter of aesthetic appreciation, shifting conceptual constructs with definitions that vary widely between different persons, different cultures, and over time.

It may help in reconciliation of these extremes to understand that eventually, they will each become the other. As we shall further discuss, the Dao encompasses a universal cycle of everlasting change in which all things eventually turn into their opposites.

When we begin to accept without bitterness, or rancor, the truth - that doing good may sometimes have evil consequences, and that doing evil may sometimes have good consequences, then the old boy will give us his effusive grin and tell us we are making progress in understanding.

Verse the third: On the perils of mere 'cleverness' – Life is not stasis.

By not glorifying high achievement, discontent is minimized.
By not flaunting wealth and luxury, crime is minimized.
All desire for the unattainable creates confusion and dissatisfaction.

A wise leader fosters hearts empty of desire and envy while filling bellies.
Strength lies in keeping ambitions moderate, and bones strong.

When the people live in contented innocence, their needs are fewer,
Thoughts of something better will not disturb harmony.
The less action needs to be taken; the more order will prevail.

The old boy has some very pragmatic advice for all governments, but his guidance also has far more widespread application and should not be limited to just that select group. Throughout the 'Dao De Jing' he demonstrates his belief that the actions signifying proper pursuit of the common good – also called 'work-on-the-self,' are much the same from ordinary citizen to supreme leader. Laozi sees the communities that form nations with a simplicity and clarity of vision we may find it hard to attune to in our overly politicized, factionalized, and polarized age.

Though it may not be immediately apparent, the gulf between the politics of today and those of 2,500 years ago is somewhat narrower than may be initially supposed. Yes, we live in an era in which many community and even national leaders, display their lack of integrity by considering dishonesty as simply a tactic to be used if the outcome seems favorable – but so did the old boy. It is also true that we live in an era of widespread amorality and self-serving greed by those public officials ostensibly working for the common good and - so also did the old boy. Laozi was witness to the same kind of propagandizing, hawkishness, deceit, broken promises, belligerent war-mongering, and political dirty tricks we are all familiar with.

On seeing our modern PR agendas, information massaging, political influencing and spin-doctoring, the old boy would surely recognize these in the similar tactics employed by public figures and community leaders since time immemorial. We can almost hear him sigh as the vociferously self-serving proponents of the rival theories of the day jostle and push for attention, and blatantly, bribe, coerce or cloud the viewpoints of those they seek to persuade - with just those cherry-picked 'facts' they consider pertinent to advancing their own agendas. While all the time, the disagreeable essentials we ought to be taking into account are thrust out of sight and ignored.

Laozi would not be out of his depth in our reality; the fundamentals of politics have not changed that much in the intervening years, and politicians, albeit with some rare but worthy exceptions, are mostly still to be found at work at the interface of self-serving amorality and dissolution - then as now. The ideal leader in the eyes of Laozi - and the leader he addresses himself to - is one who would first apply to any proper leadership role in society some of those basic and straightforward values of understanding and tolerance that are the hallmarks of any honest individual concerned to act in the interests of the common good.

The Daoist principle of 'least action' is applicable here, in the community and organizational, as well as the individual context. The trick in applying the old boy's thought to contemporary issues, is to separate the eternal principles he is concerned with, from the ephemeral principles that clutter our perception, i.e., to not let the wood become obscured by the trees.

A critical point is that reconciliation of radical extremes, and the integration of opposing elements of the self in the old boy's worldview means seeking win-win situations everywhere. Repression, prejudice, intolerance, bias, ignorance, dogmatism, vengeance, resentment; all of these represent some form of negation and are indicators that real integrity has not, and will not, be achieved. Or at least not until some form of resolution and its corresponding traits of tolerance and acceptance become the norm.

The old boy will expand further on this point later, and has a clear enough message throughout his text for the leaders within communities; if a society is structured for the benefit of an elite clique, or framed as a place where 'losers' occupy every place from second downwards, what is also created is a massive potential for resentment and disharmony. Laozi would advocate that people should be valued for what they can do rather than denigrated for what they cannot accomplish.

This is the way of harmony and the greater good, people must feel safe and valued. To avoid large-scale discontent, leaders of state also need to ensure that the modest aspirations of the majority are reflected in the modest aspirations of the government whole.

This is the first hint of something the old boy examines further in other parts of the text. He is telling us something ordinary people already know, but large organizations such as corporations and government bodies need to continually be reminded of. This is the important notion of fairness mentioned above, the idea that natural justice should always prevail against the temptation to use the power of the state or corporate body for the benefit of a few. Laozi's insistence on the virtue of actions taken in furthering the common good is in full agreement with the idea that any government that allows wealth and power to shift inexorably to a complacent elite will be surely priming the revolution that will inevitably bring about its own demise.

In the old boy's terms, for an ordinary person, internal harmony is disturbed by ambition, as expressed in thoughts of, and desires for, something which is better, but unattainable without first acquiring power and influence. It is not that the old boy is advocating that either 'rich' and 'poor' or both of these extremes be eliminated as categories of being, society needs a degree of dynamic tension between wanting and receiving to stimulate progress. Everyone needs to know that a better life is both possible and attainable, and that they may strive towards fulfilling dreams of material comforts if they wish. The old boy is about embracing these opposing ideals, not eradicating them. He does warn however, that a life focus on purely material acquisition is not the true path of the Dao and again, he speaks a lot more on this topic later.

For Laozi, a well-balanced person is one acting always in accord with, and attuned to, the common good - and an unobtrusive, benevolent government acting in the same manner is the ideal. Society is then a mirror to the wholeness of the individuals within it, and in turn, of the Dao itself. There is no end point to this process. Individuals, society, and the nature of reality itself - all are naturally dynamic and always in flux, which is a key point many leaders do not understand. Stasis is unnatural, therefore any misbegotten attempt by an overly conservative government towards an unduly stable polarization of a community into (for example) permanent and clearly demarcated 'haves' and 'not-haves' is a kind of imposed fragmentation - and that is something fundamentally in opposition to the principles of reconciliation and of unity on the path of the Dao.

In his praise of innocence and the contentment of the simple life in this verse, it is not that the old boy is advocating that people should be deliberately kept in the dark, elsewhere he is strict enough in insisting on the individual taking the initiative in the acquisition of knowledge. What he does often warn against however, is the over-blown rhetoric and the pseudo-wisdom he labels as 'cleverness,' the kind of fashionable, truncated pieces of applied logic that sometimes find an adopted context way beyond their original limited scope and sweep through society to occasionally devastating effect.

Examples of such 'cleverness' might include any area in which rational argument is used to excuse unconscionable behavior, or where responsibility is evaded, or improper excuses made for not doing the 'right thing,' or some individual or group is advocating a course whereby their profit and status may be bolstered by immoral or unethical actions – or by the lack of some required and necessary action.

For contemporary examples of this kind of inferior thinking in our societies, we only need to examine any one of the common strategies formulated to serve certain individuals or groups within a society - but which act towards the overall detriment of the common good. These examples will include; government policies abnegating responsibility and conveniently redefining the care of the needy, the aged and other vulnerable members of society as 'business opportunities.' There are also the lazy and inept politicians who allow and even encourage, corporate lawyers to draft and shape the legislation they are themselves being paid to formulate, there are educational institutions that prize financial ability over scholastic ability, hospitals prepared to offer only a small subset of the available, or required, services to any who lack the means to pay, individuals whose self-righteous rationalizations persuades them of the moral bankruptcy of the poor and needy, and therefore absolves them from blame in allowing them to starve...

All these abdications of responsibility, common in organizations and state bodies, but also found in the actions of prejudiced individuals, are illustrations of the type of 'cleverness' the old boy scorns. This 'cleverness' will require some honest and serious examination and re-evaluation within each individual self before the way of the Dao can be realized.

Understanding what the old boy really means by 'cleverness' is a valuable key to good understanding of the 'Dao De Jing.' True wisdom, the big picture view, must always heed and contend with, conventional wisdom and its assumptions; and 'conventional wisdom' includes all the prevalent beliefs and ideas that motivate individuals, organizations, and governments in regular cycles to foster the cyclically fashionable 'theories' and 'solutions' that engender widespread community support - albeit even if often only for a relatively limited time.

Some of these faddish propositions may be quite useful and positive in their effects, and some quite bad, but what differentiates and separates these passing 'clever' ideas from true wisdom and from the Dao, is their ambit. Without exception the fashionable trends in conventional thought which lead to wrong action, fail to be holistic. They propose their action based on some innovative analysis of what is always only a subset of the available data - and thereby fail to address the entirety of the problem.

While it may be stylish and popular to speak of thinking 'laterally' and consider 'innovative solutions,' and 'synergies' that are 'outside the box,' it only takes a quick glance at governmental and corporate policies anywhere and everywhere to see that short-sighted, band-aid, and advantage seeking solutions combined with some persuasive political spin-doctoring or patronage to sweeten the deal are more generally the order of the day.

It is unsurprising, given this critical failure of overall vision, that much conventional wisdom lacks in practical application the necessary scope to be fully comprehensive in answering the real need to be addressed. Like the medicine given to terminally ill patients, it eases the immediate pain, but provides no prospect of curing the malaise. In treating symptoms rather than causes, this kind of conventional wisdom foisted upon communities by their leadership, is always eventually found deficient - as the old boy sees it, there is no integration with the 'big picture,' and no advancement along the way of the greater good - which is also the common good in the Dao.

Consider for a moment a contemporary example of the type of wisdom or 'cleverness' that apparently offers big-picture solutions; the much-lauded cleverness of 'economic rationalism.' That is, economic and social policy based on consideration of supply and demand and driven by market forces and profit and loss forecasting. The key point here is that this is often the application of exclusively economic strategies - taken out of intended context - to 'solve' those social problems normally associated with a duty of care and correct personal conduct.

This model of materialistic society employs a limited subset (only what is logical/rational/economically acceptable) of an already limited subset (the purely economic aspects) of the available data on society.

The result is a de-humanizing lack od social responsibility; caring, sharing, rendering assistance where needed, empathy, community values - the good-natured acceptance of the needs of others - are all at least partially abandoned. Instead, we have a 'rational' justification for privatizing social services and public assets in the interest of profit and advantage for a lucky few - all of which serves to create a poverty-stricken underclass who will be at the service, and at the mercy, of the beneficiaries of this policy - that is, a wealthy elite who will reap almost all the benefits.

Simultaneously, this policy will also provide a convenient 'rational' justification for why financial support - in the form of welfare for the newly created poor, should be strictly limited - if not actually abolished. In this way, by ignoring the true big-picture view, moral and ethical imperatives are over-ridden by economic considerations, which has the end result of the commodification of humanity.

This is the kind of ideological babble espoused by extreme conservative pundits and expressed in cliches such as, 'What is good for business is always good for the country!' and 'We need to apply the principles of profit and loss business efficiency to social responsibilities such as coping with poverty, tackling homelessness, caring for the disabled, dealing with lawbreakers...'

Could this kind of niche thinking embody some universally applicable truth? The old boy would frown and walk away quietly and have nothing further to do with this inferior idea. Those looking to make profits from the poor and sick, cashing in on misfortune, disrespecting elders by treating their needs purely as a business opportunity - all represent a form of dereliction of duty. They are aspects of contemporary thinking the old boy would detest, even though he would surely have encountered comparable self-serving mindsets in his own era.

In this instance, by limiting the 'rationalism' to economic considerations, then even worse, by deliberately excluding and denying the legitimacy of any other ethical or moral consideration of responsibilities, needs, wants and feelings, the bigger picture is forever excluded and the whole thereby denied. There is no fulfillment, no unity, and the Dao remains unattainable. This is the kind of thinking Laozi would deride as being only 'cleverness.'

Humanity is not 'the economy,' and people are more than just 'the market.'

'Cleverness' is not just the ill-conceived idea or mistaken notion that has found some place to take root and grow in society. Some 'cleverness' is deeply ingrained in our cultural fabric and some of these entrenched ideas are dangerous. The old boy lived in an age when a ruler's whim could make or break an individual. Today, the element of chance is still a significant limiting factor in any search for ultimate truth. One need only look, for example, at what happens to whistleblowers in our Western societies to see how capricious the search for truth can be.

Though the individuals who expose corruption and misuse of public funds may be generally acknowledged as principled and moral people, though they are working towards the greater good, and even though they may be admittedly truthful and even idolized by the masses, and feted by the media, their fate at the hands of government 'cleverness' is uncertain at best and terrible at worst.

We have as examples of this in recent times, the cases of Daniel Ellsberg, Stanley Adams, Vladimir Bukovsky, Edward Snowden, Martha Mitchell, Peter Wright, and Julian Assange among many others, all reminders that telling the truth can be just as dangerous a pursuit now as it was 2,500 years ago. The old boy understood that outspoken individuals like this throughout history were frequently at the mercy of a similar fate, often in the guise of some limiting condition placed upon them by their own capricious social institutions and leaderships.

The choices can be quite stark if the social situation is not to spiral out of control, and the old boy in later verses further explores this problem, recognizing that its solution lies in the personal responsibility which needs to be taken by every individual - for that is where the impetus towards the Dao resides. The old boy agrees with contemporary thinkers including Carl Jung, who argues that organizations are always the blunt amoral tools of leadership, and the notion of genuine 'corporate responsibility' is nothing but a legal fiction, a 'cleverness' designed to minimize liability and appease the pangs of guilt in the real individuals who are responsible.

In fact, Laozi might tell us, in words which echo the sentiments of Jung, that unless there is individual responsibility taken for the actions of corporate institutions, right up to and including the state itself - we are at something of an impasse.

If our corporate bodies are promoting ill-conceived solutions, our quality of life suffers. If they behave unjustly and immorally, we are tainted as well. And if we maintain the comfortable fiction that the corporate bodies that we are members of are really entities with a 'person-hood' somehow separate from us, we implicitly accept that they can take the blame we ourselves should be shouldering.

In this way, we remain in denial of any true reconciliation of our reality.

Then, as all possibility of genuine reconciliation and integration in the unity of the whole fails, the common good of the Dao fades ever more from view.

Verse the fourth: Emptiness and plenty - Echoes of all the dead Gods.

In the unity of the whole, is a vessel which use cannot drain.
The boundless source of the known - and everything denied.

It is sharpness and its blunting, A knot and the means to untangle it,
A glare that softens and fades until only dimly realized.

Where it comes from may not be known.
It is eternal and from it the highest essence may arise.

When considering the import of Laozi's words, even a person of agnostic or atheistic tendency might benefit from revisiting the language and form of any religious teachings they may have received in earlier life. The great Dao, the way, unity, and Godhead, supreme mystery, unknown, nothingness - is a journey into self-knowledge. In the West, appropriate words to describe this finding and uniting process seem somehow lacking in secular terminology. It can only really be expressed for many by means of the vocabulary of religious experience.

Like the old boy himself and many a philosopher who came later, we falter at the outer edge of the capabilities of language.

The essence of the Dao is the same essence as that of a whole category of universal human experience. All the religions of the world and according to Carl Jung at least, all those words that end in 'ism' are types of, or potential substitutes for, a spiritual life quest. That means socialism, nihilism, feminism, capitalism, chauvinism, existentialism, communism, hedonism, Buddhism, and at the risk of being frivolous, even jingoism, are all variants on, or diversions from, the job the old boy would call 'work on yourself' – finding an individual pathway in life. Any one of the 'isms' can provide a life with a kind of passion and purpose and can be a substitute for genuine religious belief and experience. (Jung C. G., Aion, 1981)

These 'isms' are most often alternatives to the pursuit of eternal wholeness of self and can consume the energy that might be more usefully and directly applied to personal spiritual growth. They are, like conventional wisdom, sub-sets of that absolute totality, and even though for many they can be a useful stepping-stone, they are generally insufficient in themselves to embrace the absolutes the old boy is guiding us towards. For example, rationalism is itself a rejection of the irrational and, valuable though it is, is not all-inclusive and therefore inadequate to define or in any real sense grasp, the whole of the essence that is Dao.

Sartre's preferred 'isms' and the personal commitment he chose in rejecting a deity (and also perhaps ultimately the possibility of any kind of unity) were rationalism and Marxism. For himself, he judged the Dao as unattainable. The old boy would not say this was wrong, but simply that the ways are many, since the path may twist and turn and even an apparent dead end may provide some impetus towards enlightenment in the longer term. In this sense, neither harsh judgment nor complacency should be occasioned by the personal pathways that others find opportune or feel bound to tread.

Laozi encourages people to look within themselves to find the way. Insight is frequently not found in the most likely places, and there are no guarantees that the path rejected or inappropriate to one is not ultimately, the perfect way for someone else. In any event, some will deny the last step, and this too is just a part of life to be accepted.

It is because of the complexity and confusion in traditional religion and the consequent proliferation of sect, sub-sect, and 'ism' type religious substitutes that the simple lucidity of 'work on yourself' becomes such an attraction. This is where the directness and accessibility of the old boy's teachings really excel. The truth is that we, meaning that broad swathe of the peoples of the contemporary 'West' of civilization, carry the baggage of generations of complex philosophic and semantic overlays to our perception. This may sometimes cloud and perhaps confuse our discernment of the real and actual. The ideas of the great thinkers we have partially absorbed can in practice be just one more inexplicable maze we must navigate, and their signposts point in every direction.

It is little wonder then, that in every culture, thinking individuals often turn with relief from the fragmented disarray and internecine squabbles of organized religion, and even sometimes away from spiritual matters generally, towards what science offers us by way of proof and cold, hard, fact.

Yet, in turning by degrees towards the alluring clarity of the substantive, rational and scientific, the old boy would caution that we risk turning also towards imbalance and a potential spiritual vacuum. It is a crisis of insufficiency, of alienation and separation that leaves many with a feeling of loss or disorientation in the chaos of the world. In adopting this purely factual orientation we risk losing the simplicity of outlook and the intuitive connection with the natural world that is the hallmark of the genuine seeker of truth in the Laozi tradition.

When we demand proof and reject our own instinct, then we lose the capacity for acceptance. To progress, we need to somehow wipe the slate clean in favor of a more innocent and broad-minded tolerance.

'Alienation' means estrangement and emotional distance. It arises because of the separation of the individual from the entire realm of the spiritual. It can be considered, at its core, as a form of entrapment by the material. The old boy would certainly label the alienated mindset as a limiting factor on the way to enlightenment. In a sense, it is a form of extremism, despite it being somewhere not that far from the norm for many in much of latter-day Western society.

Alienation-as-separation arises because of a refusal to accept, consider, or admit that anything important or worthwhile exists beyond the defining realms of reality as it is personally experienced. For example, instead of looking for the actual shape of the whole, we draw a set of defining lines bound by what is known and proven in our lives and attempt to fit the whole into the box we have created - the impossible final triumph of rationalism and logic.

The search for a mysterious 'other' is denied in this process, some hidden validation of self and life is a universal quality associated with the fulfillment of individual potential throughout all of history. Alienated people feel a 'lack' of something. This 'something' is not just a matter of personally accepting or rejecting a particular divinity or mode of religious expression, this is a rejection of the spiritual life itself, an attempted repression of an omnipresent facet of human experience.

The fact of being an orthodox believer or non-believer of a particular persuasion is not important in the 'big picture' scheme of things, hence the proliferation of 'isms' for the diversion of us all. The point here is that despite their denial of any traditional God, even avowed atheists generally still seek some outlet for their spiritual impulse. Just as the denial of spirituality leads to alienation and the diminution of the individual, so the converse is true, any kind of spiritual commitment empowers the individual with meaning in life and gives a sense of both personal strength and personal focus.

Commitment in the spiritual sense is the equivalent of a storm-anchor, and those people driven by purely material issues are in a real sense cast adrift and vulnerable. Whether they realize this or not, they become prone to the discontents of those whose belief has failed or become irrelevant to them. They are separated from the totality of their being - alienated.

How does this come about? The Dao, wholeness, completeness of being, need not be associated with any form of religious observance or divine presence and yet is frequently and almost inevitably equated with God in our Western thought. Because traditionally in our culture this essence; the Godhead, is our mysterious other. It should be said that a sole focus on the material aspects of life removes us as surely from the Dao as it does from any traditional divinity. Dao and the Godhead both represent ultimate unity, integration, and fulfillment in the whole.

In Jungian terms, spiritual meanings and principles are realized internally or not at all, any externalized spiritual ideal turns to superstition and irrelevance very quickly. This, according to Jung, is the calamity that has struck Western society so hard in the last few generations; the idea of God as an independent entity sitting in judgment has taken hold. Many people have swapped the 'God within' for an externalized 'God the father' in some mystical 'heaven' which is not part of the self. This is against all good advice from theologians who well know the dangers. Absent Gods become superfluous in short order. (Jung C. G., Civilization in Transition, 1981)

If the concept of a 'divine being' is to be the means of the unity of the whole, then people need to see, hear, and feel their almighty leader in the most direct and personal way. Hearsay simply will not do; and yet, for many, if not most, believers at this point in history, it must suffice. So, a large section of contemporary Western society has simply ceased being spiritually involved in their traditional religions in any meaningful way - they are simply going through the motions.

When the faithful are forced to accept the substitute of empty forms of repetitive ritual for authentic religious experience something vital dies. The imitation of Christ is no substitute for the direct revelation of the innermost mystery.

Laozi's message is strongly independent and eclectic, and as usual, the old boy throws us a lifeline and cuts to the heart of the matter with uncanny ease and simplicity. To the adherents and perpetuators of form and ritual, he would say that it really does not matter whether you believe, or do not believe in a supreme or divine being. In his own era, the distinction between supreme state leader and Godhead was blurred to say the least. Laozi advises that the answers sought are to be found within, and that what is certain, is that the individual who with a shrug of the shoulders places their fate in the lap of the Gods - has ceased work-on-the-self.

The old boy will tell you emphatically that fatalistic belief in an external divinity is just a way of avoiding personal responsibility, an abdication from personal attainment of all the potential of life. In this situation the individual who is simply resigned to the will of God, loses sight of achieving full potential through the kind of self-realization the Dao represents.

This is not to say that the old boy specifically advocates atheism, the path of the Dao tolerates all honest endeavor, but if there no endeavor at all, then the way is lost. Early Christian thinkers and more contemporary theologians are both equally keenly aware of this problem when they assert that "God helps those who help themselves." Perhaps few who have heard this old saying quite realize just how vital it is. Ultimately, it is the boundary between the potential for personal fulfillment and abysmal failure.

Alienation of the spirit is something the old boy frequently references, so rather than meditate on this condition as and when it crops up in the text, it may be useful to introduce the topic here with the observation that alienation is widely experienced by its casualties as a kind of want of enthusiasm, a dulling of the senses and lack of belonging, an inability to ignite that first essential spark of motivation. The individual is blasé, world-weary, cynical, and detached. The problem is one of maintaining the individual's engagement with the ideal, keeping the spiritual quest fresh, vital, and personal.

Ideally, what is required at the outset of any journey towards the Dao is a sense of awe and wonder of the natural beauty in life - and yet alienation brings its exact opposite - a vast ennui...

To be fair, a proper sense of innocent awe is not easy to inspire in our high-tech, media-rich, and desensitized times. While the solemnity of high mass in a cavernous, vaulted cathedral may well have struck wonder into the average citizen in the Middle Ages, as a spectacle today, its capacity even to impress, much less overawe, is gravely diminished. It is little wonder that new-age churches and cults galore employ theatrical spectacle, charismatic leaders, group incantation, and devices as various as laser light shows, rock 'n roll bands and hypnotic trance to maintain the participation of their congregations – many people need the inspiration of awe to galvanize spiritual progress.

The end of work-on-the-self, and the end of any approach towards fulfillment, really sets in when a person, or even an entire religious order or community group, becomes hidebound and fossilized by tradition and ritual. For the organized religion, this circumstance means decay, and marks the failure of a fundamental priestly duty, that of maintaining the interface between the ordinary person and the possibility of the whole, the divine, the Godhead, the Dao…

Like many a bureaucracy before them, failing religious institutions have yielded to the temptation of allowing a panel of 'experts,' the theologians and other advance guard of the hierarchy, to dictate the terms of participation to the ordinary person. Because of this institutional weakness, many individuals are stuck with a supreme being that is somehow external and distant to the self, and that inspiring and previously available local 'hot line' to the spiritual is closed.

Laozi presents a way out of the quandary. The old boy says simply, stop complicating the issue and start work-on-the-self. This is all that is necessary, and the means to start and finish the job are all immediately to hand. Forget ritual and tradition. All you must do in commencement is to start to use that peripheral mental vision you already have, open your mind, and begin to resolve the conflicts within, and work always with conscious dedication towards the common good.

Of course, he doesn't promise us all an easy trip…

Verse the fifth: The breath of the universe – The cycle of opposites.

Heaven and earth are uncompromising,
For them, each living thing is superfluous once its purpose is served.

The wise are also uncompromising,
For them, no individual is vital or essential to the whole.

The unknown is a space central to heaven and earth - like a bellows,
It appears empty - yet is inexhaustible in feeding the fire,
Like a bellows, the unknown changes shape,
Creating something from nothing,
In moving, it creates, and it yields.

From it we learn that more words might mean less.
And to hold fast to the central unknown that may yet have a use.

What separates humanity from all of nature? Nothing - and we should know by now that this can be a terrifying notion. The distance between the rational human intellect and the raw and random turmoil of nature is one of the inimical polarizations of thought requiring reconciliation in work-on-the-self. And it should be noted that any person embarking on this work is severely disadvantaged should they acquire an exaggerated perception of their own extra-ordinariness or innate worthiness.

For the old boy, humility, and a humble appreciation of the insignificance of any one life in relation to the vastness of the whole, are essential primary elements of proper work-on-the-self. This is a work that has all been done before, and it will all be done again. The person who embarks upon this path now is not joining some exclusive elite, but simply working towards realizing their intrinsic potential - as they should do. Should you fail in this process of attaining self-actualization and enlightened contentment, should I fail - life will go on. The great ebb and flow of life is, like the imagery of the bellows in the lines above, symbolic of that vast universal inhalation and exhalation which is the wind of perpetual change. It is a natural process in which all things find their place for a while, but nothing is forever, and the vast cycle continues to embrace all possibilities...

Work-on-the-self is also more than just a matter of achieving some synthetic union of opposites. The old boy is telling us here that the next step in understanding is knowing that there is a natural oscillation in reality in which everything springs from its opposite. Something comes from nothing, order from chaos, good from bad, man from woman, light from darkness, elation from despair. The old boy is sensitive to these changes and is so aware of them as a continuing process, that in his terms, the night really does begin at noon - at the precise instant the power of the day reaches its peak and begins to fade.

This moment of high noon, with the sun at zenith and at the very peak of its power and influence, is the moment that decline begins and the power of the night gradually asserts itself. The onset of darkness is something which only happens after the power of the day has already been steadily waning for many hours.

Carl Jung names this phenomenon, by which all things eventually turn into their opposites 'enantiodromia,' a term which he in turn adopted from Heraclitus and which has universal application. Thus, for individuals, love is akin to hate, and one may surprisingly easily become the other, laughter when prolonged turns to tears, anger turns to tolerance or indifference, and passion becomes apathy.

Within this idea, there are much broader issues of reciprocation and cyclic change for society as well, governments, corporations, institutions, and community and state leaders are all prone to metamorphosis, undergoing radicalization or at the very least losing their stated purpose by simply drifting away from their foundations as a result of enantiodromia. It is in this way that a 'ministry for peace' may become focused on facilitating war, an environmental protection agency can become licensor and advocate for unsustainable practices, and an administration committed to the service of the people can be commandeered to the benefit of an elite at great detriment to its original charter.

If the Dao can be said to have a place, then that place is the middle ground, and when, by the inexorable process of enantiodromia that middle ground is for a time lost - generally because no compensatory process of continual re-evaluation is in place - then the Dao fades from sight and the common good, being ever more disregarded, becomes increasingly inaccessible.

The old boy continually warns us that this transfigurative process is happening all around us. As a counter to this, we need to accept conscious responsibility for ourselves and for our self-orientation in the chaos. That which is right and beautiful in the natural world is in perpetual flux, and indeed we generally all admit rationally that 'change is inevitable,' yet unless we are continually going back to basics and adjusting our outlook to the new reality, we do not always plumb the depths of any possible damage that these small incremental changes are doing to us - to our personalities, society, fundamental beliefs and attitudes, notions of right and wrong, friendship, family, morality, ethics, concept of self...

Conscious effort and some vigilance is required to maintain our personal compass and avoid a persistent and often almost imperceptible erosion of core values.

Consider further the impact of this ebb and flow of change in the environmental context of corporations and associations, institutions, and states. Enantiodromia here can be the tendency for education, under the direction of an unscrupulous leader, to become propaganda - a tool to stifle any real learning and reinforce a particular ideology. In similar fashion, the law can be exercised in preventing genuine justice from being upheld, and police powers can be perverted to the organized repression of ordinary decent people for the protection of a powerful, and sometimes malevolent or criminal few. An army can be used in terrorizing and subduing the very people they are supposed to defend - and many do so. Even medical knowledge can be subverted to harmful means, for example, in the deliberate development of diseases and toxins as weapons, or the false imprisonment on 'medical grounds' of the political enemies of the state.

All the horrors detailed above have happened before and will no doubt happen again. Rational process can and often is used to justify inhumane acts. Hence, it is no overstatement to repeat an assertion previously made; pure rationalism without a balancing human appreciation of moral and ethical imperatives, emotional and spiritual wants, fears, and needs - is itself a form of radicalism that leads away from the essence of the common good that is Dao. Logic is so useful and ubiquitous a tool that we forget that, when entirely relied upon, it denies an essential element of the human experience, and consequently any possibility of the integration of the whole. The old boy would put it more simply -a rationale, even with a set of good intentions is just not enough.

There is a constant cycling and shift of emphasis in any striving towards the greater good and both individuals and groups need to be finely attuned to this flow or risk being rashly opposed to it. Individuals more especially need this awareness, since individuals are the guiding conscience of institutions, and must in the end, be responsible for group actions.

This is why it is something of a fundamental injunction from the old boy to refuse to take things at face value and to frequently re-evaluate the truth of any given situation, even to the point of examining the prescriptive function of the language used to describe the situation.

To take a firm stand on anything and fail to re-evaluate in the light of altered circumstances is to be inflexible, and to cease to admit that change is a vital component of the ultimate whole.

Change is always - but forever - central to the ideal of unity. It is no accident that the other best-known work in the Daoist philosophic canon is the 'I Ching: The Book of Changes.' The Dao may be the pure constant, but of course, in keeping with its paradoxical nature, it is also the embodiment of all change and impermanence. (Wilhelm, The I Ching or Book of Changes, 1977)

Another consideration for the soul-searching whole-seeker on this highest quest of all, is that an aura of positive affirmation should pervade the pursuit of ultimate integration. The mind-set of the true pilgrim on the way is flexibility, determination, humility, and honesty.

The old boy would stress yet again, that it is wise to remember from time to time that even for the honest, soul-searching may turn to self-deception, unless there is frequent and uncompromising self-review...

Verse the sixth: The Mother lode – The primal one.

The spirit of the valley is timeless.
It is mother, earth, woman.
She is the first beginning of all that is.

Though the importance of first beginnings is barely noticed,
Their relevance never fails.

In Eastern literature and tradition 'yin' is a powerful symbolic first principle. It stands for earth, mystery, darkness, warmth, the feminine, motherhood, fertility, stability, devotion, and everything that is timelessly solid and basic. It is the spirit of the valley, the place of nurture where life-giving water flows, it exemplifies the productivity of the nothingness out of which all things arise, and order comes, and the energy of one who can both disengage from mundane reality and embrace conflicting principles.

By contrast, the 'yang' principle stands for heaven, lightness, strength, masculinity, fatherhood, creativity, success, power, and all that can be actualized. It epitomizes the tireless dynamism of the person who will not accept anything inferior, corrupted, or less than the whole. When you look carefully, these are the same primal elements humanity has always had to deal with. Naturally, the old boy tells us, these opposites spring one from the other and as the yang peaks, the yin gains ascendance and vice-versa.

For Laozi, the contrast of yin-yang represents a means of understanding; compare, for example our more contemporary tools of analysis in their familiar complementary duos, for example, subject and object, compare and contrast, or cause and effect - the yin-yang line of dichotomy is simply another investigative device to be used in a personal realization of the whole. The old boy is giving us the clearest picture he can of the universal ebb and flow he is inviting us to ponder, but in the knowledge that the Dao as great journey is always a unique and personal journey. You cannot simply adopt some other person's enlightenment; though you are certainly free to seek an example or inspiration in the methods of another.

Eventually, however the Dao is approached, the real work is there for you to do, and only you to do.

To effectively work-on-the-self, and thereby approach the Dao essence, one must understand something of the universe. The task seems overwhelming, but the old boy has disdain for these perceived difficulties, and in fact, a few simple steps are all that need be taken to begin on the way. Each person needs to be aware of their place in the natural order. None of us are special, or essential, and the omnipresent universal Dao is not there to care for, or nurture us specifically. We are each of us responsible for ourselves. In undertaking this task, it is not so much the case that we will inevitably encounter difficulties, but more that we must shoulder whatever burden we have decided to encumber ourselves with.

Then, when we cease to be selfish and egotistical, when we begin to appreciate that every action should be in furtherance if the common good, we discover a nurturing fulfillment in the Dao in the realization of ourselves. This process can be long and hard - or as the old boy will tell us - totally effortless.

It is up to us.

Verse the seventh: Signposts along the way - Personal virtue.

Heaven and earth are timeless.
Being unborn, they are eternal.

Knowing this, the wise put themselves last, yet they come first.
They are detached, and therefore become as one.
Having no thought for themselves, they are fulfilled.

Complete understanding comes from the ground up and is intuitively felt as well as reasoned - that is, if it is fully realized and integrated within the self. But the method or process by which this understanding is achieved is not critical, providing a few important small observances are made, including the acceptance that a process of rational self-analysis, while perhaps a laudable beginning, is still insufficient for the longer term. The old boy tells us that it does not really matter how you assess your reality providing your endeavor is honest and thorough and you do not engage in this rational quest at the expense of disregarding or dismissing any of your feelings and, intuitions. This self-reflection should be honest enough to confront, and make peace with, any dark or more painful aspect of your personal history you may find uncomfortable, distressing, or somehow surplus to your vision of yourself.

We are what we are.

The question remains though - how does one commence on this path?

The yin-yang pairing discussed in the previous lines provides the first clue, Western cultural traditions accustom each educated individual to examine and break down the various elements that constitute our world along some traditional analytical lines of cleavage. The established methods of investigation are those favored by science; they are the familiar dichotomies, some of which were previously mentioned, of cause and effect, subject and object, known and unknown, compare and contrast, logic versus emotion, and for the old boy – yin and yang, the feminine and masculine principles.

These ideas, all of which point towards a possible unity in the whole through reconciliation of opposites, are simply scientific, logical, and philosophical ways of examining wholeness – different ways to cut the cake of reality. They are all variations on the theme of discernment of the natural order - actuality if you will. And, as the old boy sees it, the methodology is not critical. Any way that you divide the cake, it still tastes the same.

So, when seeking to penetrate the mysteries of the greater good in the Dao essence, one should probably start the journey simply, with those things that are personally known and closely experienced. The old boy advises that this is a search that begins with a readiness for full acceptance and realization of things unknown and enduring.

On the way, we are all required to shift focus from time to time and consciously return to those areas of experience in which we have found no answers before. To seek the unity of the whole is to unselfishly re-examine first principles and undertake a fundamental appraisal of essential elements previously taken for granted - sometimes, it is in the most central and apparently obvious that enlightenment lies.

As always, the answers are to be found in honest contemplation of the innermost self.

Verse the eighth: On honest acceptance - Going with the flow.

The highest good is like water.
It nurtures all of life - yet makes no effort.
It flows to the undermost easily and without distinction or judgment.

In our home life, the place is the essential quality,
In our thoughts it is depth.
In our dealings with others, it is kindness,
In our speech it is integrity,
In our judgment it is justice,
In our business it is competence,
But in our actions - it is the timing that counts.

Where there is no confrontation - there can be no condemnation.

My maternal grandmother had a way of summing up any adverse situation she encountered in life in terms that would have been perfectly acceptable to a Daoist master twenty-five centuries ago. Her character, molded as it was by a lifetime of toil, was not especially unusual, almost everyone eventually runs across a pragmatic disposition like hers, but she was living proof that a formal education and a wealth of factual knowledge are not the first prerequisites for wisdom.

Two world wars, a global depression, the demands of raising a family at a time when medicine was rudimentary and it was accepted that some children would die in infancy, and the pressures of earning a living from unskilled labor during the bleak austerity years of early 20th century England honed grandmother's personal survival techniques to a fine edge. Their simplicity in everyday application almost succeeded in disguising their devastating effectiveness.

When adversity struck, her seemingly frail presence steadfastly refused to wilt under any degree of pressure, although her only apparent defense was the expression of the hopeful notion that there is always something beneficial to be gained from even the most catastrophic of events. At its most positive, the sentiment was the assertion that: 'There is nothing so bad that good can't come of it.' At its most wistful, the phrasing became the almost pleading: 'Perhaps it's all for the best in the long run...'

What was it that made her a rock and gave her affinity with the Daoist masters of ancient renown? Her matter-of-fact acceptance of the reality of her situation was the first clue. Then, there was the way she adapted to the ebb and flow of great events without consuming her energy in opposing the unopposable. She was a dependable and immovable anchor for her family. Her indomitable nature overcame physical frailty and gave her personal presence and substance, even though her whole life was a tumultuous surf-ride down the giant breaking wave of 20th century change. From the era of the horse and carriage, gaslights, and silent movies, to jet travel, computers, and lunar missions, she saw it all.

Along the way she saw the motor vehicle take over the urban landscape, tuned to early radio (and later television), and saw the world develop both weapons of mass destruction and the medical technology to save lives. She learned that the only thing certain in life is that nothing stays the same. Today's curse might be tomorrows blessing and the reverse was probably true as well. You accepted your lot, hoped, and looked for the best possible outcome, and through it all, life continued, and was as good as you made it...

The idea that concepts like 'good' and 'bad' might have shifting definitions was not something that appealed to me at ten years old.

The demarcation lines were quite clear then, with no gray areas to confuse the issue. Bad engenders worse and good only gets better. The two were as different and as irreconcilable as night and day, black and white, and cold and heat.

Years later, and now that I am no longer so confident that I can always clearly separate all that is good from all that is bad; I can still remember my absolute certainty at ten. Some perception that was previously concrete and unbending is now fluid and yielding. The question the old boy would ask with a grin is this - have I learned something, or have I forgotten something here?

Trouble, conflict, blockage, frustration, wasted energy, the very idea of opposition in general; all these negatives arise when the individual is not fully and properly engaged with the world. When anyone fights against the natural course of events, that person is the loser. In Sartre's terms, 'nothing' has come between the self and world – and a shadow has fallen. Somehow a person is distracted and gets out of tune with nature; this person has drifted away from the Dao as a great journey and accepted something less than the whole. The consequence is a lot of vitality wasted and a great deal of distraction and contention.

In this case, the old boy is directing those troubled souls who have reached this impasse to look at the environmental factors that count. The message from Laozi is unblock the view, strip away the inconsequential clutter from the mind and abandon confusion by the straightforward process of focusing on what is unpretentious and worthy. From this modest beginning the path to understanding and harmony becomes easier as the natural flow of life is reasserted.

Everything has a price however, and the easy vegetative comforts of the sedentary intellect are lost to the soul-searcher engaged in reconciliation of fundamental principles. In Sartre's terms the reality can be a harsh one, once awakened to the possibility of Dao, those on the way must embrace the whole they find for, if like Sartre they engage in any intellectual rejection of the possibility of integration, they are then 'condemned to be free,' cut adrift in a literal sense from all comforts and unable to consciously retreat back into the vacuity of a life lived before this new awareness without a profound feeling of self-loss. (Sartre, Being and Nothingness, 1993)

The old boy would, however, simply snort at the idea of anyone nurturing this kind of sense of dispossession, or considering this to be in some way a permanent and undeserved loss of innocence. The beginning of the path towards the Dao is always just one step away.

Illusion is always and only that - why treasure it when the truth, as expressed in the lines above, is also available?

Verse the ninth: The middle ground of work-on-the-self - Simplicity of action.

The vessel that is brimful is in danger of spilling.
The finely-honed blade is easiest to blunt.

The greatest treasures are a burden to those who guard them.
Those who seek great wealth and position court disaster.

To step down quietly when the task is finished,
Is the way of greatest good.

The short and simple message of these lines is that an unassuming restraint and balanced approach to daily life are qualities worth cultivating. It is no coincidence that peace and serenity are universally equated with 'centering.' In politics, the center is always where the moderates are found, and is the place where compromise is possible. In law and diplomacy all conciliation is to be found in the middle ground. Accord and harmony are characteristics of the center, while all radicalism and excess represent imbalance - a movement away from the center and towards a more extreme outlying position.

The place of understanding of the Dao is naturally at the center, but since the Dao represents the all, it is necessary to also recognize, and be attuned to the extremes - and to achieve a reconciliation of these apparent opposites before this center is reached.

In this verse and the next, the old boy emphasizes a familiar theme. He continually stresses the virtue of 'just enough and no more.' Laozi advises modesty with no display of ostentatious wealth, not just because this would excite envy and discord, but because he knows that one of the most prevalent and dangerous opponents of the unity of the whole through Dao, is the imbalance caused by all tendencies towards excess.

If any person should become wholly focused on the acquisition of material wealth, or adopt an extreme philosophy of living, or develop an attitude or behavior representing an intolerant, radical viewpoint, then Laozi's prescription for the fulfilled life simply will not apply for them. Work-on-the-self involves a keen appreciation of the concept of moderation in all things.

The capacity to seek inner truth needs an open mind and a vigilant internal vision, and these personal qualities will need to be well-nurtured along the way, as they will be tested to the full.

Verse the tenth: Moderation and acceptance are key - The dangers of intolerance.

Knowing you are both body and soul,
Can you avoid separation and attain unity?

Can you by an act of mind alone,
Become as supple as a newborn baby?

Can you clean and polish the mirror of your insight,
And make that vision perfect?

Can you, caring and taking responsibility for all,
Avoid wrong action by disregarding knowledge that poses as wisdom?
Can you, by your understanding, openness, and acceptance,
Be as the receptive valley spirit, the primal she?
Can you, in the breadth of your knowledge and wholeness,
Still feel that you know nothing and should do nothing?

Life without claim of possession,
Nurture without need of gratitude.
Leading, but not dominating,
This is the greatest good.

Laozi is speaking here of the necessity for each person on the great way to take personal responsibility for their lives and to keep an open, fresh, and agile mind. By maintaining this constant acceptance and tolerance of reality, conflict is averted. The old boy strongly advises against any attempt to oppose the realities of the world by embarking upon some idealistic quest which may serve as nothing more than a distraction from the way of the Dao. Instead, he urges the person on their own spiritual journey to seek to clear the mind of preconceived ideas and be as supple and receptive as an infant - to relax, think clearly, and take the path of least resistance without attempting to over govern or direct events.

This is again a call for moderation.

In the broader context of corporate and international relations, what pits two groups, or two nations, against each other is simply the undue influence of their respective radical elements on their moderate centers. On this greater scale, when we value freedom of speech and expression, by the process of enantiodromia, we inevitably also give free rein to the inimical forces that will employ these same freedoms in seeking our corruption and downfall.

In doing this we can be caught by our own principles, the greater good is obstructed and prevented in a downward spiral of contention. Internal conflict tends to polarize and further entrench loudly voiced and ever more dogmatic opinion, so that ultimately, support for each extreme coalesces into hostile factions - and the result is a failure of reconciliation.

When support for radical positions prevails in society, it is not just that energy is wasted on internal squabble, the way of the common good - of the Dao - is also lost. In this situation, there are numerous possible negative consequences; democratic institutions can themselves be used against democracy, laws meant to protect the people may be applied unfairly or maliciously to persecute them instead of protecting them, scientific method can be employed for destructive and retrogressive purposes, as opposed to creative and progressive ends.

Since we cannot use force effectively in this predicament, persuasion is called for, and it must be convincing. This situation in society often arises because of a failure in education and upbringing, but more precisely it is a failure of proper leadership, and may therefore become an enduring, perhaps multi-generational problem - tolerance is a two-edged sword here...

Nevertheless, for the old boy, tolerance, symbolized as 'the suppleness of the infant' - is a prime essential, even though it may seem at first to simply prolong an intractable problem by allowing its continuance. Tolerance may be defined as the learned capacity of empathy with another viewpoint and is a key requirement of social relationships that precedes any serious spiritual realization by the individual.

The abolition of intolerance is not something likely to be easily and quickly effected in any society in which it is pervasive, but it can be successfully attacked, for example by a leadership that might foster fear and distrust by demonizing foreigners to deflect attention from their own shortcomings, and by those in authority who suggest that the victim is the real culprit - insinuating perhaps that they brought poverty, homelessness, sickness, violence, or some other disaster upon themselves by behaving in some way counter to that expected of them.

This attitude, though not uncommon, does not put the common good first, it is discriminatory and needs to be addressed, as it represents serious blockage from any further progress on the 'way,' the Dao as a great journey.

Intolerance generally revolves around a rigid adherence to a set of essential principles, and prohibits action - or even thoughts of action sometimes - that an elite leadership group find either dissonant or onerous. Intolerant persons and institutions jealously guard the principles that many others might regard as being extreme and much too far from the mean, and their intolerance is often rooted in an uncompromising black-and-white understanding of the world. Their worldview, is not unusually based in their ethnic and religious identity, may be ultra-conservative, generally rejects innovation, and maybe an early precursor form of fundamentalism.

And fundamentalism of any kind is an extreme position that will always prevent progress.

The difficulty here is that intolerant, fundamentalist views generally cannot be reconciled readily since their viewpoints cannot generally be argued by intellect alone, a much more difficult re-education and re-alignment of faith is needed. This is because fundamentalism is one of Carl Jung's 'isms,' a debased, yet common substitute for the genuine spiritual quest towards the Godhead or the Dao. The proponents of fundamentalism have generally made 'the leap of faith' that makes this extreme position the central reality in their belief system.

Nevertheless, and despite the clear difficulties involved, the old boy would insist that if civilized behavior is to prevail, and working towards the common good is to become the norm, then fundamentalists must be discredited in the eyes of the majority - and have their viewpoints rendered impotent before any real further work on unity can proceed.

In essence, all forms of religious fundamentalism and the glittery-eyed fanaticism it fosters are a perversion of the wisdom as espoused by theologians of the Mosaic tradition, and certainly a perversion of the way - the Dao as great journey. Although the required 'leap of faith' is made by all fundamentalists and their strong commitment represents their 'spiritual' obligation to the cause - a true apprehension of unity in the whole is replaced by a drive towards an unnatural stasis and a focus on external goals.

The crucial acceptance and importance of continuing change is generally denied.

The fundamentalist is a die-hard conservative who takes a quick snapshot, or has a vision of, a supposed golden-era - and then attempts to freeze society, or to move society back to this moment in time for all eternity. The cyclic nature of an ever-changing reality goes unacknowledged by fundamentalists and a movement that may well have begun as the fresh revelation of a pure clean vision, stagnates and becomes irrelevant dogma. In the old boy's terms, fundamentalists have lost the primal receptiveness of the 'spirit in the valley,' and are in denial of the feminine principle of 'yin.' They have fixated on an impossible goal and denied their own selves any real unifying purpose in life in settling for an inferior goal.

Fundamentalists are excessively conservative in their views and have a tendency toward theocracy and authoritarian rule as the favored mode of government. They also are frequently in favor of the promotion of laws based on a strict interpretation of the scriptures. Unfortunately, theocracy is not a mode of government renowned for either progressive liberal policy or enlightened treatment of its peoples - quite the reverse in fact. Carl Jung is just one of any number of observers who have pointed out the sad fact that historically, any ruling elite which proclaims itself in the name of any divine being will invariably set to work to repress and terrify its peoples immediately. (Jung C. G., Psychology and Religion: West and East, 1981)

All the evidence from history is that governments with a 'divine mandate' are infinitely ruthless in seeking to exclude and discredit all opposing viewpoints. They have no compunction in using the cruelest and most ingenious instruments of torture, and far from promoting personal fulfillment, they invariably promote a set of rigid observances that stifle personal growth. From time immemorial, these regimes have invented obscenely bizarre capital punishments for even quite minor failures to observe the conventions imposed by the elite. Fundamentalist states, of whatever religious persuasion, innately oppose any variation from established rote, and they do it by ruthless domination and subjugation by force.

This is one reason why the old boy might justly remark that it is 'leadership without domination' that leads towards the greater good. The truth is that in the reality of his own personal experience, he is much more likely to have witnessed the autocratic whims and excesses of the God-Emperor at first hand than the barbarity of the fundamentalists.

In any event Laozi would say to those who seek to impose their dogma on others: Why bother? If a particular course appeals to you, take it, but do not then expect the rest of humanity to thank you, when you try to force your way on them…

Verse the eleventh: Something from nothing – The germ of change.

Thirty spokes share one hub.
At the center, is the nothingness that makes it serviceable.

Mold the clay to make the pot,
The nothingness inside makes it useful.

Cut out the doors and windows to make a room,
The nothingness created makes the room functional.

When we get something from nothing,
Profit arises from what is there.
Utility arises from what is not there.

For Jean-Paul Sartre, the individual's forced confrontation with the void of non-being is the ultimate apprehension of alienation and despair. Perception of nothingness in existentialist terms is, as was previously discussed, the shadowy awareness of a dark underside to reality, something - though strictly it should be some 'no-thing,' almost infinitesimally admitted into every consciousness. It is an uneasy realization as Sartre acknowledges, perhaps something akin to knowing there may be a maggot in the fruit you are eating.

Daoist doctrine has an encapsulating image for this being - non-being, attraction - repulsion duality; the circular yin-yang diagram denoting unity of all opposites in the whole:

The Daoist 'taijitu' Yin-Yang symbol.

Here, at the heart of the intertwined opposites, black on white and white on black, is a tiny dot denoting the inner germ of the other is visible. It signifies enantiodromia - the great cycle of eternal change whereby things give birth to, and return to, their opposites. The small dots represent the germ of being at the heart of non-being, the chaos at the heart of unity, the nothing at the heart of something and the fullness that comes from emptiness.

This symbol is a representation and reminder that, firstly, it is from the unknown that springs everything that is, or can be known. Secondly, that real understanding comes from realization and integration of the paradoxical nature of reality within the self, and never wholly from some purely rational process of absorption of fact.

Consider some implications, if (as we did once before) we first consider the lines on nothingness below as a kind of joyous affirmation, then read them again, but this time in the knowledge that the 'nothingness' is now something real; a dark and menacing presence of overwhelming power. At this point, our perspective instantly reverses. Now, it is the abyss within that we stare into, and in this dark realm we know lurks the uncontrollable elements of our worst nightmares - all the things that lead us to violence, madness, and loss of self:

Nothing can frighten me.

Nothing can disturb my harmony.
Nothing can stop me.
Nothing can hurt me.

So, are these phrases now reassuring, or threatening?

The old boy tells us that if we are honest with ourselves, and genuinely committed towards always working towards the common good, we are comforted. Jean-Paul Sartre on the other hand maintains from his impeccably argued rationalist and existentialist standpoint that in the striving towards unity that is self-actualization, failure is inevitable, and therefore the message - the very idea of 'nothingness' is threatening to the point of being terrifying. (Sartre, Being and Nothingness, 1993).

To explain this further in psychological terms, Sartre views human consciousness as essentially broken, he describes it as impossible to reconcile the public facade of self that is persona, with our conscious ego identity and what Carl Jung calls our 'unconscious shadow self.' Sartre reaches this conclusion because he rejects the irrational, intuitive and emotional in favor of a purely rational consciousness which is always negatively conscious of the impassable gulf between the internal and external modes of being – in the old boy's idiom, there is no acceptance of the reality of 'going with the flow' - the wholeness of self is denied because a part of the innermost self is denied.

For Laozi, however, firmly on the path of the Dao, and at peace with his innermost self, and having already pointed out the dangers of being overly intellectual at the expense of an intuitive connection with the natural world - the night holds no terrors. He points out in these lines that the usefulness or serviceability of anything might equally depend on what is not present as it does on what is there.

The concept of nothingness has utility for Laozi, he often extols the value of doing nothing, he is not afraid to empty the mind and contemplate the depths within, and here he is pointing out that placing all value in only those things you might be able to touch, feel, see, or rationalize is illusory.

Sometimes it is necessary to let go of that thread of rational evaluation that both benefits and constrains our relationship to the world. There is a message in the emptiness.

What if an absence of thought, feeling, desire, envy, worry, ambition - together with a total acceptance of self - could be all that it takes to achieve harmony?

Verse the twelfth: A world of desire - On avoiding distraction.

Vivid colors blind the eyes,
Voice and music assail the ears.
Varieties of taste assault the palate,
Riding and racing excite the mind.

Earthly pleasures lead one astray.
The wise person looks inside before becoming distracted by the senses,
And by doing this - can choose to let go.

This verse and the next are closely related, and here the theme of 'moderation in all things' is reiterated as one of the guiding principles in the 'Dao De Jing.' However, while the old boy values restraint and moderation, he nevertheless does not suggest that life cannot be lived with enthusiasm and to the full. Laozi does not shrink away from good living, for him the Dao is warmth and humanity, and he addresses his advice to both ordinary individuals and the great leaders of state in the full knowledge and expectation that any person holding to these values and advancing on the path of Dao as great journey might be suitable to fulfill that paramount leader's role.

Laozi has a commitment to living that is open, generous, and whole-hearted, it is also a life of purpose, and in these lines, he is speaking of the dangers of trivial distractions that need to be placed in perspective

- and not allowed to become the main focus of being. The old boy is never overwhelmed or confused by the energy, stress, or trivia of day-to-day events, but this is not to say that he is aloof from celebration, tragedy, and the common concerns of humanity. What does underlie his experience of the richness of life is his appreciation of context - the 'big picture' of the wholeness of life and of its place in nature. For Laozi, each small step taken should be an advancement towards the common good which is the unity of the Dao.

The message of being able to maintain the capacity to 'let go' given here is an insight into what exactly it is that constitutes a good and proper life for everyone from ordinary person to supreme leader.

The beginning of work-on-the-self is also the start of honest insight into what makes us what we are, followed by acceptance of that true nature. In being true to ourselves, we may have to let go of jealousies, resentments, long-held grudges, insecurities, and scathing opinions of both ourselves and others.

In working through and accepting any undesirable or unpleasant facets of our own characters, we gain not just resolution of those personal problematical elements, but also the integrity to recognize that every proper action always leads towards the common good.

Ultimately, the old boy would say that earthly pleasures should accrue quite naturally as a result of living a life consciously directed towards the greater good - but if pursuit of these pleasures becomes the primary focus of ambition in a life - something will inevitably be lost.

Verse the thirteenth: From decency to dishonor - Keeping to the way.

Favor and disgrace are both diversions.
The human body and tribulation are easy familiars.

What is meant by "Favor and disgrace are both diversions?"
One should not be too concerned by loss or gain.
When eminence becomes insignificant, acceptance prevails.

What is meant by "The human body and tribulation are familiars?"
Adversity is the human condition.
Only a lifeless body attracts no misfortune.

The wise, valuing humanity over all - can be trusted with all things.
The wise, loving humanity over all - earn custody of the world.

Jungian philosophy, (Jung C. G., Two Essays on Analytical Psychology, 1981) recognizes that a 'conventional life', the method of living of those who adopt communal values and accept the constraints and mores of respectable society is one alternative to the Dao pathway Laozi outlines as 'work-on-the-self.' Committed soul-searching can be a daunting prospect. Of course, the old boy is relaxed about this, there remain a multiplicity of alternate, albeit less direct, life-paths that might also be taken - effectively or otherwise.

What must be accepted in taking these easier options - if it is even realized by the person so distracted - is the inevitability that the possibility of wholeness in self-realization has been at least temporarily, forsaken for the material solace of the collective mode of life. But it is also true that for many people, this will suffice. The old boy would agree that his 'way' is inaccessible and unknowable for some, though there always remains the inevitability of change in the future to open the path once more.

For those who are committed though, Laozi tells us in these lines that it is these people, who are neither overly impressed by material wealth, nor easily distracted by the delights of earthly existence, who are best suited to exercise leadership.

The old boy might justly regard the phenomenon of 'career' politician and 'career' diplomat with some degree of suspicion and disdain, instinctively holding true to the adage that leadership is best exercised by those who do not seek it with ambition. What becomes of ordinary people when their supreme leaders lack the dedication of true vocation? Might 'career' leaders be as often focused on their own material self as the common good?

Laozi would have nothing of the pettiness that puts personal material wealth before the unification of the whole at any level. We are frequently reminded that when he issues his advice on the conduct of a supreme leader, that advice is as applicable to the lowest citizen as it is to the those entrusted with the well-being of the state itself. The best leaders do not have any arcane knowledge regarding the special nature of leadership, they are simply good, authentic people doing their best for all concerned. Therefore, leadership is something any individual in honest approach to the Dao might be able to undertake.

Those who are judged as the greatest of leaders are not those with the grandest of lifestyles, but those with the grandest, most all-encompassing vision. As might be expected from the old boy, his ideal supreme leader is not primarily an economist, a diplomat, a politician, a military tactician, or a brilliant scholar. The consummate supreme leader is a person who has true 'big-picture' vision, a practical focus on the common good, and a humanitarian outlook untainted by arrogance and pride - and most of all, a light and gentle guiding touch. These attributes are usefully backed by the passion and commitment that accompanies true dedication, and quite possibly, a disregard for self that might border on personal neglect. In other words, an individual who does not place self above others, and is also an honest seeker of the ultimate unity of the Dao...

The principal element in leadership the old boy implies in his verses, is not so much a strategic or tactical ability in matters politic, but a proper orientation of attitude that inspires the people to follow. The perseverance involved in practicing a contemporary 'successful' political career pales by comparison with the efforts of the enlightened leader who is inspired to unselfishly craft every action for the greater good of all of society.

Although, naturally enough, those set on the spiritual path of self-fulfillment might have little interest in complicating their lives with the trivia of political machination, the truth is that as these individuals mature and proceed to reconcile their internal conflicts and become more integrated personalities, it is precisely their disinterest in the material, combined with their natural holistic focus on the common good, which makes them potentially outstanding leaders.

So, the old boy emphasizes, those best suited to wield power and influence are those who do not want them - and those who would most hesitate to use them. In this way, justice, impartiality and the ideal of a light, unassertive and minimalist government is guaranteed. Laozi frequently advises that the wise leader must always seek the greater good of the many without regard to personal advantage. Accordingly, the very best of leaders are prepared to do what is right even at the expense of their own popularity and their own well-being.

This capacity for self-sacrifice is how the old boy would illustrate the difference between the true leader, in constant search for the greater good and thus in harmony with the Dao, and contrast this to the self-serving egotism of the typical seeker of high public office - and certainly the usual career politician, often scrambling for power and personal glory, and regularly prepared to sacrifice honor and integrity to get it.

The old boy often refers to the 'leader' in the singular whereas governments in general are plural organizations. In fact, there is little distinction between the two in the practical application of his message. In the context of his philosophy, 'one' and 'all' are mostly interchangeable, at least in the sense that the recipes for right living and right thinking are just as applicable to groups as they are to individuals. Of course, the old boy might also point out that in a group situation, there is more to go wrong.

Simplicity makes the quest easier; and it needs to be understood by group members that their groups are only the outward manifestations of the individuals who are responsible for them - they have no life of their own. One risk is that any group member may find themselves failing in the Dao as great journey by mistakenly declaring themselves blameless and abdicating their personal responsibilities to the nebulous 'otherness' of the group.

Our organizations, groups, institutions, all need individuals to give them life and purpose and to take personal responsibility for their actions. Wherever someone is attributing responsibility to the non-entity that is the group, there is a failure in the conduct of proper work upon the self. This is a particular problem in the contemporary era of course, as our leaders have enthusiastically embraced the damaging legal fiction that corporate bodies are persons, thus enabling liability to be transferred from the real to the artificial person. While this may be useful in an economic sense, it allows those who act immorally, unethically, and even illegally to pretend they are not responsible - because it was the corporate body which undertook the action, and not the persons who comprised and directed that body.

Perhaps not surprisingly, given the emphasis of the old boy on simplicity and in his recognition of the complications of group dynamics, those who achieve, or seek to achieve enlightenment by approaching the Dao, are often traditionally cast as solitary figures, giving up family, friends, and social status in their personal spiritual quests.

The great sage, the spiritual pilgrim, the rustic monkish recluse; these are all stereotypical loners at the margins of society. However, even though it might be true to say that disengagement from the complex triviality of the everyday is one fast and practical way to obey the old boy's injunction to keep things simple, it does not have to be so. National leaders with the huge responsibilities of state are most definitely not precluded from the way of the Dao, indeed they are urged to follow the path to enlightenment for the sake of their people as well as themselves.

The old boy would be disappointed should we assume that enlightenment is the strict provenance of the hermit, the recluse, or the cloistered ascetic. By now, he might remonstrate, we should know better than that. With eyes flashing under bushy white brows, the old boy enjoins us to look to the example of the unselfconscious humility of some of the great leaders of history, and some of the more ordinary working people, and to see that the world is full of quietly capable travelers on the way.

No individual is ever barred from work-on-the-self, and ultimately, complexity and simplicity are purely states of mind. The pursuit of the Dao is all a matter of individual attitude - and individual application…

Verse the fourteenth: Isolation, self-denial - And connection.

When nothing can be seen - it is formless.
When nothing can be heard - it is beyond understanding.
When nothing can be held - it is called intangible.
These three are indefinable - and joined as one.

This nothing is not-bright, not-dark.
It is not-named, not-substantial.
A shape that melts, a form without essence,
The shadow of something - vague and indistinct.

In this nothing, anything may happen.
In this nothing, no end may be found.
It is the source, an ancient beginning,
This nothing is a familiar eternal thread,
It connects everything.

To a dispassionate observer of contemporary Western culture, it might seem that it is precisely those people who enjoy wealth, power, social position, good family, education, and influence, who also seem to be most prone to feeling the lack of something elemental in their lives. This runs contrary to expectation, but we are all familiar with the stories of those privileged people who defied their apparent natural advantage to suffer pain, sadness, alienation, and depression. There is a distinct grouping of those who are blessed with status and material advantage, but who are also the natural constituents of mental health professionals. They are persons who appear to want for nothing, and yet are in some sense dispossessed...

The old boy would diagnose the problem in an instant. These are the people who have been sidetracked on their spiritual journey. Having achieved material wealth and still found something lacking, they have come to the sad realization that neither fame nor fortune is a shield against the dispossession of alienation. These are quite literally, the lost souls, and even those who enjoy huge public acclaim, distinction in their fields, money, good health, and all the trappings of success, may nevertheless be engaged in substance abuse, have low self-esteem, relationships that fall apart and poor connectivity with the world.

These people are suffering fragmentation of the self and all their wealth and influence cannot assist them in 'finding themselves' - they are unfulfilled.

No one is unduly surprised when a celebrity commits suicide, or any number of highly visible stars of stage and screen mistreat their bodies and die young. Yet, these people are, ostensibly at least, role models, and often a highly publicized inspiration to the ordinary people who value and envy their supposed achievements...

In short, many people who appear to want for nothing, and whose material needs are met, still lead sad and lonely lives. The fact that the psychotherapist has, for many in recent times, usurped the role of priest and confessor for these people is neither here nor there. The old boy is offering us all an enduring message of self-care in his advice on better living.

The perception of the essence that is the Dao is both timeless and universal, and we should never let the neologisms of later theology and the new sciences of politics, psychology and sociology hide the fact that the problems they are addressing are eternal and universal. The real question is then, when we quickly re-examine these lines with our inner vision, what is this 'nothing' these people are wanting?

In this passage above, the old boy is telling us just what this ethereal essence is, and pausing for a moment to appreciate it. It is the amorphous, nameless, fuzzy, wholeness of the Dao, but all as characterized in negatives. It is the primal urge towards the connectedness of Godhead, unity, of self-fulfillment of individual potential. The 'nothing' that people want is that tiny, unknown part of the inner self that haunts our sub-consciousness. It is irrational and frighteningly enigmatic. It is shapeless and mysterious, capable of metamorphosis into many forms. It is opaque to most inward vision and resists probing analysis. It is the source and fountain of our creativity - but also perhaps - our shame. Some may label this our 'dark side.' Carl Jung would call it our 'shadow.' The only thing we can say about it, is that, if we are honest and aware, we know it is there, even when we dismiss it as 'nothing.'

But - it is all that remains to complete us.

The universal source of the angst that causes the recklessly self-destructive behavior, and that plagues the waking hours of those trapped in what may appear as the barren deserts of fame and fortune is of course, immediately recognizable to the old boy. The way of the greater good has been forsaken. This is the individual's straightforward apprehension of their own lack of wholeness, caused by inability to grasp that final non-rational piece of their own hidden being.

The old boy has the cure for this malady, it is the sense of purpose gained by making a conscious effort to make every decision and every action contingent on its being actively working towards the common good, in other words – in beginning proper work-on-the-self.

It is ironic that those whose material needs are well and truly satisfied are sometimes more prone to experiencing this angst than others with less material possessions. But this situation is hardly surprising when you consider the dynamics of human striving towards inner peace. The first necessities for humanity, as they are for all species of life on earth, are to feed and breed.

Contemporary psychologist Abraham Maslow expressed the imperatives of life very well in formulating his famed 'Hierarchy of needs.' With this model of human development, he postulates that spiritual matters will generally only become a pressing issue when basic material needs are met, and survival is no longer an issue. (Maslow, 1987)

Maslow envisages a pyramidal model of individual growth with physical needs and personal safety as the first priorities in life. Next in importance are relationships; love and belonging, the connectedness of family, the bonds of friendship, and once these are achieved and the individual is a part of a secure community, then comes self-confidence, career, and status and respect in the community. Finally, when a person has an assured physical place in the world, the conscious mind can begin to focus more on the inner self and matters spiritual at the apex of the pyramid - and only then can the process of self-actualization really begin.

This is a progression the old boy would undoubtedly agree with, and one reason why he enjoins us to 'keep it simple' For many, total freedom from the need to provide for survival will never arise, for these people their commitment to the nurture of family and the provision of material comforts is sufficient justification and focus for their lives, and they will not seek the unity of the Dao - or at least not until they become conscious, perhaps much later in life, of that nagging feeling of something left undone, a task that still needs to be tackled...

For those with no further material needs, lack of a spiritual goal means they have nothing left to do in life - and yet they still feel incomplete, there is a lack of something vital within their being. Sartre's view is that fundamentally, human consciousness is always defined as a lack of something. In his terms, conscious awareness, being aware of its incomplete nature, always needs something other to feel complete and truly be itself. (Sartre, Being and Nothingness, 1993) In this light, it may be that those who lack material possessions are in some sense, favored by providence, they can still believe (though falsely in the longer term) that life's meaning can be achieved in simply realizing their material goals...

Laozi's advice to those in the grip of this angst of lack and loss would be given with an emphatic glint of the eye and with white beard bristling: Say "Yes' to the unknown within! Be what you are! Total affirmation of you is total affirmation of the whole. You can adopt a public persona if you wish, but you are not free to pick and choose the 'you' within. You are just what you are and remain so until your actuality is accepted. In refusing to acknowledge some part of yourself lies the source of your despair, your alienation, and your ennui. In the nothing within, that you so casually dismiss as not-really-you and not important or not needed - is all creativity, all harmony, and most importantly - all possibility of ever changing.

The old boy knows the wisdom of learning to treasure life, even with all its blemishes; the grim, the hostile, the perverse, the multitude of imperfections. This is not about becoming perfect, and there really is no choice. When you refuse to accept the smallest part of what truly is, and what you really are - the whole is forever denied.

Carl Jung was in absolute agreement with this when he made the point that self-actualization in the individual is not a matter of becoming faultless, it is a matter of being whole and complete. He uses the symbol of the 'thorn in the flesh' for all those imperfections of self that we need to fully embrace before there can be any real advancement in our personal growth and development. (Jung C. G., Psychology and Alchemy, 1981)

When it comes to this point, at which the most disagreeable aspects of the self must necessarily be confronted, this is the question that should be asked:

When you deny yourself, who suffers?

Verse the fifteenth: Glory days - A glimpse of transcendence.

From ancient times the wise were subtle and mysterious.
Profound and unfathomable - they are described, but not defined.
They were tentative, like those crossing a stream in winter,
And circumspect, like those aware of danger.
They were as courteous as the welcome guest,
As yielding as the ice in thaw,
As simple as the sculptor's uncarved block,
As empty as the open spaces,
As opaque as the muddy waters.

Yet those who can rest will see the waters settle and clear.
Knowing how to rest, they will also know the time for action.
The wise seek no fulfillment.
They are continually remade in acceptance of now.

Every culture has its 'golden age,' that often semi-mythical past when the world was young and pure, nobility and wisdom ruled, and lives were so much richer than today. Laozi is no exception, and here he recalls those great sages and leaders of the past whose mastery of Daoist principles provide us with a model for harmonious living.

Naturally enough for the old boy, we are not talking here about lives of luxurious splendor, rather he describes modest, cautious, humble, and honest people whose simple, thoughtful lives are absolutely in tune with their time and their place. These are individuals who have no desire for high reputation or outstanding ability, and yet these qualities are somehow always associated with them.

The old boy uses the simile of the 'uncarved block' here to express potential. When the sculptor chisels the unremarkable piece of stone, or block of wood, at first, we have no idea of the artistic masterpiece it can become. Likewise, the commonplace outward demeanor of the enlightened master shows no inkling of the possibilities and profound depths within.

The old boy is also pointing to the fact that in these earlier, simpler times, a clean and uncluttered outlook was the more normal state of being and might make the journey easier for those on the path of self-actualization in the Dao. In this respect Laozi was quite prophetic in that he did present his own message in a less confused and simpler time.

In later Confucian times, the work of Laozi, already centuries old, began to suffer the fate that eventually befalls all serviceable accounts of personal enlightenment. The 'Dao De Jing' became, like the Bible in Western culture, the object of study of entire and often rival, schools of thought and, just as the variant interpretations of the Bible were the inspiration for a plethora of sectarian divisions within the original Catholic framework of the Christian religion, so it was with the 'Dao De Jing.' The consequence of this for the old boy and his lean, pared down philosophy was predictable; there was a great deal of arid intellectualizing and some hardening of opinion on the meaning and import of his text.

As successive layers of complex theory and conjecture, proposed reinterpretations, and changes in emphasis obscured the principles the old boy initially outlined in such deliberate stark simplicity, some crucial elements were inevitably lost in the mountains of revision. Scholarly reputations were built and destroyed based on specific re-interpretations of the 'Dao De Jing,' factions were formed and re-formed as some viewpoints crystallized into dogmatic positions lasting for generations. Inevitably in this process, the emphasis shifted from the simple goal of reaching for the whole of the Dao to much exhaustive examination of its constituent parts, and the real meaning the old boy was trying so hard to express, became increasingly difficult to discern.

Confucianism is much more a rational intellectual exercise than Laozi's spiritually focused and simple Daoist teaching. Together, these schools of thought became sufficiently admired and respected to inspire the later insights and clean simplifications of the Buddhist Zen masters - but there was a cost. As the scholarly edifice built up around the idea of the Dao, and despite the incisive analysis of many Confucian thinkers and the sophistication of their aesthetic insights, the inevitable downside was eventually revealed. The raw power of the Laozi teaching not only became diluted and obscured in a clutter of wordy constructs and dogmatic pronouncements, but also an intimate knowledge of his ideas moved from being the province of the ordinary educated individual, to the province of 'experts...'

Laozi's dislike of 'cleverness.' in this context was far-sighted. While he would never advocate that one should literally discard all knowledge in pursuit of enlightenment, he always remains adamant that any purely rational approach is insufficient for any true understanding of the essence that is the Dao. Some of the 'rationalizations' of these numerous later scholars produced a kind of factual overlay of knowledge and conjecture on the text that was little better than mental debris in terms of usefulness.

This highlights a type of potential obstruction on the path of the Dao, something the old boy mentions more than once in the text. This is the observation that the highly educated mind, steeped in empirical method, nurtured on logic, founded in cause and effect and skeptical of all things remotely metaphysical, finds no end of obstacles in pursuing the amorphous substance of the encompassing wholeness that is Dao. Just as the rationalizations of the later Confucian school often did little to make the Laozi's overall meaning any clearer, navigating the 'Dao De Jing' by intellect alone is a losing proposition.

It is both irony and saving grace for the ideas as expressed in the 'Dao De Jing' that a person of simple education may often be more flexible and accepting of the mysterious whole and less inclined to doggedly rationalize where direct apprehension through insight and meditation on the self is required.

And so, by this circuitous route, we return to the meaning of the lines above. The old boy is telling us quite clearly: Relax, enjoy life, don't muddy the waters, accept the reality around you, no need to overthink it, be calm, be patient, and allow yourself to listen to your intuition.

When you are fully engaged and enjoying the moment that is now - you are already on the right track.

Verse the sixteenth: The evolutionary great cycle – Tranquility of mind.

Empty your mind of customary thought, belief, prejudice, and desire.
When reason stills - greater truths are revealed.
In quiet contemplation of life's diversity,
Begins the understanding that leads to wisdom.

When you can return to this source of stillness,
You will be in tune with the natural rhythms of all life,
In harmony with your own place and destiny in the world.
To act willfully without this understanding risks disaster.
But, with this awareness your mind and heart will open,
Impartiality of thought and action will be yours,

From this center springs dignity and nobility of spirit,
And from this again - the highest possible good.
You will be at one to the end of your days,
Knowing that to reach for the greater good, and be still -
Is to achieve something timeless.

These lines expand upon the theme in the preceding lines, as we have seen, the old boy disparages 'cleverness' - the mistaken notion that 'wisdom' and 'knowledge' are somehow synonymous, and the overvaluation of the type of learning which is just the aimless acquisition of facts. Here he warns against the situation that arises when some demonstrated knowledge and the articulate expression of a limited viewpoint are confused with genuine wisdom - and reiterates that there is no directly intellectual, logical, rational means to comprehend the wholeness of the Dao.

This is not to say however that it is always impossible through rational endeavor to advance some way towards the unified simplicity of the whole, the old boy would be the first to advise that the ways to self-unity and harmony are many and everyone must begin with the resources and tools at hand. There is scope to advance at least a part of the way towards enlightenment anywhere, and certainly those exploring the frontier sciences of physics, mathematics, and astronomy may already have some useful rational insights and positive ways of thinking that may assist them on the way. A sense of awe and wonder at the miracles of the universe and the natural world around us, are also very appropriate starting points.

Nonetheless, at some point on any successful journey along the way, life's essential paradox must be confronted and the polarities in its nature accepted, reconciled, and integrated. The old boy de-stresses knowledge and learning in this context not because of any innate bias against erudition or scholastic achievement, but because there is literally no point in attempting any scientific analysis of the Dao essence. Even the most highly trained mind will need to accept the necessity to abandon logic and traverse unknown mental terrain in striving towards the nature of the Dao. To succeed, one must confront the inner demons of one's own self...

This idea is not limited to the spiritual message of Laozi. All faiths and creeds concerned with some form of ultimate enlightenment, unity, or self-actualization of the individual have some point at which the follower, in choosing to be a true believer, must abandon the life-raft of conventional thinking and logic. This is a universal constant in the quest for individual fulfillment.

In Christianity as for other major religions, this moment is often described as the 'leap of faith.' For the old boy, this is not really a leap of faith at all, 'approaching the gateway to the manifold mysteries,' is more aptly, to surrender to the need to accept the reality of your own innermost self – a process which may or may not be difficult and disturbing depending upon what skeletons are to be found in the closet...

In the characteristically bleak terms Sartre would use, this can be a time of despair in facing an inner emptiness - staring into the abyss of the soul. Not that the old boy would agree on this, he is firmly of the view that this process of acceptance of the self can be significantly easier provided you are prepared to honestly examine, and then extend forgiveness to the self rather than agonizing over prior hurts and mistakes. Though the past cannot be changed - the future can.

Regarding the idea of the 'leap of faith,' there are some very strong parallels here. Just as in religious tradition the 'leap of faith' involves a personal commitment that cannot be rationally justified, so it is with the Dao. Enlightenment cannot be attained by conventional reason alone, there must be some kind of feeling, intuition, recognition of something previously unknown or repressed within the self - hence the old boy's advice at the beginning of the verse above:

> *Empty your mind of customary thought, belief, prejudice, and desire.*
> *When reason stills - greater truths are revealed.*

The old boy is giving us his vision of the great cycle of change that is the eternal natural order – and asking us to accept our place in it.

Verse the seventeenth: Strength in weakness - Power in the unseen.

The highest good is like the best government - barely noticed by ordinary people.
Next best is the known and the cherished,
Then comes that which is detestable,
Then that which is scorned.
Where faith and trust are lacking, nothing good can come.

When the common good is properly addressed,
The work is accomplished without unnecessary fanfare,
And the people say, 'It just seemed to happen naturally!'

If, when traveling in foreign parts, you should happen to notice that every available surface of every public building seems to have a portrait of the local 'dear and glorious leader' – you can be fairly sure that you are looking at someone who is not generally held in high esteem. In fact, the more pictorial representations there are, the greater the possibility that you are looking at a person hated, reviled, and feared by the masses.

As the old boy puts it, the greater good is accomplished without fanfare and the best governments rule with the lightest of hands, offering the people all the creative freedom and developmental opportunities they need for a life of contentment and fulfillment. Self-aggrandizement has no place in this design.

The global politics of the of the last few centuries have largely revolved around the development of industrial capacity, and the means to employ that power to consolidate control and supremacy. This technological might has furthered the pursuit of state imperial ambitions around the world. As governance crossed international boundaries, so in turn has the influence of the corporate bodies which have now become multi-national bodies. Along the way, the small elite bands who control these groups have become vastly stronger and more powerful.

In our day and age, we hear a lot about how 'strong' government is desirable and required, and how 'strong' leadership is needed and best for all. If we are to genuinely progress however, the old boy will quietly deny that this type of governance and leadership is the best solution. What is really needed, and what is most in tune with his ideal, is the lightest possible form of administration that can maintain infrastructure and social services for all of its people.

As always, Laozi is of the view that moderation in all things, in combination with a delicate administrative touch, is the key to good governance. Some solid support for the truth of this observance is to be found in the historical actuality that weaker governments simply do not have the power to really repress their people. Also, and for similar reasons, weaker governments must negotiate where stronger governments would not hesitate in using force, they cannot readily declare wars of aggression on neighboring countries.

Similarly, because they are conscious of the power of the people, weak governments are unable to impose harshly punitive laws on their citizens, and they do not behave like predators when dealing with the goods and chattels of ordinary men and women. Weak governments need the continued approval and support of the people and must be accountable and always at the service of their constituent citizenry. Strong governments by contrast are capable of repression and are far more commonly at the service of their controlling cliques.

In our age, strong government with its focus on the conventional wisdom the old boy calls 'cleverness,' and its tendency to over-steer on policy from one radical extreme to another is much the accepted norm. Those who really control and influence these governments are the career politicians, the captains of industry and their attendant contingents of lawyers and other facilitators, all clever, rational people - but in most cases at least, hardly altruistically motivated towards the greater good for all.

Laozi tells us quite firmly and clearly that the 'cleverness' of this ruling inner circle is something that prevents any real progress. Responsibility must always be shouldered by the individual, but here it is commonly assigned to the group. No one is accepting fault for mismanagement, and if our governing bodies are promoting irresponsible and ill-conceived solutions, the result is that our quality of life suffers.

And if they behave unjustly and immorally, we are tainted as well.

To the extent that we maintain the comfortable fiction that the corporate entities that we are members of are pseudo-people, able to take the blame and somehow separate from us – we remain in denial of any true reconciliation of our reality by failing to assume our own rightful responsibilities.

In this way the Dao ideal fades ever more from view…

Verse the eighteenth: Regression - Weakness, pretension, and turmoil.

When the greater good cannot be found,
Pretense and hypocrisy rule.
Then appears 'benevolence' and 'moral outrage.'
And 'rationality' replaces wisdom.

When families are in turmoil,
They pretend to stand together in harmony.

When governments are in turmoil,
Ministers compete in pledging their loyalty.

Here Laozi is following on from his ideas on government and communities in general in the previous lines and telling us what happens when the path of the common good is lost.

The Dao become unattainable once leadership has failed in working towards the common good, or at a more individual and personal level, when the bonds of family and community are dissolved or weakened by selfish, partisan, or ill-considered actions. Essentially, we have settled, or been forced to settle, for second-best. We are in a realm of suspicion and mistrust. Pretense and hypocrisy are all around, but we seem powerless in the face of this adversity.

Although outright conflict may have been avoided to this point, there is strong disagreement, great unease, and substantial loss of respect in this situation. All this is accompanied by a lack of loyalty and devotion. Instead of being a unified community, society is divided into contentious, and sometimes bitterly opposed factional groupings.

When this loss happens at national leadership level, it could be that the ruling person or group is cynically self-serving, or indeed, may genuinely have the best of intentions, but nevertheless be failing to make the desired positive impact. The problem is that benign intentions are simply not enough. Though given the benefit of the doubt, the leadership may not be up to the task. Even a benevolent or generous regard for other people can never guarantee that some terrible mistake will not be made. This is because, although good intent may reflect a certain sincerity, there is a lack of true understanding as to what constitutes the common good - and this inevitably will lead to the implementation of some 'cleverly' formulated, but inferior solution in the form of policy that misses the intended mark.

If the 'big-picture' holistic vision is lacking, things will certainly go wrong.

In the context of family and community relationships, the bonds within and between the groups are weakened, and genuine binding regard and allegiance is replaced by an uneasy facade of solidarity, together with a somewhat conditional acceptance of interpersonal and group relations with expectations and caveats, as well as some suspicion regarding motives, on all sides.

The old boy points here to the fragile nature of loyalty and regard. On the true path of the Dao, there is no turmoil or opposition, these things simply disappear once harmony in thought and action aimed always towards the greater, or common good is established. But, once calm is lost and confrontation looms, then the way is also lost. At times like these, struggles for power arise, both at state and family and community level, and those who are most vocal in offering their support – may also turn out to be the least trustworthy in the longer term.

The old boy tells us; the greatest of leaders do not simply deploy their vast reserves of specialized knowledge and all is automatically made right - they must make every decision in full awareness of what constitutes the greater good.

Verse the nineteenth: On the frontiers of knowledge - Dilemma.

When conventional wisdom is renounced,
And popular icons are coolly appraised.
Things become a hundred times better.

When we question our own roles, examine our own ethical base,
We rediscover some fundamental values.

When we cease our machinations, place profit in perspective,
Theft and fraud are done with.

There is more to our vocation than a thin veneer of pretense,
Look inwards for the simple truths,
Banish selfish thoughts. Appreciate what you have.

Carl Jung said that "Science comes to a stop at the frontiers of logic, but nature does not - she thrives on ground as yet untrodden by theory." (Jung C. G., The Practice of Psychotherapy, 1981)

The old boy would have no problem with that. In accepting the totality that is our real self, we accept the way things really are, we peel away obscurity, we re-examine, re-evaluate, and we try to accept that some of the things we considered, until now, to be our 'reality' may be illusory. All that we are and know, may be just a part-thing, bound by words and convention, but ultimately, something decidedly less than the whole.

In peeling back the layers, evaluating our real convictions, discarding embellishment and posturing, we can be released from the constraints of the persona we have built for ourselves. This is the beginning of real freedom.

To take this idea further, Laozi would say that in freedom is truth, and truth is a renewal of the self. However, direct experience of this revelation of freedom, as Sartre pointed out, is not always an occasion for joy and wonder, as was already discussed, it can be either ecstatic or terrifying. For a person on the spiritual way of the Dao, embracing freedom of the self is also opening the mind to the knowledge, or perhaps more properly the intuitive awareness, of a possible inner emptiness or lack, to be considered, accepted, and thus reconciled.

This spiritual 'itch' takes the form of some nagging need within, a requirement for the 'something else' that is still necessary for self-realization, a something that will finally make us into the person we want to be. In the old boy's terms, this 'something' is the discovery of the real relationship of the myriad parts of our existence, internal and external, as they relate to the whole, and how self-integration may be finally achieved - or lost.

In existentialist terms, the apprehension of this freedom is very much a two-edged sword. For one striving towards unity of self, it is the elation of being firmly on the path and within sight of the goal, and the sense of progressing towards continual personal renewal. But, for one who, like Jean-Paul Sartre, is making an intellectual commitment to resist anything which is not rational and empirical, and is thus prepared to reject the possibility of individual wholeness as forever unattainable - freedom can also be the agonizing knowledge that one has burned one's bridges. (Sartre, Being and Nothingness, 1993)

This degree of personal insight and commitment, once acquired through intellectual analysis, will effectively prevent any return to the blissful innocence of simple ignorance. The individual is self-realized as alienated, and now in a real sense as Sartre phrases it "condemned to be free" - cast adrift and isolated with the knowledge that the wholeness they seek is beyond reach forever.

It is here that the Sartrean reality approaches its grimmest of pronouncements. Since knowledge cannot realistically be un-acquired, nothing can cure this, which means in turn that the highly advanced intellect must be abandoned and the irrational nature of nothingness embraced. For those who would prize intellect above all, this must seem nothing less than the voluntary embrace of insanity. This is a very difficult situation indeed – but one which a host of creative talents have faced in the past – Nietzsche and Van Gogh among many others.

It is often said that a fine line separates madness and genius. It is somewhere around here that this fine line is drawn...

Verse the twentieth: On overthinking – The virtue of simplicity.

Where there is no knowledge there can be no worry.

What separates yes and no?
What differentiates good and evil?

If you are deterred by the fears you sense in others,
Your potential will not be realized.

Not fearing, I see people enjoying life,
Seeing families on outings, in parks and on terraces,
I am at peace with myself.
Like a baby that has not yet learned to smile, I reveal little.
Though others appear to have plenty, my needs are slight.
Though my thoughts seem slow I am complete,
Others shine while I appear dim,
Others are clever while I appear dull,
When everyone else displays purpose, I drift through life.

I place no value on superficial appearance,
And have no urge towards conformity.
Glimpsing the common good I have purpose, direction, and fulfillment.

Some commentators suggest that this passage, with its somewhat distinctive style, may be a later revision or addition to the 'Dao De Jing,' it is certainly overlooked or only partially included in some editions. Those reservations aside, the message is still quite coherent. Any bona fide traveler on the way, the great journey towards the Dao, must be prepared to let humility conquer ego to succeed in any genuine quest for spiritual fulfillment.

This requires an appreciation that intellectual ability may foster its own brand of arrogance and egocentric disdain. Over-rationalized and self-centered views of the world represent imbalance. Those hoping to approach the Dao must be open enough to accept the raw facts, the chaos, and the paradoxical nature of reality, however unpalatable this is.

The injunction of the old boy at this point is this; don't overthink the problem, be sufficient in your own self and do not fear or envy the experiences of others. When looking honestly within, no compromise can be made as it is not acceptable to simply reject what cannot be explained. If this means that some previously accepted teachings need to be discarded – then so be it... we learn as much from things that go wrong as those that go right.

By way of contrast to this dilemma facing these rational and logically focused 'educated' souls, the old boy also recognizes what may be considered as a kind of natural advantage for the ordinary person who is naturally in tune with the environment. This is something mentioned in passing several times before, the fact that the simplicity of outlook of a very ordinary life already has some of the features that those seeking their own innermost truth try so hard to attain.

In a sense, any approach towards the unity of the Dao is a quest for a return to a foundation of common values. In this respect, it should not be forgotten that the simplicity, honesty, uncomplicated integrity and direct intuition of an intelligent child or a naive young adult, represents a well-traveled route towards the unity of the whole...

With the parallel example of Winnie-the-Pooh - the 'Bear-of-Little-Brain' to guide us, we can see that the old boy respects the fundamental integrity of the unsophisticated standards of the honest ordinary person. That is because he recognizes that someone untainted by prejudice or bigotry, accepting of a humble position in life, and full of awe for the marvels of nature, is already somewhat advanced upon on the way of Dao as great journey. The community-oriented ethos, the lack of ego-driven ambition, the ability to find contentment in a modest allotment of worldly goods - all of these can be natural advantages for the soul-searcher at the so-called 'lower stratum' of society.

Indeed, one of the best ways to de-emphasize the intellectual rigor of the quest for spiritual fulfillment is probably to take an example straight out of the book of the children's fictional character, (and Daoist adept), Winnie the Pooh. (Milne, 1944)

In wondering vaguely how to organize his daily life, Pooh would simply sing a hummy sort of song, admiring the birds and butterflies, and spend time appreciating the wind in the trees as he strolled. In this apparently unstructured way, and by dint of an open mind, the 'Bear-of-Little-Brain,' would let any problematical situation resolve itself without discernible conscious effort.

If you consider that all work-on-the-self is reconciliation of opposing elements, and that opposition of the ebb and flow of natural events is a reckless waste of energy, this methodology of contented acceptance appears shrewd. After all, the more opposition encountered, the greater the work to do. But for those who are already reconciled to their situation, and who sense no opposition from nature, advancement towards the Dao proceeds essentially unopposed. It would be unkind to characterize this in terms of the adage 'ignorance is bliss,' the old boy would say that recognition of being attuned to the natural order and acceptance of the inevitability of the vastly changeable nature of existence, gives any individual an advantage in approaching the Dao.

As for accepting contradiction, why think of these things in terms of opposed force anyway? There would be no 'high' without a corresponding 'low' by which to measure it. 'Appreciation,' is balanced by 'indifference', 'righteousness' by 'misconduct,' and the two ends of a piece of string, no matter how far apart, may still be joined to form a circle...

Life is a continuum with room for both logic and emotion. 'Good' needs at least the concept of 'bad' to retain its character as good - and everything has its place. It is true of course, that between saying these words, and realizing them within the self, there is still a world of difference...

Verse the twenty-first: On searching in the obvious places first – Work and play.

The greatest good lies in only one direction.
And that way is at first vague and indistinct.

But within the shadows of your unknown self is an image,
Within the image is a substance,
And in the darkness of the substance lies an essence.

This essence is the key to understanding,
And the means to realize your proper place in the world,
From your unknown beginnings to the overflowing abundance of now...

Simplicity.

The old boy stresses repeatedly that we should not get carried away and begin to exert all our strength in energetically striving towards the all-embracing Dao. Should we do so, we will be expending effort for little reward. This is because hard endeavor and concerted effort is not a prerequisite of the way of the Dao, and everything we need to start the task of work-on-the-self is already within our grasp.

Here Laozi is asking us to trust our intuition, and focus on the inner vision, to realize for ourselves that all the answers are already to hand. We need to return to the basics of our lives on a regular basis and re-evaluate our place in the world, what we are doing and who we are.

The answer to the question, 'how best to live our lives?' is to be found in the contemplation of the unexplored, 'dark shadows' of the innermost self. This work-on-the-self is best accomplished by also understanding the occasional need to simply relax, take a deep breath and take the time to appreciate the environment, to enjoy the landscape, the weather, and the season. We need to re-charge our batteries, engage in the inconsequential and envisage ourselves as a part of nature, and not something removed from it or external to it.

In this sense, our more contemporary, objective, externalized perspectives, while providing a wealth of rational insights, may also be ultimately hindering our final understanding of the Daoist essence. Instead of considering the 'big picture,' in an objective manner we should begin to feel our subjective relationship with it and within it.

Carl Jung speaks in his writings of a "natural gradient" that transforms energy to produce what we determine to be 'natural phenomena.' This is not 'work' in any real sense, but is in accord with the idea that living a natural life is also not work, rather it is the ordinary progression of meeting the needs of a normal life. It is our cultural bias that harnesses and amplifies this energy gradient and creates the machines of industry that in turn give us consumer surplus and the Western concept of 'real work,' and along with that, the concept of the 'work ethic' that is deeply ingrained in our nature. (Jung C. G., The Structure and Dynamics of the Psyche, 1981)

This 'natural gradient' that is not 'work' is something akin to what the old boy tells us is the principle of overcoming by inaction, of simply going with the flow and doing what is needed to sustain life. But the fact is, we are all products of our cultures and, accustomed to believing that extraordinary effort will lead to extraordinary success.

Laozi will immediately advise that in terms of rendering assistance on the path of the Dao, this is wrong - nothing the old boy has to say in the 'Dao De Jing' offers support for this popular chain of cause and effect. Furthermore, we have already been warned that no amount of enthusiastic intellectualizing and energetic fostering of our striving towards the Dao will help us cross the final hurdles towards self-realization.

The old boy might additionally remind us that the very act of 'striving' is indicative of a degree of desire and neediness, which represents a form of ambition - and therefore a blockage along the way. At some point before any kind of enlightenment is achieved, there must be an end to all striving, an end to wanting, an end to all desire for the unattainable, and an unconditional acceptance of what really is.

There is a sense then in which the Dao is reached at the precise moment when we stop trying make it happen - and simply look inside and let it happen.

Verse the twenty-second: Bend before you break – The advantages of humility and acceptance.

By not opposing the natural course of events, the wise are not opposed.
What bends in the wind straightens with no damage.
To be receptive is to be capable of fulfillment,

What is worn can be renewed.
Small gains may bring major benefit,
When large gains might bring only uncertainty.

Knowing this, the wise accept contradiction, in embracing the whole.
Without being eminent, they become a model,
Without receiving acclamation, they are distinguished.
Without self-promotion, they are recognized,
Without conceit, their merit endures.

Having no disagreements, the wise have no enemies in the world.
In not opposing the natural course of events, they overcome adversity.
This ancient wisdom is the way to the wholeness of life.

When he condemns the 'cleverness' that masquerades as wisdom, the old boy does this in the full knowledge that the intellectual edifices by which people define and interpret their lives are also the filters and lenses that distort their personal realities. By 'rationalizing,' that is, by the mental processing and filtering of the import of direct experience and intuition, some cognitive content is enhanced, some added, some toned down and some is most likely ignored completely.

In addition to stressing acceptance and self-effacement, Laozi is once again here hammering home the message that by obscuring and re-shaping the essentials of experience and perpetuating an ersatz reality, an overly-developed rational intellect without an extremely open mind, can be a serious encumbrance to a genuine, honest exploration of the inmost self. It would however, be incorrect to say that the old boy is telling us here that education and knowledge in general represent a liability - far from it.

The warning here is that excessive reliance on highly developed skills in rational analysis might amount to an intellectually focused bias, an intolerance or even a rejection of the intuitive and emotional aspects of the self - and that could be an impediment on the path of the Dao. Perhaps this logical faculty engenders a certain intellectual arrogance, and possibly it reduces an individual's sensitivity to what is still to be discovered, thereby encouraging a false sense of accomplishment - in a circumstance which clearly indicates there is still serious work-on-the-self to be done.

Any bona fide traveler on the way; the great journey towards the Dao, must be prepared to let humility conquer ego to succeed in any genuine quest for spirituality. This requires an appreciation that intellectual ability may foster its own brand of conceit and egocentric disdain. Over-rationalized and self-centered views of the world represent imbalance. Those hoping to approach the Dao must be open enough to accept the raw facts, the chaos, and the paradoxical nature of reality, however unpalatable this is.

In the lines above, the old boy describes the benefits of this holistic approach to life which is founded in the rather simple and non-confrontational idea of acceptance of what is, coupled with the unselfish outlook and action that marks progress towards the common good.

Laozi is also here clearly advocating that this is not only the best way to live - it is the easiest and most fulfilling way to live.

Verse the twenty-third: A place in the cosmos – The ebb and flow of nature.

Explanations cannot always be made, or always required.
High winds give way to heavy rain that does not last.
It is the nature of all things to change over time.

And so, because everything is always and forever in transition.
Attempt no rigid definition of the possible,
- but accept the eternal in the changing whole.

Being at one is the only true expression of your nature.
You are the reflection of all your personal experience.

In acceptance of the whole - even loss will not concern you.
With tolerance and understanding - you experience glad affirmation.
If you have no trust in this - you will not be trusted either.

Change, impermanence, dynamism, an endless ebb and flow, these are just some of the paradoxical characteristics of the constant that is the Dao. No real comprehension of the old boy's message is possible until the truth-seeker begins to recognize that everything previously accepted as solid and immutable is actually fluid and in constant motion.

It is all a matter of gaining a perception of the universal scale of things.

Our understanding of time is a limited thing, geared to our bodily wants and needs, the flux of night and day, the rhythms, and seasons of a lifetime. But, as always, the old boy would tell us that there is a bigger picture to grasp. Not all events take place on the time scale that is easily accessible, recognizable, or even perceptible to humanity - there is a ceaseless background motion of which we are all generally oblivious.

Perceptual experience is all a matter of scale; a ball of tar in a laboratory appears as static as rock, but given 50 years or so, will demonstrate its fluidity and drip through a funnel into a beaker. Plants apparently rooted in their surrounds, when seen in time-lapse photography encroach, extend, and aggressively explore their surrounds, only to retract, wither and die, or colonize and flourish on a breathtaking scale. It is only the constraints of our normal perception of time and space that makes this perpetual motion undetectable to our senses.

On a greater scale yet, as the ages pass, mountains are pushed skyward by the colossal forces of tectonic movement, only to be dissolved, broken down and reduced to dust by the eroding action of wind and water over countless millennia. As the great cycle proceeds, the mountains are forced skywards yet again by inexorable continental forces and the oceans retreat and then overcome low-lying land masses in unimaginably long natural cycles.

And beyond even that mighty tide of events, we live in a universe in which the passing of tens of millennia are but the blink of an eye. On this epochal scale, raw material is sucked into the cosmic vortex of newly formed galaxies to coalesce into planets and stars that will last for billions of years; then, inevitably given the cyclic, ever-changing enantiodromia of the universe - they are engulfed again in another vast cataclysm that in turn spews out new suns and planets into the void...

The Dao embraces all this; the majestic rhythms of the vast cosmic order, and the almost unimaginable concept of timelessness itself.

What the old boy is asking us to do, given that we are sincere in our quest for personal enlightenment, is to embrace as much of the totality of nature as our minds are capable of grasping. Advancement towards the greater good is always contingent on the acceptance of the individual's place in the universal scheme of things.

It is not that the raw facts of our historical and geographic situation are particularly important. What is required to further the personal development of the individual is the humility that arises from the full realization that each human life is an insignificant speck in the cosmic scheme.

The secondary effect of this humility and acceptance is to foster the sense of natural belonging in being a small, but integral part of this vast natural cycle.

Verse the twenty-fourth: On inner vision – A question of balance.

There is no stability on tiptoes.
And big strides do not guarantee progress.
Pretense does not confer real esteem.
Nor self-righteousness admiration.

Do not use idle boasts to feed your affectation.
Accept no false regard.
Abandon the excess baggage of your conceit.
Or - you will lose sight of the path of wholeness.

Our Western cultural values predispose us in some typical, recurring ways towards an experience of predictable difficulties on the great way of the Dao. A keen sense of natural balance is what the old boy is telling us is required here. We must not automatically assume that our dedication, concerted action, and sustained effort implies that we are any closer to the goal.

While massive effort might appear to warrant some success in the approach to the Dao, the old boy has already intimated that such is not the case. Taking great pride in our efforts and nurturing the pretension that we must be getting closer to the objective is simply another form of blockage. The mystery that is the Dao essence does not reveal itself automatically to one who relies on the sophistry that a good education, the ability to employ strenuous effort, and the ability to comprehend a vast array of factual data represents a significant advantage.

In Jungian terms, the Dao essence must be approached without hubris - via both rational consciousness and via the subconscious resources of intuition that we all have inside us. And therein lies the problem, the subconscious can be a dark and mysteriously inaccessible - even a forbidding place – and yet, here, ultimately, the old boy tells us, is where the path of the Dao is to be found - within.

Jung further expressed the view that our contemporary Western mind, lacking any cultural referent, has no ready-made concepts for the goal he terms as, "The union of opposites through the middle path," and the "inner experience that could be compared to the Chinese concept of Dao." He does say however, that these ideas represent the most universal, and the most rightful realization of the purpose of life. (Jung C. G., Two Essays on Analytical Psychology, 1981)

Even to speak of the Dao essence in terms of a goal to be finally reached is somewhat misleading; the old boy would be quick to remind us that the Dao is not something to be grasped, but a path to be taken - and it is right here, right now that a step can be taken on that path.

Elsewhere, Jung remarks on the fact that the serious problems in life can never be fully resolved and that something important has been lost if this kind of resolution appears to have taken place. The meaning and purpose of life's problems is not to find any kind of ultimate solution but rather to keep us growing and evolving by constantly working at them. Life is a dynamic process and we become dulled and more rigid in our outlook without this daily challenges in our lives. (Jung C. G., The Structure and Dynamics of the Psyche, 1981)

Work-on-the-self, and apprehension of the Dao, is like this, an eternal process, an attitude of mind, and the essential occupation of a life.

The old boy might add that if this is not an enjoyable end in itself - then perhaps we are trying too hard.

Verse the twenty-fifth: Into the wellspring of the unknown - Chaos and creativity - heaven and hell.

At the beginning of all things lies a mystery.
The precursor, the source, unnamed it stands alone.
For most, it is silence, nothing, the void.
Yet, though all else changes - it remains the constant.
From this nothing, springs everything that we know.
From this unknown- springs all that is great.

This nothing is the gateway to the whole,
And though our knowledge of it ebbs and flows,
When looking inwards, it is always there.

From this source comes all greatness
From this source comes the virtue of heaven,
From this source comes the merit of Earth,
From this source comes the accomplishment of humanity.

Humanity is to serve the common good of the earth,
And earth the greater good of heaven.
Heaven serves the greatest good of the totality.

And the primal unknown joins all things naturally in the whole.

As the beginning and end of all things, the Dao is both a starburst of revelation - and a plunge into the unknown heart of darkness. It is not only the source of all paradox, but equally. the means for the achievement of unity through the ultimate reconciliation of opposites. But, before there is resolution, there is necessarily something that must be resolved.

Jean Paul Sartre would say that, to the troubled soul, the essence of the existential crisis is the despair arising from the disintegrated nature of the self. This is the soul-destroying 'other side' of the quest for unity, the frightening glimpse of an unattainable whole as experienced by those who can detect, but not quite connect, with that innermost self. (Sartre, Being and Nothingness, 1993)

Some of these folk who are faltering on the path are possibly people we are familiar with, the 'unstable' or 'easily influenced' individuals in our society, people who are of a nervous disposition, perhaps depressive, bi-polar, or just socially awkward. They are people subject to feelings of hopelessness, those who experience breakdown and self-doubt. In the worst case, these are quite ordinary people whose hopes, dreams and trust in themselves and others is literally disintegrating, as they stand, without guidance or direction of any kind, on the brink of an abyss, unable to find themselves or their place in the world.

For these lost souls, the individuals embracing hopelessness and lacking in any saving grace, all belief has been crushed and their ties with reality are frayed and attenuated. At this far 'end of the tether,' where sanity quails, and religion and morality are only an empty mockery of nonsensical ritual and futile observance, society itself appears ridiculous, repulsive, and threatening. At this final impasse, values crumble and rationality fails as the individual struggles to maintain a sense of belonging and some grip - any kind of grip - on a banal and senseless world.

No one drives us as convincingly and relentlessly into this world of disconnection and alienation as does Jean-Paul Sartre. This is particularly true of his novel, 'Nausea,' and perhaps even more especially of his major philosophical work 'Being and Nothingness,' though this latter work is less personal and much more abstract in its analysis. Both these works explore the minutiae of the human condition in the situation where everything that may be considered as solid and reliable fails. There is the anguished apprehension of chaotic nature and unresolved paradox - but all without any redeeming vision of the possibility of personal integration in the actualization of self.

One-by-one, as Sartre relentlessly pursues his theme, the life-rafts of conventional thought are sunk into the black depths of despairing consciousness. The old idols, the old values, all fall under the penetrating scrutiny of a formidable rationalizing intellect that destroys all that is solid – and then literally wavers at the apprehension of the 'nothingness' within its own fragmented awareness. (Sartre, Nausea, 2000)

Sartre (as does Jung) represents human consciousness as in its very essence disjointed. One of its parts is always an isolated awareness of the unrealized 'complete' and actualized personality we characterize here as the Dao, and that part of the self is agonized by the perception of its own lack of integrity. Sartre refers to the possibility of unity in the whole as the 'ideal synthesis', the totality of individual consciousness, and he describes this in much the same terms used by the old boy (along with many other philosophers and theologians) but in his view, this ultimate harmony is not achievable, and despair, anguish - all the elements of the existential crisis, then arise when the individual succeeds only in realizing a lack of something essential within - a missing, yet vital, integrating element in their lives. (Sartre, Being and Nothingness, 1993)

This missing element here is something the old boy can point us towards in a flash. It is the recognition of the genuine possibility of personal spiritual fulfillment through honest self-reflection – the achievement of unity in some ultimate wholeness of self-actualization. Sartre agrees entirely with Laozi, when he describes the quite ordinary human spiritual impulse as being primarily the consciousness of lacking something. Sartre labels this unity as "the longed-for ideal synthesis," and even "the missing God."

Just before he finally rejects the irrational elements of human nature (and therefore the possibility of wholeness) entirely, Sartre appears almost ready to embrace the Dao as great journey, when he asserts, in a long and complex argument, that the foundation of all human desire is a drive towards ultimate unity, a transcendent quest to surpass the brute nature of fragmented reality. (Sartre, Being and Nothingness, 1993)

Sartre also comes close to Jung in his thinking when he postulates that we each contain within ourselves a shadowy, insubstantial image of the whole - a 'something,' a potentiality of the self, that our aspiration toward wholeness is perpetually attempting to solidify. He says we are all engaged in trying to crystallize our possibilities into fact, describing this process as: "imperfect being attempts to surpass itself in the direction of perfect being…"

But here, the philosophical positions part company. For Sartre, the Dao or Godhead, or any otherwise named ultimate ideal of self-realization, is forever unattainable. It is just the chimeric externalized representation of the human desire for inner unity. In his denial, Sartre rejects both the notion of a God and of a truly unified (self-actualized) consciousness, but importantly, he never denies their psychic reality. Sartre is in rare, almost total agreement with Jung here, in that the actual existence of God is far less important than the reality of the idea of God as a genuine phenomenon of the mind.

The idea of Gods, singular or plural, is universal in human culture, and historically, it seems that as soon as people gather and form communities, some form of religion or vital philosophy arises to inspire them. Invariably, this is something that can unite the group and bring about a lifetime commitment to a transcendental quest, but also serves the purpose of defining and differentiating them from neighboring communities and in this regard can also become a source of friction and conflict.

The essence of the notion of a spiritual essence that can be called 'God' or the 'Godhead' for Sartre is simply 'all that I am,' something the old boy could hardly disagree with given that he is repeatedly stressing that the Dao essence is to be found within the totality of the self. However, given his rather bleak personal viewpoint, it is no surprise that Sartre is a hardline atheist and has no need at all for any external divinity. Nonetheless, in these reflections his thoughts are very much in tune with those of both Laozi and of Carl Jung.

Sartre says that humanity is continually engaged in an attempt (the old boy would call it 'work-on-the-self') to transcend its own limitations and achieve a unified totality of self that could almost be called 'God,' Jung closely echoes this, also accepting the notion of 'God' as a psychic fact, something, which he says is to be explored within each individual in the archetype of the self.

The philosophies obviously diverge however at this one critical point; the existentialist perspective is that the enterprise is forever doomed. Sartre, whose own consciousness was always poised at the very pinnacle of rational endeavor, concluded that "being cannot be its own totality." In his view, if the inner self was truly integrated, the individual *becomes* God and is then no longer a 'self,' and describes this as unachievable. Given this viewpoint, it is perhaps not surprising that Sartre describes the nature of human reality as an essentially "unhappy consciousness." (Sartre, Being and Nothingness, 1993)

Laozi, however, would have none of this resignation to ultimate failure. While being the first to admit that one cannot grasp and enclose the whole by any process of rational thought, he also tells us repeatedly that any connection with the ultimate ought to be fullness enough. Absolute perfection is not the goal here, and the Dao essence is not an object to be finally arrived at and seized as a prize. The Dao, the way, is both a journey towards, and a spiritual connection with – a concordance of self and nature. For the old boy, the continuing act of transcendence is its own sufficiency.

To engage in proper work-on-the-self is to be on the path of the Dao and to already have a sense of arrival in being in harmony with nature, self, and others. In terms the old boy would agree with, Sartre has simply made an intellectual decision to isolate himself in clinging to his rationalizations at the very moment the goal is in sight. In essence, the ultimate surrender to, and honest appraisal and acceptance of, the indistinct and fuzzy wholeness of the irrational center of self has not been offered.

The old boy would be saddened and point out yet again that 'cleverness' is not enough; no matter how elegantly and eloquently defined are the intellectual structures.

The Dao is not an essence to be withheld until the last, very final step upon the great way – it is the gift that begins with the taking of the first step.

Verse the twenty-sixth: On the small matters – Inner stillness and equilibrium.

In the constant is the source of the light,
In tranquility is the antidote for trouble.

The wise are alert to the hazards of the world,
Exercising vigilance in overseeing their obligations,
Showing diligence when it is due,
Then - later, resting peacefully and without worry.

Great leaders of the people, have more rigorous obligations,
Without depth in their seriousness - they lose their constancy.
Without gravitas, they lose their hold.

The old boy is firmly of the opinion that, if the small problems are properly attended to as they occur, then bigger problems will rarely arise. Each life trajectory is a feat of navigation in which obligations must be met, obstacles overcome, and distractions suitably dealt with. Each day brings new decisions to be made and actions to be considered.

Individually, these small matters may seem inconsequential enough to ignore or defer, but even a minor or apparently trivial difficulty left unattended now could have catastrophic consequences later. This the message from Laozi; complete your tasks and attend to your obligations in a timely fashion, in this way, worry and stress are avoided and calmness and harmony maintained.

These lines are a direct continuation of the last verse, in which the old boy gives us his poetic description of the attributes of the unknowable Dao. Jungian thought has its parallels here too and provides another possible perspective for a glimpse of this essence. For Jung, the pre-eminent psychologist, the 'innermost self' is to be found within the dark and oceanic depths of the unconscious mind. This is a place, as was previously discussed, very much comparable to the unknown and unnamable 'otherness' that is found in both Sartre's work and in the 'Dao De Jing.' There is a potential, barely perceived for some, and an overwhelming imperative for others, for unity and self-fulfillment in the psychic reality Jung defines as the 'God-image,' a part of the archetype of the self that is found in this area of the unconscious mind.

For Jung as for Laozi, the quest for ultimate harmony, via either the commitment to a deity or by the fulfillment of individual potential, springs from this omnipresent urge towards totality, something intuitively felt deep within the countless numbers of individuals who have achieved even some small degree of analytical and meditative self-awareness. He says that our awareness of the world comes at a cost; in becoming aware we give up the comfort of the "primal mother" – which is how he describes the original unconscious state of humanity. (Jung C. G., Symbols of Transformation, 1981)

Jung's "primal mother" and the old boy's primal 'she' - the 'yin' principle, are one and the same. They represent the unknown wholeness, the veiled mystery, and the creative source of all things. This is the area of dark unplumbed depths of the soul, where rationality confronts, and surrenders too (or is overwhelmed by), the chaotic emotional, intuitive, and irrational elements of life. This dark unknown is an essential stopover on the road to any degree of self-knowledge and enlightenment. It is the acceptance of not just what is nature - it is knowing our own innermost nature.

The most important thing these thinkers agree on is the whereabouts of this ultimate wholeness - the place where this ultimate unity is to be found. While you can look anywhere in the wide universe for facts and arguments, examples, principles and paradigms and evidence of external deities in their heavens - true integration into the whole of the Dao is an internal process of transformation and fulfillment that happens only inside you...

Verse the twenty-seventh: On the path of greater good – Finding solid ground.

The accomplished traveler leaves no signs,
The accomplished speaker makes no mistakes,
Precise reckoning requires attention.
Security does not depend on locks, but on taking care,
And caring creates a binding that is stronger than cords.

The wise, having a care for all humanity,
Will abandon no one.

The wise, having a care for everything,
Are the means to sustain and preserve all things.
This is called 'following the greater good.'

Who is the follower of greater good?
The wise person who is teacher of the bad.

Who are the bad?
The raw material used in making the good.

When the value of the teacher remains unrecognized,
And the value in the raw material is overlooked.

Then intelligence is not tempered by caring - and confusion follows.
This is a mysterious and essential truth.

We are all enjoined to act in furtherance of the common good, and we should make all our actions contribute towards it. Although there are no guarantees given, to do this consistently is to stay on the path - the Dao characterized as great journey - the way. It might lead to enlightenment, or to blockage, or even, given the capricious nature of the universe where chance reigns, it could still turn into something terrible.

The old boy would shrug and probably say, 'Bad luck! Perhaps you will do better next time.' This apparently empty expression of sympathy is not frivolous, it is a recognition that the mighty ebb and flow of the universe is not going to change because of your success or my failure on this way. Life will go on. We are all both teacher and taught.

The old boy might also add that frustration and failure are not generally terminal. We are always free to learn from the mistakes, and to abandon one path and renew the quest on another if it all goes wrong at the first attempt.

The verses above are also about the set of skills the old boy sees as the essentials for those on this spiritual way. When we ask ourselves, how are we to be sure that we are on the right path and that our actions continue to serve the greater good? He might answer; sometimes, there is simply no substitute for going back to the basics and asking silly questions. This is the mental equivalent of checking the foundations of the house before building up another level - of course it seems rock-solid, and it has served you well so far. But will things always be that way? In the words of the old boy "precise reckoning requires attention."

Once you start to query what was previously the undisputed truth - and even those recognized benchmarks by which other truths are gauged, it is surprising how often certainty falters. It may seem fruitless for example to start questioning the true positions of the points of the compass, but on inspection, a surprising amount of solid ground turns to treacherous quagmire. North, South, East, and West are well fixed in most minds, but just how concrete are they?

The compass informs me that, from my current Australian viewpoint, that what I think of as being a large part of the 'West' - the USA, is to my north and Far-East. And what I think of as 'Far-East' is actually due north. The 'real East' is a place firmly situated in my geographic north-west.

Similarly, the 'Middle East' is where it always was, way over to the west, and confusingly perhaps, so are the countries once known collectively as the 'Eastern Bloc.' Europe to be sure is 'Western' and situated to my west, but I still need to travel a long way north and then pass through the 'East' and the 'Middle East' to get to it. Of course, if I was in the USA, 'Western' Europe would be well to my east, and I would find that the Far-East was over to my west. Things are obviously not what they seem, and our relative perspectives are obviously particularly important in determining what may be any kind of 'ultimate' truth.

It is not that the compass is wildly unreliable, though we know it is imperfect when we are far north or far south. What we need to understand here though, is not just that compass points are unreliable, but that the same lack of reliability is seen in many situations; the names we use to define and categorize things can let us down. The labels we attach to things, even proven, certain, rock-solid, totally dependable things - can be subversive. Language itself can betray us. 'The West' may forever be only the west, but the label itself has been shown to be insubstantial and misleading in carrying a mass of implied meaning, where only strict definition was expected.

The old boy is right in insisting that the whole, the Dao, is unnamed and unnamable. The truth is that what is named is corruptible, as older labels are prone to decay, and with decay they warp and twist. What is named carries a lot of 'baggage' in the sense of psychological, linguistic, cultural, and emotional overtones and undertones. The very fact of Jungian enantiodromia (which asserts that everything springs from its opposite), implies that no label can be trusted as definitive and unchangeable for all time.

In seeking precision of understanding, we must be aware that change is inevitable, and in the case of our facile definitions, conscious of the probability that some, perhaps all, of the labels attached to concepts that we hold dear, and the truths that we hold to be inviolate, may be equally slippery and untrustworthy. If our Gods can metamorphose into 'isms' and our demons to psychological 'constructs' and 'traumas '- what else might be transformed that we consider solid and inviolable? This is a question to be discussed further in following verses.

Yet, despite the unreliable nature of the rigidly defined world around us, humanity seeks solid ground and pursues the immutable guiding principles that are often supposed to be life's eternal fixtures. Safe anchor, foundation, and focal point, there must be something to hold fast too, or lives are pointless. Meaning, ambition, drive, all these fail, and the will dissolves unless there is some fundamental direction and purpose.

This then, is what the old boy offers us in the verses of the 'Dao De Jing,' a simple, but accessible means to give direction and focus to an individual seeking purpose - by holding to a few simple guidelines on the conduct of a good life.

Verse the twenty-eighth: On the uncarved block - The multitude of forms.

Discover the power of the masculine,
Appreciate the caring strength in the feminine.
Then, knowing that the good flows like water to the lowest points,
Be the stream of the universe.

Before long, in your truth and your constancy,
You will uncover the innocent enchantments of your childhood.

Knowing what is white,
And yet admitting the role of the black,
Be an example for humanity.

In becoming the true ideal, unwavering,
Return to the infinite realm of the good.

The wise know the meaning of honor,
But are constrained by humility.
The wise become the vital channel of the universal stream.

As individual truth and wisdom grow,
Less and less artifice is revealed,

Returning to nature, the wise are restored in full,
Like the wholeness of the uncarved block.
The uncarved block has the potential of a multitude of forms,
But each cutting and shaping limits further potential,
So, the wise shape, but do not divide the whole,
And in this way - unity is sustained.

This verse continues the theme from the preceding lines. Laozi tells us that our perceptions should be untinged by dogma or prejudice. One thing that might aid us in this respect is to acknowledge that the dualistic nature of Western cultural tradition often results in a mindset in which the very substance of our being is expressed in polarized terms. All of us tend to define our world in terms of what is known or unknown, conscious, or unconscious, what is good or bad, and what is proper or improper behavior. We all know that if we are honest with ourselves, we are each of us, all these things, and if this is accepted, we can begin to reconcile these polarities within ourselves.

What then is so difficult about the path of the Dao? Is it not simply working towards the common good and accepting all that we are on a universal scale?

Before thought and experience, and at the very beginning of life is the primal state of pure potentiality. The infant (or even those souls living closer to nature and sometimes disparagingly labeled 'uncultured primitives') may experience the pure contentment of living, and lack of all conscious distraction from the reality of the Dao essence in a direct manner.

This state is something the old boy would call 'Pu,' and he would add that the associated image we have already encountered here is that of the uncarved block. An experienced sculptor with talent, vision, and life experience could sculpt that block into any form imaginable, but at the beginning it is just the pure and unsullied potential of creative being.

If we are to achieve some sense of purpose and gain some small insight into the mysteries of the central unity of self, the old boy has warned us more than once that we are firstly required to accept the indefinable and unnamable essence that permeates the wholeness of life. Yet it is apparent that, just as soon as we catch a glimpse of this totality and attempt to encapsulate it in words, it slips out of reach - and perhaps this time we risk losing it forever...

We are continually seeking to attach our temporary labels to this essence, but having named the unnamable, what has been achieved? A fleeting glimpse perhaps, some peripheral realization, like a moving object discerned at the edge of our vision - no more than that. We must accept that any static definition will never do justice to the ever-changing essence that is the beginning and end of all things. The integrated wholeness of the Dao will always transcend any perception we may have of it.

As an aside, this insight reveals to us one of the historical reasons many of the ancient Gods and even some contemporary religions have declined in relevance or faded away entirely. Carl Jung speaks on this phenomenon of the 'death of God' in several places in his writings. Once a religion becomes codified and a priesthood established, every aspect of the forms of homage expected is eventually named, defined, categorized, and ritualized until worship become a static, stale observation of form - and finally meaningless to the point of inspiring only boredom and indifference. It is to avoid this ossification and maintain the ever-evolving nature of life and living that the old boy insists the Dao is "that which cannot be named."

Re-examining our labels is a necessary part of the task we set ourselves in keeping our minds open. We need to periodically re-visit our definitions and impressions of the fundamentals to prevent them from being tainted with unwanted overlays of meaning.

The consequence of our not undertaking some kind of regular and fundamental evaluation of these basic premises is that we may, quite gradually and unknowingly, lose sight of the intuitive realization of the Dao as a great cycle of change, and thus, drift ever further from the ideal. In a very real way, enlightenment is only a continual renewal of a primary understanding of transience, and an acceptance of the dynamism in the way things really are.

First steps along this way are necessarily small ones.

For example, acknowledging that the truth that is known may be only a small portion of the totality, and that our 'wisdom' may be only the disturbing insight that nothing of great note has yet been learned. These are ideas worth some consideration, especially for those accustomed to accepting certain 'core' truths and long held values as immutable. There is always some value in asking questions.

Even a cursory investigation of things changeless and truths held dear reveals uncertainties and inconsistencies galore. At both the macro and micro ends of the universe, scientific rational explication generally becomes vague and unsatisfying, and the accepted models can crumble with unnerving ease.

Common sense and reason offer but a partial paradigm of reality. Worse still, there is evidence to suggest that the 'laws of nature' will never be definitive; there are chaotic and uncertainty principles at work that introduce an element of random chance at the heart of all things despite our best efforts to construct order from the confusion.

We know that some elements of the irrational must become acceptable before the great way is embarked upon in earnest, but this is not to say that reason should give way to the occult. It is just that there needs to be a healthy appreciation that logic does not always prevail in the universe, or in our lives. This chaotic aspect of the universe was meant to be - it is a part of the Dao as a great journey.

The old boy is serious when he says that the whole, the Dao, is the source of all paradox. This is the place where things cycle into their opposites. Laozi would also be the first to admit that there exists the element of chance which is also a part of the irrational, and this also must be accepted - although it can work for either good or bad. All the way through Daoist teaching runs this thread of impermanence, the dynamic ebb and flow of transformation.

The old boy will repeat this mantra until we are all certain of it.

We must not allow ourselves to become complacently assured of having covered all the ground - the only true constant is the absolute certainty of change.

Verse the twenty-ninth: The world is out of our control – Accepting transience.

Do you think you can improve the whole of our universe alone?
You cannot do this and still maintain tranquility.

This is a sacred whole.
Whatever can be done to change it, will ruin it.
Whoever tries to conquer it, will lose it.

There are followers and there are leaders,
The breath of life comes sometimes easily - sometimes hard.

There are cycles of both strength and weakness,
Now you are the destroyer - and now the destroyed.
The wise avoid all extremes, all excesses, and all complacency.

There is no mysticism in the Dao, no expectation of blissful religious experience, just a ready and willing acceptance of things that are. Carl Jung shows support and high praise in his writings on the old boy's message when he describes the essence of these Daoist teachings as "the middle road between the opposites," and the "goal of life" as the following of this path without veering towards the extremes. Laozi's thoughts he characterizes as "sublime philosophical lucidity," for Jung these verses represent the pinnacle of spiritual enlightenment, making calm all the apparently chaotic disorder of nature with both intellectual and intuitive wisdom. (Jung C. G., Psychological Types, 1981)

The essence here is that the old boy is not trying to change the world, or trying to show us how to change it. It is what it is, and that is all.

Our compelling needs and desires, our ability to change our environment, or exploit it for material needs beyond the point of subsistence, our ability to build sometimes insurmountable barriers on our borders, and to unfairly engineer our social communities – all these for Laozi are 'clever' ideas, humanity arrogantly seeking to dominate nature - and therefore they are aberrations, obstacles on the way. Life and good living are not about having and holding beyond what we really need. In the longer term, we need no legacy other than the knowledge that we did our best in every situation and were happy in so doing.

Although great leaders may erect massive edifices to the glorification of their own power and might, and consider themselves thus immortalized, ultimately time will sweep them away. But even long before that finally happens, they will have become irrelevant, except perhaps in some old-fashioned historical sense - barely noticed physical manifestations of what was once considered awe-inspiring power. In the end, the ego-driven project is all wasted effort, and less than a speck on the canvas of time.

A lot of energy may be saved in avoiding extravagances, for unlike the wholeness that is the Dao, all the accomplishments at these radical extremes are ultimately transient echoes of energy misplaced in taking an idea a step too far.

There are no promises made by the old boy, but he is telling us that a ready acceptance of our place in the world, and the ability to ride out the inevitable negative events that everyone must experience at some point in a lifetime, will give us a start on achieving contentment and harmony with those around us.

Before we try to improve something - we would do well to remember that from another perspective, it may already be perfectly suited to its purpose.

Verse the thirtieth: Snatching defeat from the jaws of victory – War and ruination.

When advising a great leader of the way to unity
Advise caution in the use of their power.
For massive force will always meet massive resistance.

Where opposing troops meet - is the wasteland,
And pain and hunger will follow the war.
Therefore, use minimum force and aim for a swift conclusion.

There is no glory in proceeding after victory,
Nor in intimidation when the fight is won,
There is no honor in being arrogant with the defeated.

Where wisdom prevails, results are achieved the natural way,
And not through violence.

Force used for aggression and not protection,
Is force used against the natural law,
And that which goes against this greater good will not survive.

The advice Laozi gives us here and in the verse which follows seems as relevant now as it would have been to the warlords of ancient China.

If we consider the question; Has humanity advanced at all since the old boy's time? We might respond, 'Yes,' certainly regarding the accumulation of scientific and technical knowledge and ability, but if we also ask; have we changed much for the better in our innermost natures? Are we healthier in our outlook? Are we smarter people? These questions are more difficult to answer. Of course, predicting the replies would be a matter of contention, but the probable answers might average out to, 'No,' 'Not very much,' or, 'Not really.'

Our governments use force at every level of society as much as, or more than ever and they do not cope well with disaster. Contemporary news bulletins are predictably dreadful; hostilities have generally broken out on a dozen fronts, there is drought in Africa, flooding in the East. Everywhere poverty, disease, and hardship are seemingly on the increase.

There are terrorist atrocities and executions reported. The warring parties, rebels, guerrillas, freedom fighters, insurgents, sectarian members, liberation armies, splinter groups and militias have all advanced on several fronts. In the affected areas, bombs, mines, bullets, and preventable diseases continue to extract their toll in human misery. Malnutrition is on the rise, mass graves have been discovered, ethnic cleansings continue - and all the while, government corruption and factional infighting are preventing the effective distribution of aid...

It is difficult to imagine our situation is in any way better or much more civilized than that prevailing for the old boy around the year 500 BCE, and it is equally difficult to deny that the old boy would certainly recognize at least some of the scenarios above...

The stark and cruelly uncompromising images that accompany these stories of oppression, misery and desperation are indicative of just how much the great way of the Dao has been lost to so many. Pot-bellied toddlers with match-stalk thin arms and legs, the haunted, careworn faces of the prematurely aged squatting barefoot in the dust, palpable anger, distress, pain, hunger and injustice.

The camera captures the inhumanity of it all, burnt-out cars and grim-faced police with flak jackets and batons, soldiers with riot shields and heavy guns, the brutal ugliness of automatic weapons casually brandished by boys not yet old enough to shave. Devastated urban landscapes, with broken families leading shattered lives in the ruins, shantytowns with open sewers, and listless, scabby, starving children in rags. Blood-splashed streetscapes, littered with the debris of lives wrecked beyond salvation - misery, amputation, laceration, and desolation...

Alienation and torment everywhere.

Meantime, all around the world the dispossessed are on the move, filling the temporary refugee camps that seem ever more permanent as the years go by, living squalid lives of hopelessness, pain, and fear. The casualties of confrontation, of squabbles over oil, power, territory, gold, mining and forestry resources... All these exiles survive miserably under cover of cardboard and plastic, or peer out from behind rolls of razor wire with dead and hopeless eyes.

For a few fleeting seconds nightly, we see them on the newscasts, trudging dispiritedly with eyes downcast across bleak landscapes, carrying meager possessions in prams, handcarts, and wheelbarrows, along roads pocked with bomb-craters and littered with the detritus of technological warfare.

These dispossessed are the desperate edge of humanity on the run. They are the flotsam of conflict, people who have abandoned everything except perhaps a tiny flicker of hope. They are prepared to cross high mountain passes and barren deserts in search of something better, putting at risk the lives of themselves and their families in the hands of unscrupulous traffickers in human misery.

They are often outside the law and can expect little help or sympathy.

They cross borders at the dead of night. When necessary, they carry their young, their frail and their sick upon their backs. They take to the ocean in leaky boats for destinations they have barely heard of, to live with people who despise them as 'illegal immigrants' even before they meet. In the face of need, they join the dreary roll call of people staking their lives on finding sanctuary in a world ever more battle-hardened and compassion-fatigued...

All the above has happened many times throughout human history, and all of it is happening, or will happen again soon. So, it is no wonder that the old boy repeatedly emphasizes caution and restraint in the use of force in both personal and state affairs. Can there ever be an end to these violent cycles of destruction and misery?

This kind of desperate situation arises following a gradual buildup of intolerance in those in the community who see religious groups, or ethnic minorities, or perhaps an influx of immigrants as competition, or a form of invasion - as a threat to their job prospects, housing prices, religious identity, cultural heritage, and sense of community integrity.

The increased pressure of a growing resentment of these 'outsiders' supercharges the conservative reluctance for change and raises expectation and a growing determination that the current way of life can, should and will be preserved regardless of the detrimental effect that might have on those unfortunate - and probably desperate minority elements that seek to share their lifestyle and good fortune.

This becomes a perfect breeding ground for confrontation and hostility.

Further problems may then arise as the potential is real for this intolerance to become a perversion of the spiritual quest. Patriotism and nationalism can seduce ordinary, good, people into committing acts of inhuman cruelty and even into becoming cold-blooded killers. These two harmless-sounding and often praised words, 'patriotism' and 'nationalism' are both 'isms,' and these two 'isms' especially have the capacity to replace the true spiritual impulse and block the path of the Dao - while at the same time appearing to fill a life with clear purpose and engendering an illusory sense of belonging and fulfillment by working towards some propagandist's idea of the 'greater good.' When this happens, the proponents of racial purity, and ad-hoc vigilante activism have a greater voice in society and racial tensions and the incidence of discriminatory practice and violent action soars.

In this verse and the next, the old boy warns us that all those people willingly surrendering to the call of arms and pledging themselves to the destruction of an external enemy have, at least temporarily, ceased work on themselves and lost their way. Therefore, if battle is undertaken at all, it should be undertaken as a last resort, with a heavy heart, and with only that force sufficient to restore peace and good order. There is no joy to be had in inflicting death and destruction and the greatest of leaders are those who will sincerely mourn the death of the enemy and extend forgiveness to those defeated.

Those who embrace intolerance, seek punitive retaliation for natural acts of self-protection, and deny others the privileges they themselves enjoy - have lost the path of the Dao, which is expressed always in action furthering the greater good for all.

Verse the thirty first: On weeping at the death of an enemy – False purpose.

The weapons of war are the tools of fear,
They are detested and avoided by the wise.
And used in sadness when all else fails.

To glory in the conduct of war,
Is to relish in the destruction of humanity,
In this way the greater good is lost.

The place of the follower is on the left, the side of rejoicing,
That of the supreme commander, on the right, the side of mourning.

So, a great victory should be observed in sorrow, as a funeral.
There is no joy in killing.
The victor should properly weep for those killed in defeat.

Continuing the theme here of the previous lines, Laozi stresses that every call to arms that is willingly and enthusiastically answered, represents a hunger for confrontation and conquest which is at odds with his message - and a clear deviation from the path of the Dao.

The problem is that when it comes down to defending family, village, culture, and nation, that call to arms can have a compelling force.

For young men especially, that force may be irresistibly seductive – a chance to prove one's mettle, strike a blow for freedom, make a mark upon the world...

This sinister attraction and even glorification of death and destruction, is even stronger when it is glorified by a cynical leadership, appears in an environment of widespread discontent, and at a time when there are people who drift through life without real purpose. In this context of unfulfilled hopes and frustrated endeavor, war can masquerade as something noble - an ultimate unifying purpose - and perversely it can fill that void in people's lives that should rightly be filled in striving towards spiritual integrity in the realization of self.

That is the chilling reality of a holy war, a jihad, a crusade, an inquisition, and the xenophobia of the racial puritans and the ethnic cleansers. These are all types of personal mission with the potential to become a pseudo-spiritual quest. In the very act of impelling people towards confrontation and self-destruction, the rising determination to fight a 'just' war can bestow an illusory and temporary sense of purpose and fulfillment that may truly feel like the path to glorious personal fulfillment and self-realization to those who would commit themselves wholly to its cause.

The old boy is showing us in these lines this dark flip side of the Dao as great journey of enlightenment, and how it may become the distortion and falsification of the transcendent impulse towards self-unity, aimed instead towards confrontation, violence, and oppression.

Laozi's advice to great leaders, and his assessments of the uses and abuses of power are as good now as they were millennia ago, and as ever, his advice is as valid for the leadership of nations as it is for individuals facing lesser adversities. Any kind of open confrontation is always a failure of communication and negotiation, but it is also a failure of personality; someone, somewhere is making serious mistakes regardless of whether blame is accepted or not.

Carl Jung summed up the situation in psychological terms that neatly parallel the thoughts expressed in the 'Dao De Jing,' in a piece written as humanity was embroiled in the tumult of a World War. In it he laments:

> *"Once more we see people cutting each other's throats in support of childish theories of how we create paradise on earth."* (Jung C. G., Psychology and Religion: West and East, 1981)

Jung goes on to suggest that the first world war was the wake-up call to the world that whole nations could succumb to mass psychosis, have their freedoms abolished, and their entire populations mobilized to murderous effect - if their leaders are prepared to employ the controlling totalitarian practices used by theocracies in whipping up an irrational religious frenzy in their peoples.

The bigger picture of war is always appalling no matter how worthy the cause may appear to be, and the old boy would agree that Jung is right when he proposes, "mere reason" is not enough. Wholly irrational wars are fought by supposedly rational beings for supposedly rational ends. Laozi tells us that any war which is not a purely defensive war is a consequence of failure of leadership, and that death and destruction are the price we pay for that failure.

Worse still, when the war is finally over, there are no winners, only tragedy, massive loss, weakness and grief on all sides. The old boy is of the opinion that we are not yet mature if we can still attempt to seek glory in destruction or feel any elation untinged by sorrow in victory. He might also add that neither are we capable of self-fulfillment until we can feel genuine sympathy for the vanquished enemy. Pain, hunger, loss, desolation, misery, and sorrow are the only sure outcomes for war.

No one benefits, except perhaps for a few avaricious individuals and corporate bodies.

And, although any national leader can unleash the might of their armies to devastating effect, the old boy tells us that it is only the very greatest of leaders that can successfully lead a nation to victory through restraint.

Verse the thirty-second: Something hidden, something found – The one within.

As the greater good remains forever unnamed,
An uncarved block does not reveal all its possible forms.
The natural cycles of ebb and flow yield to no one.

Yet if our great leaders can understand this natural flux,
The whole world will be united in harmony.
Happiness and equity will prevail for all, though no decree is made.

Divide the wholeness, and you must then name its parts.
But in the division lies confusion.

The wise know when there are names enough.
Knowing the time to stop naming averts disaster.
Let the greater good flow like a river to the oceanic whole.

The old boy is back to first principles here, as with lines that echo the opening lines of the 'Dao De Jing' he returns to a perennial theme, the 'uncarved block,' symbolizing, the simplicity of things in their natural state - but also unlimited potential in the possibility of greater things to come. From the rawness of the uncarved block of stone or wood, the inspiration of the artist can produce works of astonishing creativity, great beauty, and high value.

There is power and potential in apparently unremarkable beginnings, and Laozi's advice to leaders, and indeed to all those people on the path to self-realization, is always to tread lightly, acting with compassion and patience in the knowledge that all actions taken need to be in harmony with the flux of natural events, and that restraint and serenity allows achievement without using force.

In this way we quietly shape our future and stay on the path of the Dao, all without much in the way of exertion, but by being conscious of the best thing to do right here and right now.

This process, which the old boy calls 'work-on-the-self' has its precise counterpart in contemporary psychology in what Carl Jung dubbed, the 'process of individuation.' This term for the development, reconciliation, and true understanding of the innermost self, is exactly the same idea that the old boy continually returns too. Jung's writings usually contain useful perspectives on the old boy's subject matter, and here is what he has to say on the topic of individuation:

> *"Self-reflection - or what comes to the same thing - the urge to individuation gathers together what is scattered and multifarious, and exalts it to the original form of the One, the Primordial Man"* (Jung C. G., Psychology and Religion: West and East, 1981)

Jung goes on to say that this "self-reflection" is consciousness expanding and unifying, and helps in resolving paradoxical conflicts within the self.

The timeless universality of the old boy's teachings can be plainly seen here, the 'One, the Primordial Man' is Laozi's 'uncarved block,' the 'scattered and multifarious' are what he calls the 'myriad things' or 'the ten thousand things' and 'individuation' is 'work-on-the-self,' - that honest internal reflection and acknowledgment of self that, he continually reminds us, is our key to any actualization of self.

In his advice on "the naming of parts" the old boy returns to the theme of unity in the whole, reminding us that true understanding is not the automatic result of a determined dissection of the object of study followed by a catalog of the component parts. While this process yields some interesting information, if taken too far, the object thus dismantled will be unable to be restored to good working order.

As always, true value lies in the synergy of the integrated whole, which is always something more than the sum of its parts.

Verse the thirty-third: On knowing yourself – A kind of immortality.

Those with great knowledge hold high office.
But those with self-knowledge are higher yet.

Those who can overcome others have some strength,
Those who overcome themselves have great strength.

Knowing when you have enough is being rich,
Perseverance is the badge of purpose.
Endurance lies in holding fast to purpose,
To live this way is to be remembered and to live the best of all possible lives.

The fact of having a great reputation for scholarly wisdom would have meant little to Laozi. To be overly concerned by external opinion would be to become enmeshed in petty and selfish considerations, and in a situation quite at odds with his injunction to always engage in proper work-on-the-self. He does, nevertheless, prize those qualities of the individual which might bring just such acclaim.

Building on Laozi's work, later Daoist scholars advanced the view that perseverance, endurance, selflessness, restraint, and self-knowledge were the key to longevity - the living of a healthy life long past the average age of infirmity and death. The old boy makes no such promises. Instead, he offers us a different form of 'immortality,' an enduring legacy of remembrance, by those who matter, as being a good, wise, and influential person.

The qualities the old boy applauds; unselfish regard for others, proper consideration of actions undertaken, and honest reflection on the nature of the self, are the essential base elements of a life well lived. In persevering, in making every action an authentic contribution towards what is best for all, we create meaning, thus making all the time we have left in life purposeful. We give our lives direction and importance through maintaining our own integrity - by always doing what is right - and always working towards the greater good in every possible way.

One further point the old boy would make here is that we should not have to sacrifice our contentment, or any potentially happy moments in the here and now for some possible moment of self-realization in the future.

The 'now' is where we live our lives. Though we may be actively working towards a change we see as beneficial, the Dao we seek is the path towards that change, it is not some distant goal yet to be reached. We should maintain calmness and composure, take one positive step at a time, and enjoy the journey without being excessively eager to get anywhere at all.

The reason for this is self-evident - 'now' is the only time we have left.

Verse the thirty fourth: On orientation – Being content with what we have.

The greatest good reaches left and right,
An invisible essence supporting all of life,
It is quiet accomplishment.

Remaining unnoticed, it is called small,
But as a resource for the entire world, it can be called great.

Because it is truly great,
It really does not matter if it is named - or remains nameless.

It is appropriate to note as an aside here that when the old boy wrote the 'Dao De Jing,' he wrote it as a single continuous text. It was later scholarship that grouped, edited, and sectioned his ideas into the eighty-one verses we are mostly familiar with in the many contemporary translations.

These separations in the original unified text were a matter of convenience and clarity to assist later generations of scholars to dissect the work and put their individual interpretive focus on the individual parts - as opposed to the whole. And, if by now we have a feeling for what the old boy might think of this enterprise, we can be sure that it would not be unmitigated approval.

Laozi himself tells us repeatedly that we cannot totally understand any complexity by the simplistic process of examining and naming its constituent parts - though he does encourage an intuitive understanding of aspects of the Dao by the experience of brief moments of insight and illumination. Capturing the occasional transient glimpse by quickly switching perspective is often effective to get at least a degree of partial understanding. The whole is never fully embraced in this way, but often caught in part - fleetingly, in an unexpected sideways glance of sudden realization.

So despite the injunction, there always remains some basic need to resorting to analyzing the parts to understand the whole, and as long as the limitations of this method are understood, there is still something to be gained. The eighty-one stanzas of the 'Dao De Jing' are themselves, all artificial divisions, although the 'way' – the great journey of the Dao – is all about reconstituting and uniting the whole. So, when these later researchers began to analyze and 'overthink' the import of the old boy's words, this process eventually led to a diminution of the Daoist ideal. As scholars increasingly became authorities on narrow areas of the text; focusing for example on cultural comparison, semantic symbolism, and historical context, they were ever more inclined to celebrate form over substance.

In this way began a familiar historical shift, and one that has plagued every religious tradition and every quest for spiritual illumination since time immemorial. The old boy's philosophy was shifted by later scholarship from a clear individual quest for self-actualization to a more ritualized and mindless observance of customary form and ritual – effectively a set of instructions for good conduct to replace the intuitive awareness and sincere investigation that is genuine work-on-the-self - something that makes an effective contribution to the common good.

This is of course, precisely the same fate that has overtaken many religious groups, who have moved incrementally from the awe-inspiring experience of connecting with the divine, and the facilitation of every individual's direct involvement in a great mystery, to the mundane -

simply advising their adherents to follow the rules and regulations laid down by a bunch of theological 'experts.'

Beyond this degradation of ideas, a further latter-day complication is that in many instances throughout the Laozi text, the artificial divisions between the verses do not mark the divisions between one discrete idea and the next. Themes are often continued in a seamless, unified flow of thought over two or more verses; as for example, shown in the two verses above and in many other instances. There are also many points of return where an idea previously expressed is reiterated but given new context or perspective.

There must however be some point of analysis, a cutoff point at which thoughts can condense, so in practice, we take a leaf from the old boy's book and work with what imperfections we have.

Accordingly, with the thoughts expressed in these last two verses, the old boy is giving us a series of brief glimpses of something which, in its totality, we are told we can never fully grasp in any purely rational sense.

Laozi is again highlighting the paradoxical nature of the essence, which is both light and dark, big, and small, masculine, and feminine – 'itself' and its own opposite. Bearing in mind his views on the topic of examining and naming the individual parts without comprehension of the whole, we might, when considering these lines and our own 'understanding' of the Dao essence, usefully recall here the ancient Eastern parable of the 'Blind Men and the Elephant,' variations of which are often told to children in many diverse cultures around the world - but which still bears repeating here.

As the story goes; six blind men, who lacking vision, could have no real idea of an elephant's real size, shape, or texture, were one day at the roadside when an elephant approached. Upon hearing it nearby, the blind men decided to investigate, to see if they could gain an impression of what the creature might be like through their sense of touch.

So, the first blind man approached and reaching as high as he could up the elephant's back and flanks, he announced: "The beast is huge and high, it is just like a wall!"

But the second blind man, who had his hands on the elephant's tusks disagreed immediately, saying "Impossible! I can feel it! The elephant is hard, rounded, smooth and sharp like a spear!"

At this point, the third blind man moved forward and felt the trunk of the elephant and said: "I tell you, you're both wrong! The elephant is strong and muscled, rough in texture and just like a powerful snake!"

Bemused by this, the fourth blind man now also approached and feeling the elephant's leg said: "Why do you say these things? I can feel that the elephant is strong, thick, and round, just like the tall, solid trunk of a tree!"

At this the fifth blind man felt very confused, but moving forward managed to grasp the ear of the elephant, announcing then: "I really can't understand what you are all saying! This elephant is made of a thin, tough fabric! It is like the fan belonging to a lady!"

Hearing this, the sixth blind man thought perhaps he was being tricked and feeling his way, he grasped the elephant by the tail. He then said: "Now I know you are all crazy! This elephant is just like a piece of rope!"

Of course, they were all correct, and this old tale is relevant in our own context with its parallels to the old boy's message on comprehending the Dao. In trying to encompass the 'elephant' that is the Dao with our limited understanding - we are the blind men. We get an enlightening glimpse here and there. Perhaps there is a quick flash of localized insight and understanding, and yet the whole still escapes us.

The path we are set upon involves putting together and reconciling all these disparate elements into a single whole – the big picture view. We can advance this, as did the blind men, by gaining as many different perspectives as possible, and will benefit by accepting contentment with any new awareness we gain. But inevitably, we will never personally realize the entirety that is the Dao.

The old boy will tell you it does not matter. We do our honest best, and we are satisfied with what progress we make.

Ultimately, we are not seeking an encyclopedic knowledge of the elephant that is the cosmos – we simply seek to know enough to be at peace with ourselves.

Verse the thirty-fifth: Illumination - A unity of heaven and earth.

Capture the harmony of the innermost essence of the whole,
And the entire world will seek you out.
When liberation, tranquility and happiness in unity are found,
Both mind and soul are nurtured.

The greater good is not something that can be tasted, seen, or felt,
Yet lacking substance it is sensed and known,
As inexhaustible nexus, happy union.

All lives contain the possibility of the sudden breakthrough moment, of Eureka!

This is the inspired instant at which the final pieces of the puzzle slot into place and enlightenment dawns. Daoist, Buddhist, and particularly Zen literature is full of accounts of enlightenment striking suddenly like a thunderbolt to produce that longed-for moment of understanding and completion when the exclamation is – Yes! Suddenly it all makes sense!

Underlying these words, and this moment of spontaneity, is an abrupt appreciation of context and some vital stab of insight, a perception of precisely how the set of impressions and associations that uniquely define the here and now fit together, and exactly how 'I' fit into it. A new mental template clicks into place, the big picture is revealed, exasperation, frustration, blockage, all disappear – and the light finally dawns...

Orientation through the chaos of the everyday world is all a matter of choosing, or making for oneself, the precisely 'right' referential framework appropriate to each person. This is why the old boy insists that every individual's way to the Dao is different.

The simple, but sometimes hard-learned fact is, we are all the singular product of our own unique environment.

Human habitats and living environments are not simply interchangeable and colorful backdrops to the lives of the people who live in them, they are ambient factors with a character molding impact that is seared into the psyche of the inhabitants. Environment determines an individual's beliefs, attitude, understanding and ability.

People are the sum of their experiences, and experience is shaped by circumstance. Just as every set of life experiences is unique, there can be no single and universally applicable road to spiritual fulfillment that is the Dao. This is why Laozi stresses that the ways to personal realization are many, and all are to be found within the self.

Verse the thirty-sixth: The pulse of the universe – Alternating lows and highs.

Understand the extent of a conviction,
Will it stretch it to fit the whole?

All that is powerful will ultimately fail.
So, strengthen the foundations,
But know that you are implying a weakness.

When infirmity follows supremacy.
And the soft and weak defy the strong.
The subtle nature of contingency is discerned.

As fish are hidden in the depths,
Real power is hidden in the world - not signaled by weaponry.

One perspective the old boy returns to frequently in his writings on the great journey towards unification of the self, is the idea that the wholeness which is the Dao is a kind of dynamic tension between sets of opposing states. Sometimes he uses the metaphor of the bellows, a cyclic emptiness and fullness, for the universal ebb and flow, the image of the Dao as the lungs of the cosmos, each giant inhalation followed by an expiration of breath before the wheel turns again…

Within this eternal rhythm, all polarities are contained, and all differences reconciled. It is light and dark, plus all that is good and everything evil. It is love, hate, life, death, man, woman, passion, indifference, logic, intuition, sanity, and madness...

Although Laozi's ideas are often and commonly interpreted as a kind of 'union of opposites,' it is more precise to begin to think of this as a great cycle of steady but inexorable change along a continuum. Nothing is ever completely still – except perhaps for our thoughts when harmony prevails. Light follows dark, cold follows heat, rain follows drought and ultimately everything transforms into its opposite by this eternal recurring progression of enantiodromia.

In these lines, the old boy is speaking of this dynamism and elasticity which permeates the reality which to many of us, seems solid, stable, and fixed. Though we may say 'enough is enough' and attempt to stabilize and shore up the foundations of our institutions and beliefs, to preserve our cultures, traditions, and ways of understanding the world – in the great scheme of things, our conservatism is destined to fail.

Everything that was once strong becomes weak and infirm, and that which was once vulnerable becomes a prevailing force. We may persuade ourselves that we are masters of our own destinies, but in the grand cycle of the ages, time turns mountains to dust and shrugs off our petty concerns and miniscule ambitions.

Laozi asks us in this verse and the next, to keep this principle of 'change as the only constant' in our minds. This is because, when we fight against this constant, our energy is drained and diminished. No one, and nothing can alter, stop, or even slow down this universal overarching progression.

All things will turn.

We can be consoled that, when we fail, our perseverance means that this is only a temporary point on the road to accomplishment. But conversely, when we are materially enriched, this is only the acquisition of even more material wealth that will eventually be lost.

When we receive praise and high honor, this is just a precursor leading towards the inevitable moment of our being regarded with indifference - and eventually forgotten - just as being overlooked is but the antecedent to receiving regard. All of this is only a problem if it we let it be a problem.

What is required is that we take a breath, relax, and accept things the way they are. When we have nothing to lose, we lose nothing.

When we need nothing, we are content – what more do you want?

Verse the thirty-seventh: On transformation and equilibrium – Natural law.

Although inaction is pre-eminent in unity - nothing is left undone.
Those who wish to lead - should observe the natural cycles,
Heeding the gradual, natural transformation of all things,
And then discover how in simple affirmation,
Want and longing subside in tranquil clarity.

In the whole is the potential for everything - the desire for nothing.
When the people live this way, in stillness.
Then comes the freedom that brings peace and harmony to all.

In some earlier versions of the 'Dao De Jing,' in which verses 38 to 81 appear at the start of the text, this pronouncement is the old boy's last word. So here, not surprisingly, we see the results of successful work-on-the-self, when having returned to simple eternal values, and in the absence of longing for anything at all, a condition of harmonious serenity prevails. All we had to do was recognize and appreciate the natural cycles to assure ourselves of a fulfilling life well lived.

Enlightenment arrives without fanfare, as the dawning of a new and tranquil consciousness.

Our personal experience gives us knowledge of the world, and according to Carl Jung, it also gives us power. The old boy would not hesitate in agreeing here with Jung when he says that "everything beautiful and majestic in our culture" is the result of a single individual being struck by a propitious idea. (Jung C. G., Civilization in Transition, 1981). Each of these propitious ideas represents a moment of creative vision that reveals one small aspect of the Dao. Yet for anything more than the most fleeting glimpse of the Dao, our senses alone are insufficient. In Jungian terms this is expressed as follows:

"Human passion falls within the sphere of conscious experience, while the object of the vision lies beyond it."

Jung goes on to say that while knowledge is acquired through our senses, it is our intuition that guides us towards the irrational, unknown and mysterious elements of life. He presents the view that most cultures have intentionally kept this realm of uncertainty secret - often shrouded in mysticism and concealed since time immemorial. In our contemporary era, we are in a sense more shielded than ever from this irrational and chaotic side of nature – protected by our increasing reliance on science and reason to create our ordered reality.

Nevertheless, even though we may consider ourselves to be living a life of orderly reason, there is still this disorderly background to existence that may intrude at any time to disturb any life in unpredictable ways. This is the often barely discerned fear of chaos that haunts our dreams.

It is in facing this fear of the unknown that, according to Jung, enlightenment is born. (Jung C. G., The Spirit in Man, Art and Literature, 1981)

Every person seeking the unity of the whole is required to perform work-on-the-self, to delve into the darkness of that internal motherlode of chaos and creativity that sometimes drives our night-time dreaming – and, in doing so, to find their own independent ways to resolve their particular and personal set of contradictions.

This may be a long and arduous process for some, involving great diligence and some sacrifice. Or it may be as simple as saying; 'Enough is enough! Now is the moment to stop the naming and describing of parts and think about the integrity of the whole.' Or it may even be, 'Now is the time for some relaxation and recreation, we'll let things work themselves out and accept whatever comes from within.'

However, as we approach that deepest and most unknown part of our humanity, we necessarily must begin to confront our hidden fears and uncertainties. In essence we are bypassing, and for the time being at least, abandoning, that rational element we consider to be our real and actual innermost self. In doing this, we open ourselves to the emotional and intuitive reality of the 'real' innermost self.

Although it seems incongruous to phrase the experience in medieval terms, our contemporary vocabulary of experience can be inadequate at this outer fringe of experience. What we might face at this moment is the primordial fear of loss of our souls, a kind of demonic possession, or descent into madness if you will - we loosen our grip on the rational, to embrace a dark unknown, and all without the sure knowledge of any safe return...

It is no wonder that Jean-Paul Sartre, the supreme rationalist, and intellectual giant rejected this course, but perhaps the more towering the intellect, the greater the challenge. For those who already are attuned to instinct and intuition, and who prize their experienced 'gut-feeling' - and are open to the phenomenon of the sudden epiphany - the way may not be so daunting.

In the end, we choose for ourselves how this journey will go.

If our experience on this path is blockage or frustration, then conceivably, it is at least partly because we still feel that we are not ready – we still feel that we do not yet fully deserve the gift of insight and harmony.

On this road, we must accept our faults and weaknesses as well as appreciating our strengths. In this process, we inflict on ourselves whatever penance or trial by ordeal seems appropriate for us as a rite of passage.

The old boy however, does not insist at this point that there is any penance due or any high price to be paid in redemption for past sins - and if pressed - he would certainly recommend doing it the easy way.

174 - JACK PARKINSON

Verse the thirty-eighth: Inner passion – Impressions of high virtue.

To live by the highest good is a mode of being.
It is not the consciousness of trying,
Or the observance of the rules of goodness,

To try and to observe are both acts - something is left undone.
But in being is completion - the inaction of the whole.

Living by the greater good leaves nothing undone.
Benevolence acts, yet without much thought of personal gain,
Kindness acts, yet leaves much undone,
Morality and justice act, but expect an observance in return,
Then, when persuasion fails, ritual demands the use of force.

So, when the greater good is lost from the state, benevolence prevails,
Until true benevolence gives way to kindness,
Then, when kindness is compromised, justice and morality rule,
With justice and morality abandoned, empty ritual gains ascendancy.
Since ritual is but the emptied coffer once filled by greatest good,
Confusion and disorder gain mastery in the state.

Knowledge without wisdom,

> *Being a flowery adornment to the greater good,*
> *Is where foolishness begins.*
>
> *The wise know that wholeness is found in the depth and substance of reality,*
> *And never the thin crust of superficiality,*
> *As nourishment is in the fruit and not in the flower.*
> *So, the wise in rejecting the other - are accepting the one.*

These lines are the first of that portion of the 'Dao De Jing' called 'virtue,' and in some early versions of the text these are the very first lines. So, not surprisingly, these stanzas represent another dense, multi-faceted declaration of the values the old boy is here espousing.

Right and wrong; good and bad, what constitutes proper living? Our ideals and standards are shaped in part by the vernacular in which we interpret and express our experience. What this means in practical terms is that our belief systems are widely differentiated and what appears as normal and everyday to one person may seem wildly and ludicrously exotic to another.

It may be useful to digress briefly here and consider an observation originating in the world of anthropology and subsequently extensively covered by contemporary ethnographers. This is, in essence, the idea that our entire Western cultural mode of thought and being is a wholly artificial construct - yet one that we have come to regard as entirely 'natural.' Furthermore, it is demonstrably possible to live what might be termed an entirely irrational and totally illogical life, but – a life which still has all the validity of internal cohesion of value and structure.

The classic example for this alternate mode of living comes from the work of the renowned British anthropologist E. E. Evans-Pritchard, who, when studying the Azande people of the Southern Sudan in the 1920's found himself living in a society in which there was literally no such thing as illness, natural death, or bad luck. This was a world ruled by witchcraft and magic oracles, an entire community in which it was accepted that all misfortune and natural disaster - without exception - was attributed as being the result of malignant sorcery. (Evans-Pritchard, 1990)

The observation that many cultures (if not most) believe in at least some elements of mystic or magical occurrence is not uncommon of course, but what greatly surprised Evans-Pritchard, and in its explanation caused his work to become a classic of descriptive anthropology, was the fact that the Azande people were inclined to fully determine their conduct in daily life in their society in ritual, but strangely non-rational ways. Not least of these was the oracle they consulted by observing the effects of a natural poison called 'Benge,' which they force-fed to hapless chickens before killing them and then examining patterns in their intestines in order to determine what future action to take.

The second remarkable thing was that, despite the outlandish and bizarre nature of this oracle, and of many other Azande convictions to the European mind, Evans-Pritchard gives us an account of a remarkably coherent and stable system of implicit belief - although it is a system based wholly on witchcraft and magic. The Azande were content in their ordered lives, yet, by any estimate of Western normality, randomly motivated and completely irrational in their views.

This observation raised, and continues to raise, some fundamental questions concerning our own beliefs and how we might be able to take a detached viewpoint of the things which we consider unequivocally true - and might in turn question them.

Evans-Pritchard found that, when he finally surrendered totally to his local situation and 'went native,' completely abandoning all science and logic as the determining factors of his working life to fully adopt the apparently senseless determining values represented by the way of the Azande, chaos did not ensue. In fact, life went on, smoothly and without interruption. Making no attempt to organize his work and household routines by any conventional means, Evans-Pritchard allowed the entirety of his daily life to be organized by prophecies and dictated by the random effects of poison on fowl – with everything he did each day the result of following advice on ritual procedures as interpreted by the local oracles.

Contrary to expectation, this radical course brought no huge upheavals, no conflicts that were irreconcilable, and the orderly rhythms of his household did not descend into chaos. Furthermore, he found on deeper examination of local dogma that the beliefs of the Azande were not just resilient to any criticism he offered them on the grounds of logic and rational explanation - they were apparently impregnable. In other words, the Azande neither wanted nor needed to think in terms of his mode of Western logic and rationality.

He also noted that the Azande regarded the Evans-Pritchard scientific mind-set as quite odd and peculiar, and they simply refused to waste their valuable time on the 'bizarre' logical objections and alternate considerations he raised, which to their mind were so obviously futile. When Evan-Pritchard tried to catch them out with his logic he failed - miserably. He found that there was no circumstance he could contrive that lacked explanation in terms of their own belief - their worldview was complete.

Given the fact that the Azande view of the world could not and still cannot be proven wrong, and that any judgment made about it was entirely subjective, who could truthfully say that the Azande were wrong and Western science right?

Commentator Max Marwick wrote of this phenomenon:

> "...the parallel between science and witchcraft ... may be closer than we have hitherto assumed ...both scientists and tribesmen ...hold theories of causation, both derive specific explanatory hypotheses from these theories, and both carefully apply recognized tests to these hypotheses." (Marwick, 1990)

The Azande, along with all the other peoples of the world in social groups that are not built around a defining superstructure of logic and reason, still need to cope with all the exigencies of life, and somehow, unlikely as it may at first appear, their own belief system, based entirely on divination and sorcery, made this perfectly possible.

What will most surprise those raised within the confines of the Western cultural mode of thinking and relating to the world is just how easy it can be to live without logical or rational justification for one's conduct. 'Right' and 'wrong' are both labels frequently applied in erroneous context. A thing is not right because we usually do it that way; and it is certainly not wrong because we never do it that way.

In reaching understanding and reconciliation of opposites, as a part of the quest for personal fulfillment through the Dao, it sometimes helps, as previously noted, to be able to slip without too much effort from one specialist vocabulary of experience to another. Already we have discovered, language itself can be a limiting factor in gaining a genuine understanding, of the Dao. The languages and idioms of psychology, philosophy, the occult, and of religious experience are all relevant to that all important big-picture view.

To illustrate this idea further, as Carl Jung pointed out that, although we are disinclined, in our modern day and age to admit being possessed by demonic forces, we still seek therapy for our 'neuroses.' In this case, the terminology has been updated, but historically, or so Jung tells us, nothing has changed but the language of expression. Similarly, in Jung's writings, the theologians 'spiritual salvation' which for Laozi is Self-realization in the Dao, is re-branded as 'individuation.' Similarly, 'spirituality' is consciousness of the God-image within the archetype of the self. (Jung C. G., The Symbolic Life, 1981).

As we have previously seen, the terminology of description can be slippery, and we need to accept some fluidity when the Dao is variously labeled as; the greater or common good, the Godhead, the archetype of self, the integration of personality, the whole, self-realization, self-actualization, the supreme life force, and ultimate unity – to name but a few of the possible designations. Acceptance is needed in this, after all the old boy begins by warning us that the Dao is nameless and amorphous, our labels here do not define, they provide only a point of brief illumination.

To take a further example, 'wisdom' may also be not quite what it is commonly perceived to be. While we tend to associate this quality with the ability to absorb a vast corpus of knowledge, the old boy would equate it more accurately to the direct cognition of the great natural ebb and flow of life. This understanding of 'wisdom' is so far removed from our ideas of scholarship and factual 'knowledge' - that Winnie-the Pooh has it in abundance by simply observing the grass, trees, and sky in his small rural idyll...

There is a purpose to these considerations of ways in which we routinely impose static definition to describe and relate to our environment. The dark and negative side of all this is that inflexibility can be our failing. Even though the idiom and vocabulary of the quest for understanding changes, our first instinct is to hold onto the bedrock of our belief. The path towards our own personal realization may not be a straightforward course, it twists, turns, contradicts, and denies, if we are not careful, we will hang on - like a limpet to a rock – to our familiar patterns of reason and our own narrow, specific interpretive framework as filtered through the lexicon of our early experience, and in doing so, may miss something important.

The old boy would certainly recognize the principle that, 'A rose by any other name would smell as sweet.' This is why he asks the truth-seeker on the path of the Dao to consider carefully what is meant in the verses on 'virtue' above, by his description of the downward spiral of disintegration represented by this sequence:

Greater good... benevolence...
kindness... justice and morality...
ritual... confusion and disorder...

Such a question always has more than one good answer, or it would be impossible to discuss the Dao in so many different terminologies of knowledge and experience. But a good start in answering might be made with the observation that any settling for second best in place of acting always in the common good is not the hallmark of the committed seeker of ultimate truths.

Knowing as did the old boy, that language and habituation to the norms of culture might conceal as much as reveal, how shall we answer the original question: Right and wrong, good, and bad - what constitutes proper living?

The essence of this answer is something the old boy pushes though he will be ignored by many and unheard by even more; the greater good lies in choosing substance over form every time. Whether you are a Western empirical scholar schooled in logic, or a respected oracular haruspex among the Azande, educated in divination through inspection of the entrails of dead animals, your authority, your personal dignity, and your integrity rest on your commitment to following your own instinctive, often unconscious feeling of doing exactly what you know is right. The old boy will also warn you that simply doing only what is acceptable, or just what might be expected of you - is not enough for any serious seeker of the whole.

The instinctive impulse to choose substance over form is something that comes from a maturing within and represents a significant turning point in an individual life. This expression of commitment to the greater good of all - in the Dao as great journey, has a counterpoint in the language of Western theology, there it is variously known as, 'receiving one's vocation, 'opening to divine guidance,' or 'hearing the voice of God.'

In psychological terms it is 'listening to the inner voice.' In secular terms the analogous expression is - 'living life with an honest passion.' While we may praise perceived virtue, and admire the virtuous, this is a second-best way of living. If we are truly on the path to the Dao – we must follow the heart as well as mind and seek the common good everywhere.

This is the downward spiral we see in the lines above; when virtue is lost, we still may hope to at least have benevolence, and when that is lost in turn, we may still fall back on kindness and righteousness. When we lose that in turn, we look to the regulating powers of justice and morality, and when even that crumbles, finally, we may slip into unthinking ritual and from there to confusion and disorder.

The final words in this verse are the old boy's repeated reminder to us to focus on the present and not the future. If we have experienced ourselves as kind and benevolent and now aspire to the greater good, we should remember that the Dao is not a goal – it is a path, and once on it there is a sense in which we have already arrived.

Any strong ambitions we hold onto will delay our way along that path.

Verse the thirty-ninth: On fragmentation in the group - Integrity in the one.

These are the attributes of the whole from time immemorial:
The heavens, by virtue of their wholeness are translucent.
The earth, by virtue of its wholeness, is firm and solid.
The spirit, by virtue of its wholeness, has strength and power.
The valley, by virtue of its wholeness, is full.

All the multitude of creatures are by virtue of their wholeness, alive.
The wise leaders of the people, by virtue of their wholeness
- Maintain the integrity of the state.
These are all united in the whole.

Lacking the whole that makes it translucent, the heavens might darken,
Lacking the whole that makes it solid, the earth might split apart,
Lacking the wholeness of unity, the spirit might lose strength and power.
Lacking the whole that gives fullness, a valley might run dry and barren.
Lacking the whole that gives life, the multitude of creatures might depart this world.
Lacking the whole that gives them wisdom in their authority, leaders might ruin the state.

All that is greatest is founded in the humble.

The high draws strength and stability from its roots in the low.

So, the greatest of leaders are barely known - isolated and non-interfering,

Taking solace from being humble servants of their people.

Not wishing themselves rare possessions - they are as unassuming as unrefined stone.

Laozi is telling us here how the world, and all of nature, functions harmoniously and arises from humble beginnings. But he also shows us how things may malfunction, and the Dao be lost. We are invited to meditate on these processes; what is the greater good? What is it not? It is certainly not a set of observances. It is also not painstaking adherence to the letter of the law, and it is not the ready, thoughtless acceptance of rule and regulation. In fact, it is not the zealous application of anything at all. Rather, it is the expression of fulfillment in appropriate action, and the proper mode of being of one striving towards the common good of the Dao.

We, meaning the peoples of the approximate 'West' and 'North' of the world, mostly think of our institutions as broadly reflecting our own standards and principles, and we may generally also credit ourselves with being progressive, humane, compassionate, and tolerant. We sometimes forget or fail to notice that there is always a dark and complementary downside to things positive and affirmative.

The individual seeking fulfillment must, at some point, face and accept any weaknesses and unpleasant aspects of the discovered inner self. This necessity is mirrored by the need for the leaders and members of corporate bodies to take full personal responsibility for finding and addressing the weaknesses within their organizational structures. This injunction from the old boy to the great leader applies at every level up to and including the state itself.

In a group or community context, which is more usually the way our leadership is constituted, the old boy's message is exponentially more significant and more imperative and he expands on this elsewhere in the text. Many people mistakenly think that they are responsible *to* an organization, but then fail to realize that as a member, they are also responsible *for* it. Without the active oversight and control of its members, any organization has no morality, no conscience, and no sense of restraint - and yet still may have immense power and influence that can be misused in a host of damaging ways.

As was earlier mentioned, it is a purely legal fiction that organizations have some measure of 'personhood' independent of their affiliate membership and are autonomous entities capable of taking responsibility for themselves - they are not. The reality is that all the groups and organizations sanctioned by community leaders to exercise social, commercial, or political power are mindless and amoral vehicles for the furtherance, good or bad, of the ideas of the strongest and most influential of their constituent members.

It is also true to say that in the face of member apathy, incomprehension, or perhaps fear of censure or reprisal, even the most well-meaning of organizations can have their agendas commandeered in the service of some unscrupulous or sinister intent. Working towards the greater good requires an appreciation of the interplay of roles and responsibilities between individual and institution, and importantly, an acknowledgment of the culpability of individual members in all failures of the organization to adopt the highest possible standards of practice.

Blaming the organization for 'its mistakes' is like blaming the heavy, blunt instrument at the crime scene - but not the individual who wields it with murderous intent.

Organizations follow the path of the greater good only to the extent that they are so guided by their members. Without good guidance, they can, and they do, get out of control. Historically for example, there are numerous instances of organizations charged with responsibility for state security exceeding their briefs and committing criminal acts of authoritarian oppression. When the membership begins to believe their own institution has genuine power - some autonomous function that does not require their active participation or intervention, the old boy would warn that it is perhaps time to feel anxiety about precisely what, or whose, interests that body is serving...

A closer examination of the actual roles of those groups whose activities we generally accept without question can produce startling results. The old boy was no stranger to the power struggles of factional leadership and might remind us from personal experience of government, that our contemporary liberal democratic institutions ought properly to be our servants and not our masters.

Laozi also prompts us here and elsewhere, to reflect on just how good our leadership is. Are the institutions of state, really providing the service they are meant to provide. How well do they serve the common good? Do they assist the needy? Are they discriminatory? Are the people properly considered? Do the populace lack shelter, medical care, access to justice, education, and support services? And importantly, who are the specific individuals responsible in these institutions of state?

Society, as represented by its institutions, always retains the capacity for a viciousness and brutality mostly undreamed of by its constituent citizenry – unless and until that capability impinges upon them directly. We may imagine ourselves in a comfortable niche in a liberal and humanitarian environment, but the old boy generally advocates a continued wary vigilance of leadership. At best our institutions are unprincipled, and at worst they are so motivated by partisan considerations of profit, status, and power, that they become predatory and, rather than nurturing, are quite inimical to the wellbeing of the ordinary person.

We can be deceived and threatened - and even destroyed - by the very organizations we create to protect ourselves. Through these institutions, authorized by some paramount leadership we may be only partially aware of, our lives can be ruined in an instant. We can be forced to fight wars we want no part of, we can be compelled to accept decisions that impinge with massive negativity on our lives, and we can be forced to accept and implement action on, decisions that we may consider unjust, immoral, and unfair.

Carl Jung was one of the great thinkers of his time, and one who knew something of the psychology of organizations and leadership in community and commented with great insight on the phenomenon of these societal groups as amoral juggernauts, denying natural justice and capable of carving a destructive swathe through whole societies. Jung characterized these institutions of society as potentially dangerous, quasi-independent entities generally lacking scruples, conscience, and sense of liability for actions performed. He wrote that:

> *"Any large company composed of wholly admirable persons has the morality and intelligence of an unwieldy, stupid, and violent animal. The bigger the organization, the more unavoidable is its immorality and blind stupidity."* (Jung C. G., Civilization in Transition, 1981).

Consider the wars, terrors, pogroms, and repressions launched by national leaders on their neighbors, or even - and more chillingly - on their own constituent minority elements. Then also consider the fact that if there is to be some final, devastating, and totally unnecessary holocaust, it will be brought about by some institution within society claiming it is acting rationally on behalf of its members - almost all of whom might claim they do not really want it and are not themselves responsible for it.

It is in this way that the group may sleepwalk its membership towards catastrophe and destruction...

And, in this direst of situations, even though each member of society may protest the insanity, and truly feel their individual righteous innocence, the deed will still have been done, and the destruction will still need to be dealt with.

Behind the benevolent countenances, behind the ethical facades and the noble mission statements the old boy warns us that our leadership is capricious. All corporate bodies and indeed, all governments, no matter how altruistic, base their ultimate authority on their well-established capacity for violence. Our corporate entities expect ordinary citizens to toe their established lines and non-compliance generally brings retribution swiftly, surely, and usually - severely.

As it was for Laozi in 500 BCE, and has remained the case throughout the intervening millennia, great leaders, and their governmental groups, commonly and recurrently safeguard their own power base at the expense of the basic liberties, rights, and well-being of their citizens. Without exception, all governments quite unambiguously offer a sliding scale of violent penalty for infractions of the rules by their citizens.

At the lesser, more communal level, organizations exercise their power and influence to take whatever punitive measures they can to deter those they consider 'wrongdoers' in opposing their enterprise. If we have listened closely to the old boy, we should also be keenly aware that 'right' and 'wrong' and 'good' and 'bad' are often pre-emptively legally defined by governments, and not unusually, those definitions may be in defiance of previously accepted norms.

Additionally, market rules and regulations are frequently dictated by powerful corporate bodies and elite groups with partisan concerns. Clearly, the odds are heavily weighted against the ordinary individual citizen no matter how just the individual cause.

In the international arena of course, the entire existence of the state revolves around familiar games of threat and counter-threat with external governmental bodies similarly set up to protect (and threaten) their own citizens. And while the deadliest weapons of war are brandished, and the direst threats issued, everyone on both sides of the hostile divide may still maintain that they themselves stand for peace, truth, and justice - they will probably even both claim that God is firmly on their side...

Laozi was the product of an aggressive and confrontational era when capricious autocratic government was the norm, and supreme rulers could justify their excesses, and the far-reaching destructive consequences of their acts of pure impulse, by claiming a divine mandate. For the old boy with direct experience and observation of the fickle nature of leadership, the less government there is, the better things are. He has little or no trust in government or leadership to ever protect their citizens fully. He also has every expectation that the whim of some deluded or malevolent leader could at any time devastate any citizen's life.

The old boy knows and warns from direct experience that community leaders may enable institutional violence which might strike the individual at any time from out of the blue - and at any level from the trivial to the cataclysmic.

Anyone surveying the historical and contemporary global political scene will probably find themselves hard-pressed to deny that the old boy's gloomy assessment of state and institutional power throughout the 'Dao De Jing' is as accurate now as it was then. Yet despite this evidence, there are still those people who are generally more afraid of living without 'strong' government than living with it. This may be partly explained by our Western cultural appreciation and admiration of strength and power and partly by the observation that true freedom, as Sartre expressed it, can be a terrifying apprehension of isolation and vulnerability (Sartre, Being and Nothingness, 1993).

A strong leadership relieves the follower of the burden of responsibility and allows them to exist in a child-like state of passive acceptance of whatever comforts trickle down from the elite classes above - and possibly allows an indifference towards events in the political sphere. Obviously, the old boy would have none of this regressive attitude which disavows personal responsibility and fosters disengagement, but he would also agree that this way of living is far from uncommon at any point in history.

Carl Jung said on this matter that as the size of any group increases, some of the unique qualities of the individual are lost - including morality - which he attributes to the individual's very personal sense of correct action and wrongdoing. The result is that every person becomes a worse version of themselves in a group context. Because they are a part of the group, they feel relieved of much of their individual responsibility.

The problem here of course is that a duty of care when it is attenuated throughout a large group, becomes so diminished as to constitute almost complete disregard. (Jung C. G., Two Essays on Analytical Psychology, 1981).

Why do we even need governance? The popular wisdom is that people group together to form the communities that become states in an affiliation to safeguard lives and property from potentially hostile and predatory outsiders. However, Laozi is clear on the dangers.

Once this over-arching governmental power is created, there is then a need for it to controlled, and its ambit clearly defined and limited. Without this deliberate weakening of the power structure, it will take on a life of its own, and not necessarily one which is beneficial to the constituent citizenry. The old boy's verdict is that for the state as for the individual, the ultimate balance and the ultimate unity is found in the moderate center, with suitable exercise of humbleness and restraint crucial to keeping on the way of greater good for all.

It is in keeping with the old boy's view then, to say that a weak government is infinitely preferable to a strong one. The nature of enantiodromia within the ebb and flow of the Dao, is that injudicious exercise of massive power will, over time, inevitably attract massive resistance, and retaliation. However, if the government is inherently weak and uncertain, this is far less likely to occur. Also, weak governments do not empire build or bully their neighbors, moreover, for a weak and more vulnerable government, consultation is key, as sensing and reacting positively to the real needs of citizens is clearly the best survival strategy.

The old boy would therefore approve heartily of some of the systemic inefficiencies of real democracy, although perhaps not so much of some of the contemporary oligarchies claiming they are democratic. The idea that governments should be saddled with an officially sanctioned and elected opposition for their full terms would surely delight his sense of natural justice. He might also remind us in this context that this fundamental provision of true democracy also fits naturally with the Daoist principle that stresses the reconciliation of opposites as the means to understanding and initiating proper action for the greater good.

In deliberately introducing weakness at the heart of the process, in the form of obligatory public consultation, and a forced rapprochement for every step taken, tendencies towards radicalization can be slowed if not entirely thwarted, and the focus of governmental concern remains on its citizenry, and thus somewhere around the middle ground - the place of unity and the Dao.

As the verses above demonstrate; from this apparent weakness springs the strength and unity of nations. This is the beginning of a template for the moderation of any corporate organization that Laozi would surely have affirmed.

Of course, it would not be the way of Dao if the old boy's central maxim in all this did not encompass a measure of paradox - our institutions are always stronger and better when they are deliberately weakened from within - and naturally, we should not forget that the highest of our institutions are still only the servants of the lowest of the citizens.

Verses the fortieth and forty-first: On the power of the positive – Progress is a force.

The greater good turns, returns and circulates,
Always taking the path of least resistance,
And all that there is known comes from something,
- that arises in nothing.

The wisest students seek the whole with all their resolution and ability.
An average student seeks it only when the thought arises.
The foolish student laughs out loud at the thought of seeking.
The greatest good will always earn the laughter of the foolish.

So, it is said that in journeying towards the whole:
The brightest of guiding lights may appear dull,
The quickest way forward may be a return to beginnings,
The easiest of ways might seem cluttered with obstacles,
The highest essence may be found at the lowest point,
That which is pure may first appear as unclean,
Abundant merit may at first seem insufficient,
The strength in merit may be seen as weakness,
The reality of merit may not be recognized.

The whole has no boundaries.

And the greatest work takes longer to complete,
The highest of notes are hardest to hear,
The greatest of forms has no shape.
The greatest of good is concealed within the unnamed.
Yet the journey brings all things to fulfillment.

The old boy here begins with a very short verse which contains a claim that for centuries afterwards seemed to be quite easily dismissed as the poetic license of an ancient mystic, yet which today, seems fully in accord with the contemporary scientific disciplines of physics and astronomy. This is the idea of the Dao as a field of universal energy in which something may quite literally arise from nothing. Here Laozi is also giving us another illustration of that aspect of the Dao, which is the heartbeat of the universe, here revealed as an endless rhythmic pulsation, or eternal wheel of cyclic energy.

The discussion of 'the student' that follows is of course applicable to all who will listen. The old boy knows his message of a self-actualized life lived with respect to all living things and an awareness of the rhythms of nature is simply not for everyone, even though the potential in each person remains and is real. But just as in every school of learning, not every student is a good, or even capable or willing scholar, so in life there are those who will never take a footstep along the path of the great way, and those who will stumble at the first steps.

We live in a world in which traditionalist viewpoints frequently wield formidable power. It is human nature to protect and treasure a long-held belief or custom, and few people are genuinely thankful and joyful to see the guiding precepts of their lives proved either illusory, or simply wrong. Consequently, the cycle of change which is the hallmark of the path of the Dao is often opposed by those who see sufficiency in what they already have and hesitate to tear down their hard-won models and methods of understanding and coping with the world in order to cope with a new reality.

For this reason, revolutionary ideas, regardless of their truth or possible beneficial aspects, are often derided, and even frequently feared, censored, blocked, and repressed. The religious establishment for example, tried to deny and suppress the idea formulated by Copernicus that the Earth revolves around the Sun, and Darwin's work on evolution, despite its early acceptance into mainstream science and its central role in modern biology, is still a bone of contention for some sectarian branches of the church even today. Mendel's work on genetics, the first theories on the spread of disease by germs, and the efficacy of a sterile environment to combat infection – were among the many scientific theories ridiculed at first, then later shown to be correct.

Sometimes, the opposition to an idea is fueled by a desire to hold onto a cherished belief or dogma, or sometimes because there is a perceived need to maintain the status quo, or even possibly some religious, commercial, or political advantage in suppressing the breakthrough. It is a matter of record that at least a half dozen scientists who later went on to win the Nobel Prize, initially had trouble publishing their ideas and found themselves rejected by the arbiters in their fields.

In fact, it is more common than not, that new and revolutionary ideas will meet strong and sometimes implacable resistance. And again, even if a new truth is recognized, some people will prioritize lesser, but to them, more pressing concerns. There will also of course, be those who simply fail to appreciate the gravity and importance of understanding a new theory fully before issuing a condemnation of it, or lack the inner focus or curiosity, that might motivate them to further exploration.

The old boy would not miss the irony inherent in any indifference to his message - in a universe where the eternal rhythm of perpetual and inexorable change is the only true constant – we are often reluctant to accept it.

Although the path of the Dao seems strewn with obstacles and pitfalls for the unwary, there is no need to feel overwhelmed or daunted. No one should believe that work-on-the-self is either a difficult or a straightforward progression, sometimes we listen and learn, and sometimes we do not. Sometimes we feel strong and capable, and sometimes we do not. The path is always an imperfect work in progress and encountering the absurd along the way is just as natural as experiencing the most profound of epiphanies.

Acceptance and patience, as well as an ability to find humor in adversity, will ensure that somewhere along that way is a place for everyone who wants it.

Verses the forty-second: On violence and opposition – The softly-spoken warrior.

The one comes from the greatest good.
And from that one - the two.
From these two comes multiplicity.
And from multiplicity - the whole of existence emerges.

The whole of existence is a blending of mighty principles,
The harmony born of the receptive in partnership with the creative.

Although insignificance and unworthiness is not associated with great renown,
The best supreme leader will describe themselves this way.
And, by being thus diminished, grow in stature.

What others have also told you, I shall tell you now:
Those who care overly bold, or choose violence - are punished by violence.
This is an essential and self-evident truth.

In this verse and the next, Laozi first reiterates how all of reality springs from the paradoxical whole of the Dao. He also offers two visions of handling adversity. When hostilities seem unavoidable and the battle unwinnable, the best of leaders are circumspect in their actions.

They will quietly and calmly deflect, bide their time and ultimately, through patience and a refusal to waste energy on futile opposition, they may still win the day. The unworthy leader by contrast, will lay the blame for trouble on the opponent, incite hatred and aggression, and commence along a calamitous path of death and destruction that, 'win' or 'lose' brings disaster to all concerned.

The old boy prizes the kind of personal self-sufficiency that can harvest the natural abundance around us and does not seek personal gain beyond what is needed for a life of contentment and honest endeavor. In his world, hostile confrontation is almost always avoidable and always indicative of failure of proper work-on-the-self. In particular, he rejects the use of unnecessary force. Violence of any kind is not only repulsive, but also something that will eventually rebound upon the perpetrator.

As always, the greatest of leaders is not the larger-than-life warrior who conquers all by harnessing the power of the people in forging weapons of war, and then wielding them mercilessly against a recalcitrant opponent, Laozi's model of a leader achieves the objectives with as little controversy and opposition as possible, mostly via an understated, self-effacing process of quiet progress through negotiation and consensus.

The greatest of leaders are those you scarcely ever hear about. Working for the common good is unremarkable and rarely captures attention. Therefore, when anxieties concerning the actions taken by the leadership are uppermost in the minds of the people – the signal here is that the path has already been lost.

Verse the forty third: On quiet achievement - And a meditation on faith.

The softest and most yielding thing in the world,
Flows easily to envelop and enclose the hardest.

The apparently insubstantial cannot be denied entrance,
It diffuses into everything solid and material - all pervasive.

To teach the great truths without defining statement,
To achieve a great work from non-interference.
This is something understood by few.

The description in these lines of these facets of the Dao essence, is also the old boy's key to achieving victory through inaction. In quiet acceptance, through patience, and by continuing to do always what is right without direct confrontation, all conflict evaporates, and the vital energies of life are retained. Injury, loss, and destruction are avoided and as the world turns, new opportunities will inevitably arise.

Dynamic spirit of stillness, omnipresent non-substance, shadowy whole, indistinct source, amorphous unity, veiled truth, the ever flowing, yet rock-solid base of all that is. Irrational source of fulfillment, shapeless constant and unnamable beginning of all things... What we hear and see of this Dao essence is always paradoxical and never categorical; our insights are like a series of short glimpses at the peripheral edge of vision.

Carl Jung once said that transcendent objects could only be described in terms of paradox (Jung C. G., The Spirit in Man, Art and Literature, 1981). Laozi would say that in the whole, the Dao, is the beginning and end of all paradox - they would not be in disagreement.

For the old boy, an honest acceptance of self and others in the context of the natural world all around is truth and harmony enough. Peddlers of wholesale religion generally 'teach the truth' in other ways, by assuring the Godless that all that is required for wholeness - to live in the joy of the divine light - is 'faith.' It does not sound like very much to ask, and surely even the meanest among us can muster a modicum of this 'faith,' especially if the prize is to live in peace, joy, and harmony forever...

'Faith' we are told earnestly, is all that we will ever need. Rarely is anything said about how we can give what we do not have. How does one, in practical terms, go about acquiring this faith, and should one even attempt to do so? The old boy would probably tell us that faith is a slippery concept that often masks deception – both of self and others. The truth is that, notwithstanding any declaration that may be made in apparent affirmation, genuine 'faith' cannot be mustered by any normal act of will that remains totally sincere.

Ultimately, faith is something received - not manufactured or assumed.

Though the old boy is never a cynic, he would undoubtedly question whether very much of the professed 'faith' in our societies was really that primal flow towards unity in the Godhead that indicates a life well lived, or something much less than a spiritual quest, perhaps just an intellectual abandonment of sorts, a conscious decision to adopt a community approved pretense, and a relatively easy fallback position from genuine work-on-the-self.

Life is never a straightforward progression, sometimes we may seek some lesser, interim goal, or maybe we will adopt an 'ism' to masquerade for a while as an ultimate purpose in life. In this respect, the characterization of 'faith,' if it is not outright dishonesty and role play, is to be absolutely convinced of a truth, and yet, to hold this belief entirely without evidence.

For many of the 'faithful' then, their declared 'faith' is an inferior thing, perhaps the mental equivalent of shrugging the shoulders and accepting the advisability of an each-way bet. What harm can it do? One may pay lip-service to the ideal, worshiping your God, pursuing the Dao, or accepting the creed, perhaps embracing the words of a prophet, or accepting Jesus - yet still lack any real involvement, or sense of work-on-the-self. This is something in the manner of the Christian who burns incense at the Buddhist temple, or the agnostic accepting the last rites - 'just in case…'

Laozi does not ask the individual for anything that is not within their power to give. All that is required of the seeker embarking on the great way is the will to continue, and the openness to accept the truth, the whole truth and everything that is the truth.

In the Jungian scheme of things, organized religions are characterized as 'psycho-therapeutic systems' and any controversy concerning the 'actual' existence of a deity is of little importance or relevance compared to the undeniable reality and universality of what Jung calls the 'God-image' that resides in the normal healthy psyche, and is the same phenomenon that the old boy would describe as the 'unnamable.'

Jung would no doubt dismiss the relentless materialism of those who seek (or profess to have) a scientific proof of the presence of God, and those who might feel naively impelled to probe the heavens with powerful telescopes looking for the pearly gates. The concept of God in his terms, is a psychological necessity that is quite unrelated to the question of whether any God exists. He elaborates on this further when he says that:

> *"Proof of God is not only impossible but also unnecessary – the important consideration is the very real idea of a divine being that is present in*

everyone's mind, whether consciously or not." (Jung C. G., *Two Essays on Analytical Psychology*, 1981)

The people who insist on the exclusive existence of only 'their' God as a part of their cherished system of being are simply wrong in Jungian terms. As with Laozi himself, Jung's interpretation of reality includes a process of self-realization that does not have to depend on any external divinity. Both the transcendental impulse towards a unified wholeness, and its means of fulfillment, dwell in the unconscious recesses of each individual mind.

Interestingly, in this sense, one may live a life steeped in the wisdom associated with religion and spirituality, and yet still be, by any strict definition of the word, a confirmed atheist - the old boy himself is fully in accord with Jung on this and would have no problem accepting this viewpoint.

It is not necessary to be 'religious' to understand the essential meaning of religion and its most fundamental function. It is the same goal outlined in the 'Dao De Jing'- to give life purpose and, through inner contemplation, to seek the fulfillment of the individual in integration with a universal whole. When we surrender our 'reality,' our rationality, to the Dao, or to the pursuit of the God-within by any other name, we are sinking into the uncharted depths of the self.

And, when we re-emerge - we are reborn.

This process is however, not without its hazards, as every person considering this course instinctively knows. The process of rebirth and salvation always implies some preliminary self-destruction or abandonment.

The alternative to a genuine 'leap of faith' or, 'answering to the call' or 'total commitment' is to simply adopt the creed and observe the forms as many of those counted as the 'faithful' do in practice. There are benefits in this lesser commitment, and it can be made before any final binding pledge of the self to fully commit to taking the way towards real personal fulfillment is made. While this lesser way is not yet the direct way to the Dao or the Godhead, it can have its life advantages, for example, in enabling practical community assistance by strengthening bonds with a peer group who are protective of family life and supportive of individuals who piously demonstrate group values. Despite the potential for hypocrisy, this can be hugely valuable to an individual or family group, even if secretly, no ultimate commitment of the self has been made.

There is a strong moral component to every religion, and each adherent lives by an adopted code which was (originally at least) designed to promote the greater good for all. This is something that offers community and family groups some basic protection and a sense of belonging. This sense of belonging is also why most religious commitment is simply a matter of geography. Rather than making any considered individual commitment, our innate tendency is to simply adopt the God of the environment of our youth. Primarily, we take the simplest course, bow to family and community peer pressure, and worship the local deity just as everyone else around us expects us to do.

So, in this sense, even a purely ritual religious observance lacking true commitment can have its advantages in solidly embedding the individual in the protective embrace of his society. Although this level of participation is so common as to be near the norm for millions of 'worshipers,' in the longer term, this ritual adherence alone will not suffice for enlightenment on the way of the Dao.

In the old boy's terms, this choosing of form over substance represents a lesser solution, and a deviation or obstruction on the true path towards the realization of self.

However, while the case may be made that a ritual observance of form is an inferior way to achieve life's full potential, in practice, the prevailing circumstances may dictate actions and real choice may be limited. There may for example, be a social penalty to be paid for any perceived failure of religious observance within a community. In this situation, the espousal of this form of moral commitment, and the real-world consideration that often drives an insincere or superficial adoption, is the fear of ostracism and reprisal.

There is an undoubted potential for the apostate to become a pariah, a rejected member of society and possibly the victim of the brutality and barbarism that history, both ancient and recent, shows us may befall the non-believer in many societies.

While it may seem hypocritical in the extreme to maintain the pretense of belief without feeling true commitment, in the verse above Laozi reminds us that the soft overcomes the hard. When the environment dictates the course, the wise will conserve their energies, accept the inevitable and bide their time. Patience wins the day, and even mighty conquering armies wielding overwhelming force will eventually settle in the lands they take and be absorbed - in this manner becoming the substance of the very society they sought to subjugate and rule.

It is always best to be flexible and wait - ultimately the right moment will arrive. In this sense, the individual who rejects the local forms of worship and defies the local order to become a free thinker, may not be the most prudent person. The old boy would shrug at this apparent impasse and repeat that the way of the Dao is not meant to be a battle. Pragmatism rules. The reality of a situation needs to be accepted. If patience is exercised, who knows what opportunities may later present for a harmonious integration of self.

Ceasing opposition and bending to a force which cannot be opposed prevents strife, thus, compliance is advisable. But even this 'halfway house' principle of adopting ritualized procedure over genuine substance may not always be trouble-free. Laozi would sigh and confirm the truth that anyone can be persecuted, both for having a belief and for not having a belief, or for not expressing that belief in an appropriate public form.

In fact, even when the final undertaking of faith is made in the most sincere and heartfelt manner, the potential for complication is not diminished. There is a surprisingly thin dividing line between the tranquility of the sage imparting his message of enlightenment in tones of quiet assurance - and the zealot seeking forcible religious conversion by carving it into the flesh of his non-believer victims in lines of blood.

Verse the forty-fourth: On self-sufficiency – When enough is enough.

Your good name or your good self - which matters more?
Your good self or your great wealth - which matters more?
To gain or to lose - which is more troublesome?

Accumulating riches may lead to great expense.
Amassing goods may lead to heavy loss.

The wise know when they have enough.
In knowing when to stop they avoid disappointment and find harmony,
Being in harmony, they avoid misfortune and endure.

Where do we begin? Which way should we go? How are we to value what we have?

The world often seems full of illusion, nothing is what it seems, and life is full of unresolved contradiction. How is a person to be sure that they are not deceived, and that they are truly on the right path? In these lines, the old boy reiterates the superficial importance of fame and fortune as prime motivations for a well lived life. Harmony, he assures us, is to be found in realization that the trappings of wealth and success are simply incidental to those who are set on the path of the common good.

As we have previously considered, to be on this path is to become consciously aware of the promptings of the spiritual impulse - something hidden in all of us. Heeding this impulse places us firmly in the realm of creeds and convictions. Traditional, organized religions always provides some guidelines for the perplexed, but will also most often suggest to the weary traveler on the way that they place their faith in the deity and accept whatever outcome is ordained.

This may be good advice for some, and is certainly not something the old boy would entirely disagree with insofar as any sincere step in the direction of self-knowledge is good, but the degree of that genuine commitment is important. As time passes, if the conviction is real and honest, the way is not lost. If the genuine 'leap of faith' has not been taken however, then eventually a certain inner hollowness and a lack of something vital will be experienced.

It is at this point that awareness may dawn that this is simply one more frustrating dead end. Unless further honest work-on-the-self is undertaken there will be no proper integration of self.

For the old boy, a simple, humble appreciation of nature and of life itself is sufficiency enough. Even though religions are considered, in almost all societies to be the great arbiters of good and proper living, Laozi tells us that true wisdom arises from internal reflection and reconciliation of the inner self. In this sense, much as it was (for example) for the early Christians – the physical church is largely superfluous, functioning only as a meeting, or congregation point for like-minded people.

Despite this, he would still freely admit however, that many individuals might usefully draw upon church teachings of proper conduct and the community experience of shared family values for strength and guidance in determining how to enjoy a life of contentment and a proper focus on the common good.

As always, there are both positive and negative aspects to be considered here. There are a multiplicity of competing churches promoting a host of conflicting versions of the 'one true message.' Not unusually, they teach doctrine which may be quite antithetical to the simple pursuit of the common good that is the old boy's ideal.

Within the various church hierarchies, there is much controversy, and substantial discrepancy between the various sects, on what constitutes 'right' and what is truly 'wrong.' If there had not been some overly broad areas of disagreement then Protestantism for example, could never have split into the many hundreds of denominations it has now become. Established religions around the world today are in many cases, in an advanced state of fragmentation, with often rancorous rivalries between the splinter groups of die-hard fundamentalist persuasion, and the more secular groups who attempt to oppose often draconian religious edicts and the antics of the new evangelists whose intrusive edicts and dollar focused religion-as-business attitudes threaten to upset the established secular order.

This dissolution of faith is part of the modern-day dilemma of religious church orders, organizations that frequently place favored dogmatic interpretations of scripture above the principles of unity and reconciliation. Which of course in the terms we are now familiar with, means they are placing form over substance.

To express this in the terms that Carl Jung uses, individuals in this situation of purely symbolic and ritualistic adherence to their religion have lost touch with both the immediate reality of the spiritual experience and with their reason for being. Jung maintains that the fundamental basis for individual independence and self-governance is not reliant on either moral values or established beliefs. Rather, it hinges on the intensely personal encounter with a higher power that counterbalances the rationality of everyday life in the world. (Jung C. G., Civilization in Transition, 1981).

In other words, the congregation do not take it lightly when the priesthood intervenes with all its bureaucratic pomp and ceremony to form a barrier between themselves and their direct experience of the Godhead.

For Jung as for Laozi himself, the 'higher power' is the reality of the true nature of the inner self. His thoughts coincide closely with the old boy's advice, which as ever, is self-contained. Those seeking the unity of the Dao need no external deity, all that is required is to start with the simplest things, our own selves, and our real place in the world. Furthermore, should this exercise prove confronting in forcing us to abandon some previously treasured, but complacent self-assessment, this will be all to the good in the longer term. We will now be in a better position to experience the paradoxical freedom that comes when one is able to recognize and accept one's own limitations.

As the old boy reminds us in these lines above, knowing precisely when to stop is an insight to be prized.

Verse the forty-fifth: On the middle path - In praise of the average.

The greatest perfection may appear as ordinary,
Yet never outlive its usefulness.

The greatest totality may appear inconsequential,
Yet use will not diminish it.

So, the straightest way may seem to have many turns,
The greatest skills appear unpolished,
And great eloquence seen as a combat with words.

Movement overwhelms cold, as stillness conquers heat.
In calmness and tranquility, the whole of the world is put in order.

In looking inwards, and in realistic assessment of the mixed-up jumble of instinct, emotion, knowledge, and experience that is the inner self, sooner or later the soul-searcher on the path of the Dao might begin to realize that some confusion and misunderstanding is an inevitable part of a normal life and is nothing to fear.

It might also then be realized that without these spontaneous and uncontrollable elements of the self, the impressions, feelings, and thoughts which suddenly flash into consciousness, there would be no surprise, no amusement, no sudden impulse of joy, and no laughter in the world.

To be able to say, 'I really don't understand that, but I can accept it and I can feel happy about accepting it,' is to take a first step on the way. Even a neurosis, though characterized by Carl Jung as a sign that a person has lost touch with their innermost self, is also indicative of someone who, "...has not yet found a new form for his finest aspirations" (Jung C. G., Freud and Psychoanalysis, 1981). There is a positive side to everything.

Sometimes appearances are deceptive, things are stubbornly not what they seem, and our judgments seem flawed. Sometimes we miss or are unaware of things around us. Who is routinely alert to all the textures of the world, to the warmth of the breeze, the kaleidoscopic colors of cloudy skies, the smell of fresh rainfall? When the imperfections overwhelm, and frustration saps the energy, perhaps it is time to relax.

We do not need to agonize over absolutely every little detail. Fulfillment is not the reward we reap for sustained effort and extraordinary feats of endurance. The goal is always at the moderate center of all things, and we must never forget that the principle of least effort for best effect is the old boy's guiding precept.

We should not fall into the trap of thinking that the Dao is something rare and strange, and to be gained only by a deserving and industrious few as a reward for exceptional effort. That would make it rare and extreme, and it is not – the Dao is found at the moderate center of things, and in the simplest things, and despite the experiences of some, may be gained by anyone with the most modest of efforts.

When thinking about what this 'moderate center' is, it may be useful to take an analogy from contemporary scientific research - think for a moment, about what extraordinary beauty is. True beauty is not rare, it is found in nature, all around us, all the time. So, to be more specific, what is it that constitutes truly exceptional physical beauty? Science has recently considered this question in an empirical way, with some fascinating results.

In an experiment conducted some years ago (Trujillo, Langlois, & Langlois, 2014), psychologists attempted to discern the nature of physical 'beauty' by experiment; displaying snapshots of hundreds of faces, both male and female, and then getting their subjects to grade them based on their attractiveness. They then used computer technology, to 'average out' the shape, size, and position of facial features such as ears, nose, eye, mouth etc., to build a composite picture of the average face of each region.

At this point, they had their subjects view those 'averaged out' pictures as well.

This research has since been duplicated by several researchers, with some disagreement, but an overall consensus being that physical beauty is not found at the radical extreme of human experience. Somewhat contrary to expectation, the conclusion reached was that 'beauty' is the average for your area - and the more average a person's features are, the more attractive they are invariably judged to be.

The old boy would surely be pleased to know that the moderate center, which is the place of the Dao, is also the place of the most profound beauty.

In a similar way, the greatest of skills are to be found in the commonplace and mundane areas; the effortless ability and mastery of the artisan, the tradesman, the athlete, and the artist – in other words, ordinary, average people who apply themselves to a task with a dedication and perseverance that is more a driving passion to excel rather anything that might be called 'work'.

The Dao is something like that, a middle place where opposites are reconciled to create a breath-taking vision of a calm and restrained perfect wholeness that is in fact - quite ordinary.

Verse the forty-sixth: On confrontation – The misfortunes of war.

When the greater good prevails,
War-horses plow and fertilize the fields of the state.

When the greater good is lost,
The war-horses gather by the borders while the fields are neglected.

There is no sin greater than to covet beyond reasonable need,
No disaster worse than discontent amid plenty,
No greater misfortune than riches gained at the expense of others.

Real contentment is to know when enough is truly enough.

The wealth of the state is far better employed to better the lives of the people than it is in financing hostile action abroad, but the failing leader who is enviously observing the riches and good fortune in neighboring states may still lose the way here. What does a national leader do when their mission is failing and the path is lost? Suddenly, the leadership is vulnerable. Opposing factions seem to be gaining traction, there are generalized rumblings of discontent for which support is growing among the people. There is dissatisfaction everywhere, and even normally close associates in the ruling elite are distancing themselves. Multiple disasters are looming, and in consequence, power and authority are waning.

The embattled leadership no longer feels able to push through the planned austerity measures and increases in taxation, and the whole situation is further complicated by apparently uncontrollable corruption, regular scandals, and widely criticized bureaucratic incompetence within the circle of the governing elite, as well as the fallout from several rashly implemented policies...

To add to the woes, the growing unrest is sparking more frequent public demonstrations of outrage, and now some sort of diversion is urgently needed to draw public attention away from this growing problem. The leadership is increasingly desperate, but they reason that the situation could be rescued - if only they can persuade the people to rally behind some noble uniting cause – and preferably one that will force rival and dissident factions to also toe the line...

Unfortunately, as Laozi well knew after a lifetime of witnessing warring factions, there is a ready answer to this quandary. Historically, the 'best' solution is to start a war. It may sound outrageously excessive, but it is a classic, long-established strategy, and one that has been in frequent use since time immemorial. The first step is to identify a suitable adversary or adversaries. Once this is done, everything that goes wrong, or has previously gone wrong - is now pronounced the fault of this iniquitous enemy.

As a bonus, anyone who continues to oppose the measures the leadership is taking is now derided as either downright unpatriotic or an outright traitor. With some outraged speech-making, some trumped up charges and a slew of dark rumors, before too long, the leadership can count on the support from an uncritical, angry mob which is now solidly behind it - and even demanding action against 'the enemy.' At this point, the governing body can push through almost any extraordinary, even punitive measures they want to.

At the same time, they will now be asking and expecting the ordinary people to demonstrate their patriotism and nationalist fervor by compliance, tightening their belts, bracing for hard times, and providing one hundred percent backing, whatever the pain...

In the longer term, or as an alternative, an unscrupulous leader can also further entrench power by fostering a more lasting discontent against some unfortunate minority, instigating perhaps a racist or religious xenophobia. Of course, this leader will also need to strictly control the flow of information through the media and identify a steady stream of miscreants and scapegoats. After a while, a secret police force of some sort, perhaps a new office of national security, along with a network of informers will make things run more smoothly. To mollify any concerns about this, the leader can name the enforcing body as something benign and protective, perhaps the public safety and protection bureau or anti-terror unit or similar. But its primary function will be to bolster support for the new order by crushing dissent, and both spy on the people and initiate severe reprisals for disloyalty or opposition.

To aid in all this, now is also the time to beef up the military and to make sure the top echelon remains loyal by doling out favors, such as government patronage for their private enterprises. Heavily armed soldiers can now be seconded to be used as police or bodyguards, and trusted cronies can be given control of key manufacturing, media and infrastructure.

Finally, to alleviate international concerns on 'autocratic tyranny,' the great leader can even call 'free' elections and make sure (with bribery, intimidation, and control of the ballot box) that no rival is able to win in the polls. If someone does look capable of beating the leader, they can always be accused of something nasty and illegal and tied up in a court case or forced to flee the country, or failing that, might perhaps suffer an unfortunate 'accident' of an incapacitating or fatal nature.

This traditionally (and sadly) is often how it is done. Generation after generation, we are blighted by conflicts that a vast majority of the general populations of the combatant states neither want nor need. The old boy speaks to us from an era when these circumstances arose just as often as they do now and reminds us that not that much has changed.

And yet, each time these conditions recur, the way of the Dao becomes compromised, and enlightenment recedes as the 'isms' are once again embraced; nationalism, fundamentalism, patriotism, fascism, colonialism, imperialism, communism, fanaticism, idealism, racism, all leading towards an ultimate and inevitable climax – antagonism, vandalism, barbarism - schism.

In the lines above the old boy speaks of this process and of how the good times can turn sour. The ideal, where the resources of state are directed towards bettering the lives of the people, and the greater good prevails, is turned in this process, towards a time of war, when all resources are directed outwards towards defeating the enemy. This is when families are split, and good agricultural land lies idle as the population is conscripted and militarized.

Wars are often justified because they give the victor access to new lands and resources, but the old boy would have none of this inferior idea. Wars more often serve the selfish needs of great leaders or are stumbled into through their incompetence. For Laozi, a war is a waste of time, effort, and happiness. Even the riches to be gained at the expense of another in war time are a misfortune – just one more obstruction on the great way of enlightenment.

Verse the forty-seventh: On feeling the sun on your face - Live, work, play, laugh, love.

To travel widely - is not always to gain knowledge of the world.
To observe closely - is not how one learns the way of heaven,
Much effort can be expended in going far - yet seeing less.

The wise can see the truth from where they sit,
Identify the essence from where they are,
And do what must be done without the appearance of being busy.

Wisdom versus knowledge, the old boy returns to this consideration again and again. We are all easily persuaded that enlightenment requires something we need to obtain, somewhere we need to go, more knowledge, more humility, more insight, more understanding, more learning, more personal strength, more opportunity, more time, more effort, and more experience...

Equally, we are accustomed to believing that 'action' gives us purpose and direction and equates to 'progress,' if we busy ourselves with the task at hand, we will inevitably receive due recognition for our dynamism - or so we like to assure ourselves. Conversely, if we sit around idly, perhaps we are just too lazy, and never deserved the benefits of any ultimate reward in the form of a serene and well-lived life anyway...

The reality is that our work ethic is culturally instilled behavior, as often as not motivated these days by exposure to corporate propaganda, as for example, listening to the employer's imperative that 'hard work is its own reward.' Since the industrial revolution, people have worked longer and harder than at any other time in history and individual productivity has soared.

Yet despite all the advances and the often promised prospect of easier lives, all our technology and know-how have not brought us the long-awaited leisure time we once expected from it. Despite the massive gains in productivity, we still work longer and harder than ever before, with compelling statistical evidence in English speaking nations, that at least some of the living standards of ordinary families are actually decreasing generation by generation.

This raises the question; is industry serving the needs of people, or are people serving the needs of industry? Obviously, we must work to survive, but bare survival should not be a life's work. The old boy is always scornful of all forms of ill-considered and pointless action, and work is only a part of life - no matter how hard the die-hard capitalist business owner tries to make it the primary focus. If our vision is to penetrate the muddiest of waters, we must stop swirling them around first and have the patience to wait until stillness brings clarity.

Work-on-the-self, the nurturing of inward vision, also needs a place in our lives. Proper action is a lot more than just slavish adherence to a cultural work ethic. Those engaged in seeking the common good need to understand that sometimes, time spent in quiet contemplation is worth more than any sustained energy-sapping effort. One of the hardest lessons we must learn is that we are truly sufficient unto ourselves. Realization is in the self - and it is for the self. We all need space for life and family as well as career, and mostly we must seize those moments for ourselves - step back from the insatiable corporate and business time-sink that threatens to monopolize our lives and turn existence into drudgery. Time for ourselves is essential - it is very doubtful that any person on their deathbed ever regretted not spending more time at work...

What we do with our time is also important. While some people may find contentment in seeking out new experiences, fulfillment for the individual is never dependent on going somewhere, doing something, or achieving some rarefied intellectual height. Often, a simple child-like comprehension and acceptance of the world is more than sufficient. We have already considered and celebrated for example, that beloved, bumbling hero of children's bedtime stories Winnie-the-Pooh, who needed nothing special in his day to celebrate the fact of his fulfillment and achievement of satisfaction other than to simply, and sincerely, to wish all his friends "Many happy returns of the day..." (Milne, 1944)

Somehow, once we have the time, we need to deal with, and as a first step at least acknowledge, our cynicism, our prejudice, our predispositions of attitude, our accumulated doubts, our unbridled ambition, our self-deception... all in all, it sounds like a very serious business indeed, but latter day masters of the Daoist ideal, such as Alan Watts would join the old boy in dismissing this inappropriate mind-set with an understanding sigh and a grin - and tell you to lighten up! Feel the sun on your face, go dancing, take a break, watch a sunset, love someone or something, read a book!

As Watts puts it:

"This is the real secret of life - to be completely engaged with what you are doing in the here and now. And instead of calling it work, realize it is play." (Watts, 2011)

The old boy never suggests there is always a bitter pill to swallow or a hard road to travel in attainment of the ultimate essence. The size of the mountain you must climb to find the true nature of the Dao is a thing of your own making. When you can see the humor in your condition, you are already on the way...

When the human condition - your condition, causes you not recrimination, not doubt, not anxiety, not fear, but a huge and uncontrollable belly-laugh at the random vagaries of fate, then the old boy will be laughing right there along with you, with the happy tears rolling off his white whiskers - as the mental gates swing wide open...

Verse the forty-eighth: On letting go – Clarity of vision.

In learning - new facts are acquired daily and added to the sum.
In pursuit of enlightenment - the unimportant facts are discarded.

As less and less become necessary – stillness through inaction is achieved,
When stillness is achieved, all that is necessary has been done.

The world is best governed by this minimal action,
All things must take their course,
Those who interfere in this natural order,
Are not equal to the task.

Laozi asks us to view the universe as a self-correcting, self-governing, self-sufficient whole. We should not waste our time trying to change, to slow or otherwise influence the natural course of events. There is a grand cycle of dynamic transformation in progress on a scale which makes our petty concerns of less significance than the fate of a single drop of water in the vastness of an ocean

Things are as they were meant to be.

To fight mother nature and oppose those mighty forces is folly in the extreme, and something that may well invite disaster, and at the very least, will sap our energy and drain our capacity for pursuing the peace and harmony we seek.

Even though our instincts might tell us we need to be in control of events, the old boy will generally advise, 'Let it go.' Instead of reacting negatively to perceived adversity, we might first ask ourselves; why are we so disturbed? Why are we upset or stressed by events? Wisdom lies in observing as events unfold and attaining conscious appreciation of the unfolding rhythms and patterns of life.

This, once again, is where a rationally focused or over-developed intellect - even in those with a vast accumulation of learning, can sometimes still be more of a hindrance than a help. Our enormous store of human knowledge is something we draw upon to find solutions, implement plans for change, and evaluate possible courses of action. But sometimes, all that is required is that we consciously relax, empty our minds of thought, and just let it all go.

The temptation to overthink the situation is always there.

We are all still a part of nature, and our enhanced ability to rationalize and intellectualize can be both our strength and our weakness. On the one hand it makes possible all the wonders of our science and technology, on the other, it may cause us to doubt our intuitions, override our feelings, stifle our instincts and prevent us from behaving and relating to our environment in an entirely natural way. To those who would use logic and reason to seize the controls and consider themselves able to channel nature to their own ends, the old boy would raise a bushy white brow in admonition and advise that the best course is to let the world turn, and to look inside the innermost self for the answers sought.

As Carl Jung said:

> "Your vision will become clear only when you can look into your own heart. Who looks outside, dreams, who looks inside, awakes." (Jung C. G., Man and his Symbols, 1999)

Verse the forty-ninth: On the hallmarks of wisdom - Doing what is good for others, is also good for you.

The wise cannot be swayed by personal whim,
The leader's mind reflects only the mind of the people.

Those with wisdom treat those that are good - as good,
And those that are not good - the same.
In this, the greater good is served.

Those with wisdom treat those who are unfailing - unfailingly,
And those who fail - in like manner.
In doing this, insufficiency is averted.

The wise are at one with the world - the center and focus of harmony,
By this example, all people learn and find their place,
And yet the simplicity of childhood is maintained.

Here the old boy has a message that, centuries later, was to become incorporated into Christian and many other religious teachings, and which is also to be found in the core precepts of Zen philosophy. This is the self-sacrificing idea that we should try to do good even when someone is doing something bad to us. To reciprocate a hostile action with yet another hostile action means escalation into conflict and continues the weary cycle of debilitating negativity.

In other words, our virtuous deeds and proper conduct - which should aim always in the direction of the common good - are not conditional on receiving the same courtesy ourselves. In this way, we embrace tolerance, further our global 'big picture' outlook on life and accept the casual indifference and ordinary contrariness of the natural world while still managing to stay on the middle path towards our own realization of self.

Laozi lived in a time and place in which even relatively minor officials of government might have the absolute power of life and death over any ordinary person. A great leader might be worshiped as a deity by some, and undeniably had almost God-like powers over the people. Even lesser leaders might still inspire awe, terror or revulsion, and every level of leadership was always deserving of a wary respect.

In view of the excessive powers that they could wield on a whim, and the punitive excesses that were possible by those charged with the direction of community and state, the old boy frequently couches his message as advice to these officials who more than anyone, could affect the lives of others for better or for worse. As always though, the message is scalable, and the advice proffered will invariably have relevance to people at all levels of society.

The deficiencies of the average 'great leader' are depressingly familiar to us, not just from the examples from bygone times, but right up to, and including, the mixed bag of presidents, monarchs, warlords, oligarchs, premiers, commanders-in-chief, prime-ministers, governors, and other executive ranked personnel to be found on the world stage throughout our past and more recent history.

It must be said however that, although politics and high office within the state is a field in which venal mediocrity often rules, and although it can foster the worst excesses of human greed, ambition, cruelty, and ruthless self-aggrandizement – there have been some genuine great leaders. These were people who, though possessed of the human failings we all have, nevertheless demonstrated their own overall orientation towards caring, selflessness in action, and working towards the greater good for all.

Here Laozi presents his thoughts on some of the rare qualities which characterize the behavior and normal conduct of those state officials who are among the very best of their kind. Not unexpectedly, the well-developed political abilities of wheeling and dealing, smearing the opposition, misleading, or deceiving the electorate and pork-barreling for advantage are not among the desirable traits. Nor are cynical political ploys such as gerrymandering, spin-doctoring, playing the 'shift-the-blame' game, trumpeting the good news while sweeping the bad news under the carpet, and failing to adopt any firm position on any controversial topic (right or wrong), until the PR risks are thoroughly assessed and damage control is in place.

All of these are things that also had their counterparts in the environment Laozi knew, and the old boy would recognize - and consider regrettable - that part of the political landscape in which individual career ambitions and the accumulation of personal power and influence take precedence over social responsibility, genuine justice for all, considerations of ethical and moral behavior, and the nurturing of well-being in the citizenship - all of which are of course, the real work of state.

Since the old boy insists that progress comes always from individuals accepting personal responsibility, we can never expect any institution to make a great leap forward - unless it is at the behest of some guiding individual with progressive vision. So, until more people begin work-on-the-self, the great way remains littered with obstruction, and the greatest of great leaders remain a select few.

The old boy's message, in short, is one that is equally applicable to everyone. Whenever we may feel that it is right to treat someone unfairly, unjustly, or even without due respect and courtesy, the damage done is something that will inevitably rebound upon us as blockage and obstruction on the path to self-actualization.

Harmony and true satisfaction is to be found in acting always towards the greater good, and no good at all will come of vengeance or persecution.

As the old biblical saying has it; "Don't kick against the pricks."

Verses the fiftieth and fifty-first: A tantalizing vision – Of imperfect reality...

Every life may strive for unity and wholeness - or accept dissolution.
One third of humanity are affirmative of life,
And one third condemned to live it.
The middle third passes unremarkably from birth to death,
But, having valued their mortality over total being - in turn accept their condemnation.

Those who know the value in their total being - walk without fear,
They expect neither aggression nor misfortune.
And so, appear to live a charmed existence.
Having committed to the fullness of life
Death has no hold over them.

All that is - begins with acceptance of life's vital essence,
All that ensues - is nourished by goodness,

Substance gives a form to what is good,
Contingency gives it shape.

All living things depend upon the indivisible one.
To respect and honor this natural order is not required,

Yet it is wholesome to do so.

From the formless aggregate of this wholeness - life is offered.
From this totality comes nourishment and growth,
And from that - maturity and attainment,
And from that - quietude and sanctuary.

In giving without taking,
In serving without recognition,
In guiding yet not dominating,
The greatest good is revealed as primal virtue.

In these lines, which are all very much on the same theme, the old boy gives us a vision of the Dao that is enticingly close, something accessible to all persons in all situations. The enlightenment and self-actualization we are seeking may be just a heartbeat away, and everything we might possibly need for its attainment is already to be found within our grasp. Yet, here again the old boy is telling us that many, even most people, will almost certainly miss out. Much of humanity will never find this kind of harmonious unity in the integration of the self in their lifetimes.

Laozi's words in the first few lines above, will find resonance in the lives of those many individuals who are trapped and live lives of barely conscious toil - those whose awareness of the world is stunted, and whose mental horizons are limited to considerations of the immediate problems of subsistence. In modern psychological parlance, these are the people who are barely surviving and are trapped near the bottom of Abraham Maslow's famous 'Hierarchy of needs,' which was first encountered in examining the meaning of the lines in verse fourteen - and because of this, their engagement with the day-to-day struggle for survival precludes any serious pursuit of spiritual needs – at least in the immediate term. (Maslow, 1987)

This is a fact that the old boy is resigned to, something that must be accepted as a simple truth. There are many people who simply cannot seek, do not seek, and may never seek, transcendent goals. This is not a criticism, and these are not people who deserve to be disparaged. It is though, solid and damning evidence that we are not as advanced or altruistic a civilization as we may sometimes think we are.

Cultured though we may consider ourselves to be, there yet exists within our societies, a stratum of each community whose needs regarding the acquisition of life's fundamentals remain unfulfilled; food, water, a livable income, a roof overhead, basic job security, sufficient self-respect to become an effective family and community member. For some, the recurring and urgent considerations of daily survival at this vital level of bare subsistence may effectively occupy a whole lifetime.

These then, are often the innocent victims of society, whose necessary focus on survival and whose minimal status within the community leaves little time for considerations of the spiritual. Meantime, another group the old boy mentions here, while not condemned to scrabble for a bare existence, are still happy to accept a brief, and materially focused life, before inevitable dissolution. These are possibly the people mostly tied to the limited position dictated by their particular 'ism,' those with close mental horizons who will never catch more than a distant glimpse of the bigger picture, but may nevertheless be kind, benevolent and productive members of society. They could be the flotsam and jetsam of the community, but equally might represent decency, the righteous core of productive individuals and church members living lives of quiet virtue.

Nonetheless, unless they change their life focus with some rigorously honest introspection and self-evaluations, the old boy is ultimately not for them.

For those who do accept the challenge of self-fulfillment, and of 'valuing their total being,' the old boy offers his tantalizing vision. These people, if their quest is a genuine appreciation and fostering of the greater good as applied in every situation, have an exceptionally good prospect of appearing to their contemporaries as blessed by contentment and good fortune. Without appearing to be forceful or overly aggressive, everything good seems naturally to flow their way. Without becoming strident, their opinions will be valued. They will be seen as fair and decent advocates of truth and justice, people valued for their good judgment, and people whose advice is sought and appreciated.

Though they are not ambitious, these people are often widely esteemed, and considered to be natural leaders who command respect when it matters. Yet even among this group, the ones who initially take up the challenge of forming that personal connection with ultimate things, a significant number may still eventually fall by the wayside and settle for lesser consolations than a perceived - but distant - promise of unity of self into an as yet unrealized cosmic whole.

One thing that should be recalled here is the old boy's advice that the actualization of the self is never accessible by the adoption of a particular form or process, it is more readily defined as commitment to the higher principles of the common good and the exercise of absolute personal integrity in working towards that common good. It is the consummation of our individual reality, but it is in no way perfection - because we are all still human and prone to error.

The old boy is here to assert that it is the best you will get – a life at peace with itself and with nature, contented, assured, and always focused on the greater good. A life which accepts the imperfect reality of self and others – warts and all.

Verse the fifty-second: On the light of understanding – Holding back when appropriate.

Think back to the beginning of all beginnings,
The uniqueness that is the mother lode of our world.
When you recognize the mother,
Then know her kind.

When you can relate all things with their source,
You will know the essence that can shelter and protect your life.

Use no unnecessary words,
Be on guard against false perceptions.
And knowing stillness – live a full life.

In being diverted by the inconsequential,
In indulging idle sensation,
And in so doing, being busy – life's potential is abandoned.

Have awareness of the world around,
Do not fight the ebb and flow of nature.
Use the light without to illumine the sight within.

Remember - insight into truth prevents misfortune.
When learning the perseverance of constancy.

In this verse and the next, Laozi, beginning with the phrase "use no unnecessary words," gives us an account of some of the possible obstacles in the search for the whole, and some of the ways in which we might mistakenly take the wrong path by failing to hold back from some small temptation. He describes the pitfalls of those on the way as many and various, and in these lines details just some of the possible diversions from the way of the Dao as great journey.

What is it that happens to an individual when considerations of personal status, wealth and material possession take precedence over the higher ideals of fulfillment within the Dao, and the ideal of personal integration? The old boy has no doubts on the matter at all. This is a negative, self-destructive mindset that fosters the growth of intolerance, injustice, cold-heartedness, and inhumane action.

When this ideology is applied at the higher corporate and state level, that is when individuals in prioritizing personal gain, fail to take full responsibility for their organizations. The consequence is of course, that these institutions become corrupted, and prejudice, injustice and inequality become systemic.

There is also a further warning here on the make-work of inconsequential action. This is effort and energy expended on any non-essential task, it could be the kind of work which is often undertaken reluctantly in order to deflect any criticism of idleness - but which lacks any real value. Or perhaps, it is the kind of pointless tinkering that gives the appearance of useful activity but is an adopted facade of productivity that simply wastes time and effort without yielding any positive outcomes.

In this context it is useful to recall the old boy's advice that the ultimate unity is never accessible by the adoption of a particular form or process, it is not a mode of doing things, unless there is also insight to understand the relevance of the action. 'Busywork' takes the time and energy that could be spent on work-on-the-self or work perhaps more aptly described as work undertaken with full commitment to the higher principles of the common good.

The way of the Dao represents the consummation of our reality in both its internal and external aspects. It is most definitely not some ineffectual role-play or dilettante intellectual dalliance.

Verse the fifty-third: On predatory leadership – Subjugation and servitude.

When striving towards the common good and to unity, a little sense will suffice,
The greatest way is the easy way.

Yet - although there are by-roads seductive for many.
Do not be tempted to stray.

When some live in opulent grandeur,
While weeds choke the crops, and the ordinary people go hungry...
And when high society wears exclusive finery,
And ceremonial occasion diverts attention from the real essentials,
And when the finest foods and rarest wines are reserved for the few,
And those few having strayed - have possessions neither used nor appreciated.
While all others live with need...

Then the robber barons have taken over the state,
And the great way to unity has been lost.

The old boy is here scathingly outspoken about the ostentatious wealth of those wealthiest members of society who both control the resources of the state and wield the ultimate power of life and death over the people. He condemns the urge towards the accumulation of ever more wealth as a form of meaningless greed and often makes the point that accumulated wealth beyond what can be spent, is truly a hindrance. For Laozi, a pile of treasure is an encumbrance to a good life, something that must be perpetually guarded and kept secure - so that simply holding onto it becomes a stressful source of anxiety.

For him, great riches are a constant source of worry and distraction.

These views of the old boy have some strong parallels in some of the New Testament Christian teachings as well as in socialist political ideology, the excessive accumulation of material riches is often chracterized as a form of robbery, since this wealth must ultimately be sourced by taking unfair advantage of the toil of an exploited underclass of workers. This deviation from the way is compounded by a lack of empathy for the plight of the underdog, since there can be no genuine serving of the common good from someone who enjoys the finest foods and a life of opulence while the poor starve in miserable circumstances.

So, in choosing the path of enrichment at the expense of others, these community leaders are lost to the path of the Dao, and will not progress further along the way of self-realization until such time as they can look honestly at themselves and abandon the ornate trappings, and selfish gluttony of their privileged lives, and prioritize the common good by ensuring that the needs of the people are being met.

The old boy is not an ascetic as such, he just wants those in power to serve the needs of the community before wallowing in their own indulgences. This kind of admonishment of those with wealth and power, is unusually forthright criticism from Laozi, and might have brought some retribution from those in authority unless he very carefully picked the time and place to make public these ideas.

Comparing the old boy's situation and our own experience here and now, reveals that despite this injunction, nothing much has changed in society at large. Too often, a privileged sector of a society falls prey to the temptation to use some slight or passing advantage to entrench their fortunate position in the community at the expense of some lower stratum of society, thereby semi-permanently tipping the balance of power in favor of their own comfort and personal enrichment.

The fact that these materialistic people have abandoned the way of Dao, and any hope of personal fulfillment in falling victim to their own greed may be of little consolation to the citizens whose wealth will now be pillaged in taxes and whose labor may be forcibly diverted - perhaps for generations, to the enrichment of this chosen few.

This situation, where the polarization of advantage and disadvantage arises repeatedly in different societies and within different nations, was perfectly familiar to the old boy, and has re-occurred many times throughout history. Yet today, as it has always been throughout history, there are still leaders of state publicly recognized as weak, self-serving performers, and with extensive records of favoring an elite, fostering cronyism, and using legislation as a tool to perpetuate exactly this form of injustice.

Despite this, it is often seen that even these most apparently culpable of institutional leadership failures will proudly, stoutly, and invariably maintain that they have done their very best in attempting to fulfill their duties to their people, and mostly they may even believe this to be true...

The old boy can tell us why this happens. Firstly, this is a failure of vision, the leadership are failing to see the 'big picture' and have accepted something less than the ideal of always working towards the common good in formulating their decisions. Possibly the rulers are genuinely benevolent in intention, but simply lacking in the necessary personal qualities - certainly they will lack genuine honesty and integrity and therefore have deviated from the path - whether knowingly or not.

In some instances, the governing elite is possibly seduced by some passing trend in political ideas, something like the commonly adopted precept that the 'good of the economy' is the same as the 'good of the people.' Or perhaps they have simply opted to selfishly take advantage of their privileged position to indulge in personal enrichment at the expense of ordinary folk.

Growth in the overall wealth of a nation, as the old boy strongly indicates in his words above, is actually an extremely poor determining factor of the overall strength and health of a state. The key factor is not the total amount of capital or income within the system - it is in its beneficial distribution. How wealth is apportioned is a far better determinant of overall well-being than the gross statistics.

To take a contemporary example, while stock markets may soar and property portfolios experience boom conditions, and while new millionaires and billionaires are created in a regular stream, and even while many businesses expand and prosper – all may not be well. Unfortunately, it is not so uncommon that boom times do little or nothing for the lower strata of society. Possibly, unemployment, poverty and homelessness increase in tandem with national growth as jobs are lost to technological innovation or global outsourcing.

For those workers competing for fewer jobs, the quality of life diminishes, discontents multiply, and the gulf between rich and poor widens. Low interest rates, favorable exchange rates, and the record dividends paid by multi-national corporations are of little import to the ordinary working poor, struggling minorities, or the multitudes of sweatshop workers supplying rich countries from squalid third world factories that may be lacking in even basic health and safety for the employees.

The economy is important, but it is still something much less than the whole. Harmony, security, justice, tolerance, tranquility, peace of mind; these desirable things arise when the leaders of societies recognize an essential truth - and in doing so, raise their eyes from their financial bottom lines to a consideration of what makes us human.

We are not just a demographic in a market sector - we are a people with lives to lead.

Verse the fifty-fourth: On proper action - To know others, first know yourself.

Knowing your roots, knowing your origins - this is your reality,
What you hold tight will not slip loose,
And the lessons of history will not be lost.

Give life to the totality within yourself - and achieve fulfillment.
Energize unity within the family - and achieve abundance,
Vitalize community values in the village - and contentment will grow,
Activate unity within the state - and there will be goodness in plenty,
Awaken harmony in the world - and virtue will be all pervasive

Be honest when looking at yourself,
Apply family values to family issues,
And community values to community issues,
Consider the national issues when looking at the state,
And the absolute picture when looking at the world as whole.

In proper contemplation lies the enlightenment that serves the common good.

Action is justified in its scale by the context in which it is taken, and what is appropriate at state level may be quite wrong in the context of community or family affairs. So, what then is the 'big picture?'

Correct action as the old boy sees it, is a matter of first discerning the actual context of events. Understanding is key since an ill-considered action may have devastating consequences. Unless all the relevant facts have been carefully considered, how can an appropriate decision be made, a policy implemented, or an approach formulated? Wisdom lies in tailoring the solution to the problem, and foolhardiness in trying to make the problem fit the preferred solution.

Carl Jung was a great believer in the pre-eminent importance of the individual in society, just as was Laozi himself. For Jung it was axiomatic that all the great events that constitute world history pale to insignificance beside the inner life of the individual. He further remarked that all the monumental and momentous happenings in the world have their beginnings in the thoughts and hidden resources of ordinary people, and that we are not just the passive observers of events - we are the makers of our world. (Jung C. G., Civilization in Transition, 1981)

The rules to be followed in determining the criteria for individual action are few:

Never mistake the visible symptoms for the hidden problem, do not waste energy on a lost cause, and be totally honest and fair in your dealings. Also, be aware that, although it may not be that difficult to fool yourself - the fool will still be you.

Correct action is all a matter of self-nurture, if we cultivate our insight honestly and habitually, then the path of the common good becomes just our natural mode of being.

Also important is to remember not to fight against what is natural (nature will always prevail) and to always listen to intuition, while at the same time, being sure to have all the facts. The goal is peace and harmony through acting in the common good, and all other considerations are secondary.

Finally, have regard to the cliche that those who do not learn by their mistakes are inevitably condemned to repeat them.

This last point is made with respect to the fact that cliches attain their oft-repeated status because they generally contain the kernel of some vital truth.

The old boy would likely also remind us here that an effective community leader must have an ongoing appreciation of the fact that the powers of state are given in service of the needs of all the people. To avoid the seductive lure of personal aggrandizement, it is helpful to retain a keen awareness that no amount of privilege, prestige, or wealth can bring personal fulfillment, unless the central issues of personal reconciliation through work-on-the-self are addressed.

In this context, Carl Jung also speaks tellingly of the Dao essence as the "spiritual adventure of our time," and remarks to the effect that to be on the path of the Dao is to be exposed to the something indeterminate and undefinable. He further makes the point that individuals do not hold metaphysical beliefs – but rather they are influenced, held, and controlled by them. (Jung C. G., Psychology and Religion: West and East, 1981)

In a very real sense then, one becomes the Dao.

Verse the fifty-fifth: On vitality - The potential in simplicity.

One who knows the virtue of the greater good is like a newborn boy,
Unperturbed by his environment,
Unafraid of life's dangers,
Untouched by the pressures of earthly living.
Soft-boned and apparently fragile - yet his grip is strong.

Knowing nothing of the union of the sexes - yet he shows his virile potential.
Shrieking his small discontents yet not becoming hoarse - he is in total harmony.

Harmony brings constancy and constancy the inward vision,
Acceptance saves the weariness of wasted endeavor.

Add your energy to the natural rhythm,
And take your strength from the whole.
Those fighting the great ebb and flow will not succeed.

Laozi here uses the image of the baby, as compared to the sage, to examine some of the paradoxes to be confronted on the path of self-realization. The symbolism here is reminiscent of the earlier chapters in which the 'uncarved block' represents the infinite possibilities of final form. The 'newborn baby' described here also represents raw beginnings; unlimited potential for growth, power, strength, and vitality - yet at the same time, and in full conformity with the paradoxical nature of the Dao, the baby represents weakness, vulnerability, fragility, and insensibility. The last lines are a reminder of the great universal cycle, the ebb and flow of light and dark, birth and death, growth, and decay.

It is no accident that Laozi tells us often that the Dao essence is not a goal to be achieved but a path to be followed. The concept of 'enantiodromia' which Carl Jung borrowed from Heraclitus, is remarkably congruent with the old boy's description of the universal cycle as encompassing all polarization. Since the whole of creation is in perpetual flux, and everything changes inexorably into its opposite, if the absolute pinnacle of perfection is ever reached, the only possible next step is downwards…

As always, the best course is to not to rush things, enjoy the here and now, stay true to the self. There is no need to hurry or push forwards, this leads only to stress and anxiety. Simply go with the flow and try not to overthink life's problems, or allow ambition to disturb harmony with thoughts of things not yet achieved.

When the mind is relaxed and at peace, our natural energy will be asserted.

Verse the fifty-sixth: On lucidity and integrity – Trust and respect.

The greatest truths are often deliberated in privacy,
The greatest deceits are often widely preached in public.
Accordingly, use no unnecessary and meaningless declarations,
And be on guard against those that you may hear.

Let your sharpness become well roundedness,
Untangle your thoughts,
Value what you know about yourself,
And not what others know about you.
Be at one. Act for the common good.

Having done this - no extreme can sway you,
And your thoughts will have value for all.

Here the old boy is issuing a few simple, but nevertheless vital guidelines for those considering the elusive nature of the Dao. Firstly, the Dao is not some distant goal. There is no need to seek wisdom in faraway places and ransack the libraries of academe for the essential missing pieces of a life of fulfillment.

In fact, everyone on the great way should be honestly considerate, but innately skeptical in matters of public debate on proper living, and the urgings of those they may meet on the way who preach the prospect of salvation to their followers. The very fact of becoming a 'follower' in itself implies some dependence on an external authority, whereas the old boy promotes a healthy self-reliance as being key to honest and productive work-on-the-self.

What is needed by each of us is a well-rounded appreciation of the possibilities that lie within, and an open commitment to accept the whole of the reality of our own inner being, and place in the world – be it ever so humble. When we take on the responsibility for our own development in this clear-sighted manner, Laozi assures us that good things will generally happen.

Interestingly, the naturally humble, less sophisticated, and more self-effacing may well have the advantage here, since the movers and shakers in our society are more likely to be embroiled in egotistical concerns and therefore may not so readily embrace the humility that comes more naturally to other, less status-conscious people.

One of the problems we might face is that our (Western) cultural tradition has given us very little education in the benefits of cultivating a modest or humble outlook on life. We are generally all encouraged from childhood to regard ourselves as special, and not to shy away from informing others of our abilities and triumphs. For this reason, a natural and ingrained respect for the wisdom of society elders comes far more easily to those of the more collective Eastern tradition than it does to those raised in the individualistic traditions of the West.

In this regard, it is also true to say that Western society is more likely to prize youthful attributes and consider the elders of society as 'old and out of touch' rather than as revered seniors possessing the wisdom of hard-won experience. In short, people in the West are generally more ego-driven and less inclined to seek to sit at the feet of a master, as is more acceptable and commonplace in the Eastern tradition.

C.G. Jung wrote in some detail on this difficulty and in a somewhat uncharacteristically pessimistic vein, saying that there is a reverence in the East for great wisdom, and also a readiness to believe in the possibility of a paradoxical transformative experience - although he himself is of the view that this is something which will involve the sacrifice of many years of a lifetime to achieve. He contrasts this with Western tradition, in which it is rare to express total trust in any superior Master, and even rarer for someone to accept the reality of receiving enlightenment from a mentor or spiritual guidance figure such as this. Our Western educational tradition leads us to view the 'Master' figure as possibly untrustworthy and harboring some ulterior motive, or even possibly as a charlatan undeserving of support. Therefore, when faced with this difficult task of approaching the Dao, Western peoples begin to doubt themselves and thereby find the path of self-development to be as unpleasant as "the path to hell." (Jung C. G., Psychology and Religion: West and East, 1981)

Despite this pessimism, Jung does not close the door on individual transcendence towards the Dao as the reality of self-actualization for Westerners, he just insists that we do not try to reject our own Western identity in the process. He is firmly of the belief that becoming more familiar with Eastern culture can help us connect with unfamiliar parts of ourselves, but that any subsequent rejection and denial of our own history would be foolish and could lead to a detrimental loss of identity. In effect, it is only by staying true to our own roots that we can fully understand and appreciate Eastern culture. (Jung C. G., Alchemical Studies, 1981)

Once again, the two very different perspectives of Laozi and C.G. Jung are in perfect accord, since the old boy also advises us more than once that we must accept the truth of what, and who, we really are to advance along the way of the Dao.

To return here to the further import of the lines above, it is fair to say that in any list of great world leaders of integrity, the same names will appear time after time. In no special order, the list will generally include: - Martin Luther King, Mahatma Gandhi, Nelson Mandela, the Dalai Lama, Mother Teresa – to name but a few. To this base list might be added many more names, inevitably including many quite controversial contenders; the artists, monarchs, entrepreneurs, sporting celebrities and politicians who have inspired respect and admiration – at least for some among us.

After that, there remains almost unlimited possibility for potential additions to the list. Not everyone will agree with every inclusion of course, and it is also possible to take issue with any person on the list and point out that their characters were hardly flawless. They were human, with all the failings that implies. They made mistakes, had defects in personality, or were associated with ill-considered deeds, and if we look at them carefully, we reach the conclusion that none of them were perfect - each had their quirks, foibles, and human frailties.

The quality that unites them in this list is the quality the old boy is talking about in this verse – integrity. Despite their sometimes quite visible failings, these are generally people considered to be of high principle and resolve. They are persons for whom words such as honor, justice, honesty, decency, virtue, fairness, dedication, morality, scrupulousness, perseverance, and commitment seem (perhaps with some dissenters) to apply generally and quite naturally. For anyone on the path to self-realization, this kind of integrity is something that they will need to nurture in themselves and in their dealings with others.

The interesting thing about the word 'integrity' is that, in addition to having that essential meaning the old boy would agree is 'nobility of spirit,' it also means 'whole,' 'undivided' and 'unified.' In other words, this word - 'integrity' - marks a place where the Dao essence resides. Those on the path of the greater good are not deceptive, and do not attempt to trick others with 'cleverness.' Those with real integrity are noticed in the community. Their advice is sought, their leadership accepted, and they inspire respect. True integrity brings a great leader universal acclaim that is acquired without much fanfare.

Laozi is telling us here that those who have untangled their thoughts and confronted their reality possess that quality of integrity. They seek no favors or flattery; they are secure in their own self-worth without needing or seeking recognition for it.

They are on the path of the Dao.

Verse the fifty-seventh and fifty eighth: On wisdom and leadership – Justice and law.

How do you win the people? - With fairness and justice.
How do you win the war? - With resourcefulness and surprise.
How do you win the whole? - Without strife.
You will know this when you recognize no conflict.

As rules and regulations proliferate within the state,
The people become poorer.
When the populace seek to arm themselves,
The state is troubled.
When novelty and artfulness occupy the community,
Discontent becomes rife.

When the citizens trouble themselves in learning the letter of the law,
Theft and lawlessness are becoming a scourge in the state.

The wise among leaders do not try to reconstruct their people,
And by this restraint - the people are free to develop themselves.
The wise among leaders prefer stillness and distance to action,
And by this restraint - the people are permitted to advance themselves.
The wise among leaders do not concern themselves in trivial regulation,
And by this restraint - the people can prosper.

The wise in, their freedom from need, are an example to the people,
And in this simplicity - they approach closer to the greatest good.

When the state is governed with restraint,
There is goodness and simplicity.
When the state is governed with harshness,
There is conspiracy and equivocation.

The great cycle includes both great joy and great grief.
Elation succeeds the misery behind the happiness that follows despair.
How can we cope with this?

In seeking the whole, the path that appears straight may yet prove a diversion,
And even best intention may be put to evil ends.
This perplexity has occupied many lives.

The wise maintain faith in their personal vision - and avoid confrontation.
They connect with the world - and yet are sufficient in themselves.
They nurture inner awareness - but not at the expense of another,
They know that which has most brilliance,
Can not only illuminate - but also dazzle and blind.

These two relatively long passages flow naturally into one whole, the old boy laying out in the clearest terms what it is that makes a great leader - or a person who is fit to be one. Evenhandedness for all, kindness, respect for individual self-determination, and simplicity of action without needlessly restrictive rules and regulations are some of the key ideas - plus of course the necessity that decisions and actions are all motivated primarily towards the common good.

Justice, integrity, understanding and compassion; these are some of the old boy's ruling precepts. Laozi is just the kind of person to support a liberal humanitarian legal system where the same set of rights is guaranteed for all.

But what might these lines mean?

> *As rules and regulations proliferate within the state,*
> *The people become poorer.*

And:

> *When the citizens trouble themselves in learning the letter of the law,*
> *Theft and lawlessness are becoming a scourge in the state.*

With these lines, the old boy tells us the way is all but lost. The ruling elite are failing to rule with the light touch which marks genuinely great leadership. A confusion of guidelines and protocols has arisen as the ship of state veers erratically off-course and, in the absence of benevolent oversight, people are turning towards the letter of the law for protection.

Where previously there was freedom of action in an environment geared towards the common good, now there is unease and a sense of insecurity and threat. This is a time of doubt and uncertainty in the ability of the local institutions to properly shield and nurture the ordinary people.

Justice is not just a noble concept, it is forever intertwined with the law, and the law is not just a list of statutes. Legislative bodies are institutions of state, and the old boy has already warned us that the institutions of state are not entities to be fully trusted. In fact, Laozi makes it abundantly clear that our legislative and other community institutions can generally be regarded as stronger, and better when a weakness or vulnerability is deliberately introduced into them.

This weakness, like the sanctioned opposition parties in democratic governments, thwarts excessive authoritarian control and furthers the average person's ability to criticize, comment upon, and ultimately to influence, any ruling elite.

There are numerous examples from both historical and contemporary sources to support the view that the law does not always serve the greater good. Political prisoners, censorship, oppression of minority groups, restriction of movement and other freedoms... the list of repressive violations in the application of law goes on.

For the last century or more in the West, legislation has been a major growth industry. There are at least twice as many acts on the statute books now as there were a hundred years ago, and plenty more on the drawing board. But the question the old boy might prime us to ask is this; do we now have twice as much justice?

With each passing year, the law becomes more complex, more specialized, and more technical. The downside of this sophistication is that familiar muddying of the waters the old boy is constantly on guard against, the law becomes less understandable, less accessible, and more difficult to interpret and comply with.

Suppose for just a moment, that all those statutes were suddenly abolished, and a mountain of legislation vanished without trace, would this make any difference at all provided that you were still able to go to a duly constituted court and have a group of your educated peers decide reasonably and honestly if something was proper or improper? In many cases it probably would not. Justice is simply the correct determination of right from wrong without fear or favor. The old boy might say - why complicate it?

Throughout history however, the practice of law has not always and purely been about justice. Not only does the law frequently fail in respectability by lending itself to be used as an instrument of political control, it also frequently violates the principle that simplicity is preferable, and that explicitness and clarity best serve integrity.

When we consider the law, and the lawmakers, we can begin to see why Laozi has so little faith in the institutions of state. The law as defined in many of our complex statutes deviates from the ideal of integrity whenever it becomes something that can be manipulated by criminals and by the unscrupulous to serve their own ends.

In addition, corrupt leaders of a society can, and do, misuse the law in oppressing their opponents, and even at times their own peoples, to serve their own selfish interests. Unjust statutes can also be used to entrench a ruling elite or discriminate against a minority. Loopholes in convoluted legislation enable individuals and groups to escape retribution from actions deserving blame or censure, because - 'there is no law against it' or, 'technically, it was not illegal...'

Justice on the other hand, is vastly different from 'law.' Justice is, by definition, the proper application of wise judgment in the determination of right and wrong, and it is a quality either present - or absent. Though some written guidelines may be welcome – at a basic level it does not require a legal system at all, just the necessary respected wisdom, in focused deliberations working towards the advancement of the common good.

The old boy reminds us that the institution of the law should be the tool that assists the judge in proper determination of the greater good, not an instrument of subversion through obfuscation and improper application.

Laozi would have no time for 'the law' as an elitist club with a focus on personal enrichment for its practitioners, and certainly no respect for any legal system in which 'technicalities' might be allowed to prejudice the just outcome of a case. The very idea of the litigant with the largest bank balance getting the best access to 'justice' would be as much anathema to him, as it is (in reality) to the poor people on the receiving end of such discrimination.

For the old boy, the questions are all quite simple: Is there equal access to genuine justice for all citizens? Does the legal system adequately service the greatest good? And if not, then why not aspire to make it better?

Though truth-seekers might support the moral order and incorporate the principles of justice into the very fibers of their being; there is still good reason to be suspicious of both the law, and the people who apparently, so zealously and properly uphold its virtues. Might not the perceived 'rightness' of 'the law' be sometimes just another second-best substitute?

Carl Jung was one thinker who had his doubts.

Jung observes that the improper use of custom and law can hide deceit from view and forestall criticism to the point that we may even be convinced the right thing has been done. But even though the leadership has apparently succeeded in doing something wrong without being caught, or facing consequences, deep down, there is still a nagging consciousness of something not right, a feeling that persists despite any efforts to justify the behavior. (Jung C. G., The Development of Personality, 1981)

Laozi's message is that we need to be aware of the uses and abuses of legal action - as opposed to proper action undertaken always with the needs of the greater good firmly in mind. Given the old boy's insistence on the necessity of taking personal responsibility, and of undertaking only properly considered action, a slavish and unquestioning adherence to the principles of law might just be the kind of inflexibly dogmatic position that stifles spiritual progress for those who adopt it.

This position is comparable to the imitation of Christ, as espoused by those choosing to live in a self-righteous and judgmental way by publicly conforming to a religious system, while at the same time lacking any real religious conviction. It is form over substance again - the acceptance of second best and the abrogation of individual responsibility in merely observing the forms of empty ritual and convention.

The old boy is emphatic in offering his message of unity, freedom, and independence to every person at every level - there are no prizes awarded for blind obedience.

The success of any personal spiritual quest for fulfillment depends entirely on personal integrity; that is, the sincerity of work being done on the self, and the direct apprehension of the substance sought - but never on any purely passive acceptance of procedural customs and sacraments.

So, is the old boy advising us here to become outlaws? No, this would be to indulge in an energy-sapping confrontation with a very low likelihood of achieving anything at all positive. The message here is to be aware, and to have the flexibility and forbearance to bend rather than break. The rules and regulations of a society are often written by a select group who are assisted and guided, but not absolutely bound by those rules, but they are intended primarily for a lower-class group who are controlled and obstructed and unequivocally bound by them.

A well-lived life is a balance, it is as much about suffering hardship and adversity as it is about harmony and joy. Unjust regulation is just one more aspect of life that we need to be able to cope with. We learn a lot about ourselves when compelled to deal with disaster and discomfort, and it is when the spirit is at its lowest ebb that we are often the most reflective on the self.

Though we may feel as though we are staring into the darkest abyss, this is a time of opportunity for deeper insight and a more receptive attitude towards positive change and the awkward problem of our own inner nature.

This is when the tide turns, and renewal begins. The path is not lost.

Verses the fifty-ninth to sixty first: On tactical inaction - Conquest, defeat, and restraint.

The wise will govern the people and serve heaven with the same restraint.
With this condition - falseness is avoided and the correct way taken.
Along this course - integrity and wisdom accumulate.
As this abundance arises - all things are possible.
In this environment - there are no limits.

One, who is restrained, yet knows no limits - is a fit leader.
This is the mother principle of all government.
With these deep roots and with this firm base,
The greater good endures.

Government of a state is best done lightly - like cooking a small fish.
When government is in harmony with nature's cycle,
No evil can prevail.
Its potential is balanced by the presence of the greater good.

The wise accept the balance that brings no harm to self or others,
And the merit that accrues with this acceptance.

A large state is like a great river,
The place where every separate stream unites,
The mother principle is like the union of the streams.
Flowing to the low places - in its depth and stillness is strength,
In this submission - great power may be engulfed and held.

So, the great state, in acceding to a smaller, will annex it,
And the small state in deferring to the larger - conquers by affiliation.

To overcome with restraint requires the capacity for submission.
And in submission lies the possibility of greatest advance.
Great nations need to grow - small nations need strength in alliance.
Each gets what it needs,

But larger states must not forget this greatest truth:
Ultimate accomplishment lies in yielding.

These short verses are all very much on the same theme of leadership and relationships and are best considered together. Laozi is here continuing his advice to those in positions of power and influence and focusing on what constitutes correct governance. As ever, the message is intended for, and valid for, relationships of all kinds. One central principle is knowing when to act, and perhaps even more importantly, when not to act. Practiced restraint and absolute integrity are the characteristics of the best relationships and of the most principled rulers.

The ability to act in just the right way to further the common good is a trait the old boy places right at the top of the list of essential qualities for those properly set on the path of the Dao. These are the people who have an eye towards personal development as an ultimate life goal. Restraint avoids excess, integrity avoids falseness, and with this, the way towards absolute realization is cleared. With just these two attributes the 'deep roots and firm base' are established.

These fundamental qualities are representative of both the dynamic nature of any individual striving towards the Dao, and the primary characteristics of the very best of leaders in our various communities and institutions. Laozi recognizes intuitively, and in turn asks us to recognize, that each person who consciously chooses to do what is right, and only what is right, is incrementally engaged in making the world a better place.

Jean-Paul Sartre also argues strongly that a collective benefit is conferred in making a personal commitment towards furtherance of the greater good, saying, in effect that when a person takes responsibility for the development of self, that person, in choosing the greater good, is choosing the best for all humanity (Sartre, Existentialism and Humanism, 1982).

In making this point, Sartre here builds an intellectual monument to the intelligent analysis of consciousness and makes a point that the old boy would absolutely agree with - even, though it does come from the totally unexpected perspective of a philosophy which, having rejected the possibility of reconciliation of the irrational aspects of self into the whole, has also incidentally encountered terminal blockage on the Dao as great way.

A further consideration is that in the great universal ebb and flow of power and influence, the power, authority, and capabilities of both the state and of each individual rises and falls in a naturally oscillating cycle. The wise are advised to be aware that the enemy made today, could be the friend needed tomorrow - that by always acting with integrity, future conflict will be avoided.

The third and final verse in this triptych on the theme of leadership and guidance of the state could well be given the title, 'Victory through surrender!' A very typically Laozi expression of paradoxical reality, and one almost echoed by Carl Jung in a phrase that might have been spoken by the old boy himself: 'Every victory contains the germ of a future defeat' (Jung C. G., Archetypes and the Collective Unconscious, 1981)

Even as Laozi expresses his message of restraint and tactical inaction as guidance for actions of the most powerful of leaders, it should be kept in mind that what is good advice for the highest ranks of government, is also applicable to the lowest and most humble citizens of the land. His notions are universal, so that when he speaks for example of 'diplomacy,' we can safely extrapolate the core of meaning to the realm of community and interpersonal relations.

In this verse the old boy is looking closely at relationships between those that have power, versus those that lack it. By now, we are familiar enough with Laozi's principles to know that any enterprise which depends on the application of violence to achieve success is facing an uphill struggle, and one that, though it may provide some short-term material gain or satisfaction, has little to do with any proper advancement towards the ultimate wholeness of the Dao.

The old boy begins these lines with his analogy of the state as a great river, in the depths of which are strength and stillness. The Dao, as we have seen before, has the formless, fluid quality of water, and its natural movement implies that the result of conflict is that the greater good flows always, and quite inexorably, from the high ground of the victor to the lowest position of the vanquished.

Capitulation to a superior force - one which is obviously willing to inflict casualties and severe damage is therefore, not simply the last resort of the state (or individual) facing total defeat. For the old boy, it is a recommended tactic that avoids both the exhausting challenge of battle, and the potentially debilitating loss and consequent diminution of power a hostile engagement would inevitably bring.

Submission in this sense is a supreme exercise in patience, forbearance, and restraint. It is going with the flow and, far from implying any final or ultimate surrender, it leaves open the possibility that factors other than the capacity for violence may eventually rule the day.

It was in much this way that the ancient states of China eventually absorbed and subsumed the hordes of Mongol aggressors, and the Viking and Norman conquerors of Britain vanished, becoming in a few generations, quite ordinary citizens, workers, merchants, and upper-crust members of society - all of them losing even their own native languages in the process of that amalgamation into society...

To put this idea of submission into a contemporary psychological context; in any movement towards the common good, and in any personal search for ultimate truth, egotism is both an impediment and a tendency towards the use of force. The ego is only a small part of our internal reality, and this small part can both prevent us from seeing the big picture, and simultaneously foster the inability to submit when good sense demands it.

Through the lens of the ego, submission is often perceived as weakness.

The old boy, however, will tell you in no uncertain terms that often, the ultimate test of strength lies in accepting the wisdom of inaction. 'Ego' is in essence, a hard and brittle substance and quite antithetical towards the fluid nature of the Dao.

To those who may still harbor doubts on taking this course, the old boy might also ask this question: What happens to something hard and brittle when it meets something powerful, yet fluid - and yet the two cannot freely mingle? The answer is of course that the hard and brittle is engulfed and vanishes. The trick in allowing this to happen to the self, to sink voluntarily into the whole, is to think of it in terms of a tactical disengagement rather than a crushing defeat.

For a naturally humble person like the old boy, this may be no problem at all. The rest of us may need to learn this lesson the hard way.

Verse the sixty-second: On sanctuary and self-delusion – Stages of being.

In ultimate unity the Dao is a haven for all.
For the good - it is the refuge and sufficiency they strive to reach.
For those who are lost - it is asylum and the agency of salvation.

In achieving harmony, it is not the good or bad of previous deeds that counts,
   But the words and deeds of right here and right now.

What is the greatest gift that can be offered to the nation?
Not the rarest, most opulent of gems - not the finest livestock,
But the wisdom born of unity on the way of the common good.

Why is this valued above all?
It is the goal of all endeavor, all sustenance and redemption,
In this whole is the greatest bounty of a nation.

The Dao is ever present. While there are always those good people who are constantly and unaffectedly working in every aspect of their lives towards the common good, there are also those who appear trapped and lost and are faltering on the way. Unable to begin any meaningful work on themselves, they are held back by adverse circumstance, possibly struggling with basic survival, or trapped in family conflict, or facing some other life situation they find oppressive and inimical to any joy, good cheer, or betterment of self.

Possibly they are stifled by regulation or ambition, rendered impotent by a sense of duty, or distracted by a nagging acquisitive impulse, or a failed or negatively focused relationship – the possibilities are endless.

These are the people who feel the weight of the world on their shoulders, who have been, so far at least, unable to reflect upon themselves in any deep or more profound way and not examined or perhaps even admitted to their own darker or shadow side - those aspects of self they normally choose to bury, neglect or deny. The innermost realities of the self are at least for some, uncomfortable at best, and unrelenting torture at worst. Those who deny experiences, harbor delusion, are confused, or misled, have embraced a deceit, or simply have no idea what they should do to remedy the pain and misery of a life lacking love, happiness, hope, meaning and direction - may feel that their cause is hopeless.

To experience this level of alienation and loss, is for Sartre at least, a state of disconnection of the spirit that is not that far from normal. He says, "I exist, that is all, and I find it nauseating." This is how Sartre's describes the anguish arising from the failure to realize the self. In his novel "Nausea' the main character Roquentin, a man who has lost his path in life, is incapable of loving himself or others, and unable to make that 'jump' that would finally connect the facade of his public persona with the reality of the innermost self.

He speaks of being aware that he will never find anyone or anything to awaken passion within him. He characterizes love as an undertaking requiring energy, generosity, and blind courage. It is a leap of faith across a chasm within his soul. He is aware that the slightest hesitation means failure – and yet he hesitates, and becomes certain that he will never take that leap... (Sartre, Nausea, 2000).

There are numerous examples in literature of this kind of despairing, numbed, outraged, desperate, disgusted, futile, half-life of the soul of those individuals for whom life has become impossible; people the old boy would describe as having wandered from the path of the Dao.

Kafka for example explores the meaningless nature of life in the 'The Trial,' Camus covers some of the same territory as Sartre in 'The Fall,' as does T.S. Eliot in "The Wasteland,' among other works. In a contribution by Antonin Artaud written in fragmented poetic vein he speaks of being lost to world, facing a void, and utterly desolate in lacking all hope:

> *"A truly Desperate man is talking to you, who never knew the happiness of being in this world until he left it and became absolutely separated from it." (Artaud, 1974)*

To those folk who have reached this drab and dreary impasse and who feel that life has passed them by and that there is really nothing to hope or to live for, the old boy has this message; for all who want it - the Dao can still be your refuge. This is a sanctuary which will be always available. No matter what terrible mistakes you may have made, no matter that you feel utterly abandoned and alone, and despite the scars of self-doubt that appear to cripple your ability to progress – the path is open. There is no judgmental review of your case before you take the first step on the way, no qualitative assessment of your fitness, and no demands that you make any penance.

The path to a healthier more unified life begins always by looking within the self with uncompromising honesty, abandoning all the small deceits, facing the inner doubts and fears, and engaging with reality by making the commitment to being the best person you can be - and then taking one small positive step at a time.

With this open-handed and open-minded viewpoint, Laozi tells us in the lines above that a great leader does not simply reward only the best people. The greatest of leaders provide guidance and assistance so that even those careworn souls struggling to eke out a miserable existence on the bottom-most rungs of society are not forgotten.

Clearly, we can see here that it is also the old boy's injunction to lend a helping hand to those less fortunate than ourselves at whatever level of community they are. In this way the common good takes rightful precedence over purely selfish considerations and the Dao essence comes closer.

For the old boy, exercising kindness and compassion, empathizing with misfortune, and assisting the needy are not just acts of charity, they are stages on both the path of personal development and the way of the greater good. In that sense, they are practical and indeed essential steps to be taken towards self-realization.

For those who might believe that this is all much easier to say than it is to put into practice, and for those overwhelmed in the depth of their depression and facing apparently insurmountable obstacles in the form of past injury, grief and even perhaps the half-repressed memories of terrible events and awful suffering, the old boy would remind us that the healing potential of forgiveness and the formation of good relationships is often healing power enough.

We may usefully begin this by forgiving others and accepting the reality of any damage done to us. This will be helpful in the sense that a grudge long held is just another energy-sapping obstacle with benefit to no one. The old boy advises us at this point that somewhere deep inside that current weakness we feel - is the germ of future strength and ability – all things must change.

Next, we move onto the potentially more difficult task of forgiving ourselves…

Reconciling the reality of the troubled inner self with your adopted exterior and public identity is only as hard as you want to make it. So, in this respect, be as honest and generous to yourself as you would wish others to be to you.

There are no extra rewards for making your path towards the Dao more difficult than it must be.

Verse the sixty-third:
On correct modes of being - Abandoning the baggage.

Practice control without effort and self-restraint without regret,
Abandon the extreme and value moderation,
Forgo the exotic and savor the modest,
Have care for the small things and consideration for the few,
Seek reconciliation and not vengeance.

In making big advances - take one step at a time,
Remember that all greatness in founded in the small and insignificant.

True greatness is not for those who crave it,
The wise achieve it, but do not want it.
Ill-considered promises lead to bad faith.
Momentous issues need sincere consideration,

Do not make light of the difficulties that are real.
But, knowing that no difficulty is insurmountable,
Initiate your first step on the way to ultimate achievement.

Restraint, moderation, care, patience, perseverance, tolerance, these are the primary hallmarks of the person engaged in proper work-on-the-self - a person well on the way of the Dao as great journey. But it should never be forgotten that the Dao is not something that is rare and quite out of the ordinary, and most certainly not something to be gained only by immense effort.

The old boy will always tell you that any journey of a thousand miles is still accomplished by taking just one small step at a time. Sometimes the task ahead appears insurmountable, but when faced with this possibly daunting mission, the correct action is to tackle each small component of the whole individually, so that success is measured in a series of minor, but energizing achievements.

For the old boy, 'small' is always good, he appreciates that if the fine details are properly taken care of, and if all our actions are honest, and if real justice is served, then each step taken is a forward step towards the common good, and each of these advances brings greater confidence, self-knowledge, tolerance, and the capacity for greater pleasure in, and appreciation of, the natural world. In this incremental manner, resistance dissolves, obstacles are overcome, and quite rapidly the great journey, becomes an easier and more straightforward progression as time goes on.

And why should this not be so? When our lives are harmonious and fully in tune with the natural flow of events in the here and now - then we may safely cease to concern ourselves with the future.

After all, the 'big picture' we have been thinking so much about, is nothing but the accumulation of all these small details. Once the foundations are strong, the edifice of the whole is supported, and now, even though little effort will appear to have been spent, we have in some sense already arrived at the goal. Perfection was never the objective, just the will, and the ability, to continue the journey feeling an advancement and greater level of fulfillment with each step taken.

Laozi warns us that confusion of 'need' and 'want' can be our downfall along the way, since our consciousness of things lacking can be a severe obstacle to our progression. After all, if the Dao is enlightened contentment, then conceivably, it is right there under our noses this instant. So, if I were to disregard for just a moment all the things I want, and re-examine my needs, the goal might be realized in just the blink of an eye.

In this sense, it is my judgment, my perception, and my evaluation of my own being that decides if I become, like the old boy, a fully rounded person in harmony with the universe, or remain an aspirant, still in possession of faint hopes, futile dreams, and unrealizable desires. If I cannot rid myself of this baggage, the fact of my encountering resistance to any further progress towards the Dao is a sad inevitability.

As always of course, the old boy tells us it does not have to be an arduous task – unless we make it so ourselves. Carl Jung is another who has commented on the endless life difficulties we manufacture for ourselves. in a passage which clearly echoes the old boy's injunctions regarding the inconsequential trivia and busy work with which we clutter our lives. Jung notes that people will go to great lengths, and do absurd things, to avoid confronting their own inner selves. They may devote themselves to faddish health regimes, take up diversionary disciplines such as yoga, follow strict dietary routines, or look towards help and guidance in literature from around the world - all because they cannot face examining the truth within themselves and do not believe anything valuable can come from within. (Jung C. G., Psychology and Alchemy, 1981)

Towards the end of this verse Laozi issues a warning we would do well to heed when he tells us; "Do not make light of the difficulties that are real." Although we can approach a difficulty and tackle it by treating it as a series of smaller obstacles that need to be overcome, we are not free to simply ignore it. A problem left unsolved is like a wound left untreated, it will fester, become more painful, and cause even more trouble in the longer term.

The old boy always advises correct understanding before either proper action or inaction – but he never advises indifference.

Verse the sixty-fourth: On maintaining participation – Contexts of action.

The peace is easier to keep than to make,
Trouble is easier to prevent than to deal with,
What is fragile - easily breaks,
What is still small - can be prevented from growing.

Know the dynamics of your situation,
And to prevent confusion - build on what order there is.

Great trees grow from tiny shoots,
Great feats of engineering begin by shifting a handful of dirt,
A journey of a thousand miles begins with a single step,

Beware the judgment that fails to nurture and maintain the peace that is,
Be on guard against the discord that brings about misfortune.

The wise nurture the peace and avoid disharmony,
In preventing trouble - they also avert conflict.

Exercise care at the very end - as for the very beginning
Or failure may arise at the brink of success,
Maintain the harmony, maintain the focus - all will be good.

Desire only not to waste time and energy on desire,
Value that which you have, and which cannot be taken from you,

Acknowledge that your learning may have to be abandoned,
Seek the whole in the common good - but do not impose,
Seek inner harmony in life - but do not control,
Then, refraining from ill-considered action - you will achieve.

The first part of this verse continues the previous theme on meeting adversity. Here Laozi tells us to be always ready and willing to cope with any small difficulties that are encountered, and not to put off necessary action until a slight problem becomes a large and potentially uncontrollable one. We are also reminded that if action is to be taken, it needs to be considered action. We should never act in a shallow, ill-considered, or superficial way, but always with our honest and conscientious assessment of what constitutes action towards the greater good.

It is the little things that count, and a sensitive appreciation of context goes a long way towards making those small, incremental steps along the way - steps that the old boy tells us constitutes essential work-on-the-self. Progress here requires no dramatic gestures, no radical changes, and no flamboyant embracing of the new, or wholesale rejection of the old. In fact, all these things represent a potential for over-reaction, something which eventually may result in hindrance along the path.

What is required here is a sensitive awareness of any small undercurrents of disharmony, and the will and ability to deal with them fairly, efficiently, and promptly – and before they get out of hand. The true great leaders, and the genuine travelers along the way do not hesitate in reacting to a new circumstance, and whenever possible, they are proactive in ensuring that order is maintained, disharmony does not grow, and the peace is valued and preserved.

In this way, by taking upon themselves personal responsibility, they also have purpose, and they are always moving towards harmony and protecting the greater good - not just for themselves, but for all.

Few people act in absolute isolation, and, in the normal course of events, what we do as individuals affects the lives of many of those around us - and sometimes far more dramatically than we may think. So, effective and considerate participation in close and broader community is a requirement here. The old boy warns more than once that bad things inevitably happen when apathy takes hold. This is true of course for individuals, and groups all the way up to state level, where indifference in the population can frequently take the place of proper civic engagement.

The nation is its people, and the state is their servant. Each is needed to guide the other, and when the citizenry effectively washes its hands of the actions of its own governmental institutions, something has gone wrong, some vital connection has been broken. In this case, at least a portion of the constituency are experiencing alienation and dispossession – they have been slighted, or they feel themselves in some way no longer a part of the process. Perhaps the high officials of state have wrongly decided that the resources of state are theirs by right, or possibly, the population are undergoing hardship and oppression.

Carl Jung describes this situation as a common phenomenon of our times. The catalyst for all this discontent is a move by the leadership away from the moderate position, the middle ground, and the place of the Dao, to drift almost imperceptibly in many cases, towards some radical extreme. None of this happens without some howls of protest, and the imposition of some forceful controlling measures. As the leadership continues to lose credibility and respect, they commonly also seek to deflect any criticism for their own shortcomings by pointing towards a scapegoat in the form of some supposedly inimical exterior force.

Jung describes this as a kind of mass blindness, where each ordinary person, going about their everyday business fail to realize that the nation or state they belong to is driven by an unseen force that is terrifying and unstoppable. The problem is often attributed to fear of neighboring nations, which are believed to be evil. As the populace project their own unconscious fears onto their neighbors, they come to believe that it is their duty to develop more powerful weaponry to protect themselves. Jung admits that the problem is that there is a sense in which they are right. Everyone is in the same situation and suffering from the same fear, and mental health professionals know that patients are more dangerous when they are scared than when they are angry. (Jung C. G., Civilization in Transition, 1981)

The old boy will tell us that there are good leaders and there are bad, but even the worst of them are still generally driven by an assessment of their own selves as sincere, decent human beings. In other words, they see themselves as people doing their best in difficult circumstances, and often, from their viewpoint, rightly seizing the opportunity along the way for a little well-earned personal recompense.

However, this sort of ego-driven conceit can have ruinous effect. The resulting turmoil and instability within the community, the possible impoverishment of the people, and even perhaps the resulting disruption and devastation of civil unrest and of war – are all a result of ill-considered action or lack of proper action by a leadership failing in its duty to act in accordance with the common good.

In this respect Laozi is absolutely correct in prioritizing the great leaders as recipients of his advice. Their blunders along the great way of the Dao can and will, continue to have potentially harmful and long-term damaging consequences for all of us.

Verse the sixty-fifth: On knowing enough to realize you know little – A clash of half-measures.

Those who first knew the harmony of the whole,
Were circumspect in its revelation to others.

Knowing that a little knowledge is a dangerous thing,
And that before enlightenment comes much work-on-the-self.

To be clever and yet not wise - can be the ruination of the leader,
To be clever and not yet wise - can be the ruination of the people.

To comprehend these models is a remarkable virtue,
An understanding of depth and great consequence.

The highest virtue strives towards the whole of the common good,
And is undeterred from unity even if the path appears to diverge.
By this means the whole can be found.

Alexander Pope is generally credited with coining the adage "A little learning is a dangerous thing." But more than two millennia before Pope published his poetic work 'An Essay on Criticism,' in 1711, Laozi was making the same point in the 'Dao De Jing'

Before knowledge, there is instinct and intuition, the simple and direct apprehension of nature and of life, and all in absolute harmony with the cycle of seasons and weather, birth, life, and death. Everything is in its place and as it should be and life, though challenging, still has its simple joys.

And is this not exactly what Laozi is telling us we should be aiming for?

The underlying message is that self-actualization in the Dao is just as accessible and possibly even more readily accomplished by the uneducated laborer in the field than it is for the scholar and would-be great sage poring over the confusing variety of the wisdom of the ages in a great library. In this sense, a lifetime spent examining and dismissing endless rational arguments, and prolonged reflection underpinning an acquired wealth of penetrating and enduring insight, might only serve to bring the sage back eventually to just that uncomplicated insight that was already there - way back at the beginning...

It is not that the old boy is an advocate of keeping people deliberately ignorant, or that he opposes scholarship and learning. This is just an acknowledgment of the way things really are, Laozi is going with the flow and avoiding fighting against the nature of things as he so often asks us to do. He is also keeping alive the idea of the Dao as a path towards self-realization that anyone can take - and at any time in their lives.

There is no problem here with the acquisition of knowledge as such, but the old boy will take issue with the confidence with which it is brandished as enlightened truth. Often it is the partiality of that information received, or the incomplete nature of that education, that may lead to an illusory sense of possessing a rational grasp of topic, and a corresponding tendency to incline us towards discounting our instincts and feelings and disregarding our intuitions in favor of this more logical and rationally justified process.

Laozi is concerned that the folk who have absorbed just a smattering of data without any real understanding of context, and perhaps been impressed by some ideological viewpoints - but not exposed to the counterarguments that may afford even greater clarity, may now consider themselves qualified enough to be highly opinionated and justified in their world views - simply because they feel able to mount a basic rational defense of their position.

Overconfidence in one's own judgment implies a disposition towards rash decision-making and ill-formed arguments, and the drawing of unfounded conclusions. And those who are in this situation are also those most prone to dismiss criticism and counter-arguments without fair examination. Lacking open-minded tolerance, they are not yet ready for the honest self-evaluation necessary to take a first step along the path the old boy is leading us towards.

These lines also bring us back to echo a point made in verse fifty-six; although within our current educational models, children are rarely taught the virtues of modesty in Western society - as for example, they are in the East – this is a quality which has real value here. A modicum of humility needs to be learned by those who seek self-realization, and the old boy continually stresses the need to be humble and self-effacing. So, those people who know a little, but not yet enough to realize how little that really is, have an ongoing problem.

This kind of rational half-educated consciousness, stuffed with facts and masses of supporting data, but lacking any profound insight into how any of it relates to life's meaning, or to the individual's place in the world, is apt to take itself way too seriously.

Here again is the 'cleverness' we have encountered before. It is no coincidence that we live in the age of psychotherapy, our own 'cleverness' is something we can easily become conscious of, and even profoundly uneasy about, as there is usually a corresponding and underlying lack of real confidence and satisfaction and deep down, perhaps the feeling that there should be more to life.

In the face of this 'cleverness' we may be uncomfortable, but yet not quite aware that we should be trying to resolve the conflicts within the self that lead towards a genuine sense of life's purpose.

There is yet another viewpoint to be considered on this topic of learning. From a practical point of view, for any leadership, a more educated population is inevitably also a more fractious population. Democratic standards are founded in the ideal of a good universal education, and they depend on an informed, literate, educated, and engaged populace – which will of course then demand that its leaders listen to its concerns - including those suggestions for action not always welcomed by ruling elites.

Accordingly, leaders of every political persuasion have routinely suppressed information and attempted to limit or control learning at some point in history, and in almost every part of the globe. This process still continues today with numerous examples highlighted in our news broadcasts on a regular basis where disagreements on media censorship, school curricula, teacher guidance, and the banning of books are the perennial battlegrounds of competing ideologies.

What the old boy is really getting at here is that, once education is commenced, half-measures taken are a point of conflict. This might be termed a clash of knowledge versus wisdom, and any person on the path of the Dao needs to be conscious of the fact that sophistry, or any superficially 'clever' philosophizing, without true reconciliation and a profound understanding of the paradoxical nature of the conflicts within the self – is doomed to failure.

Verse the sixty-sixth: On apex and bedrock – The path follows the watercourse in the valley.

The rivers and the seas fill the valleys and low places,
And in the ocean - they find their wholeness and unity.
Being the lowest point of the world, the ocean rules supreme.

Know this when seeking to guide the state -
You must have humility in giving service.
Know this when seeking to lead the state -
The greatest of all leaders - are followers of the will of the people.

Therefore, there is no repression in the rule of the wise,
And no obstruction to the will of the people.

Then the leader earns loyal support and the respect of all,
And in never being confrontational - is never confronted.

In this verse, the old boy is making the point here again, that the Dao, like water, flows naturally towards the lowest point. We need to regularly re-evaluate what constitutes our understanding of our 'highs' and our 'lows,' since he also tells us elsewhere that strength and power are not things naturally residing in the high places. Mountain tops are in fact cold, bleak, barren and hostile. They are gaudy, magnificent, awe-inspiring, and challenging environments, but true strength lies necessarily in the lowest - the secure foundations of things supporting all that is above.

This, Laozi tells us, is the Daoist ideal of the 'spirit of the valley.' It is a place which, far from being just an empty space, or a gap in a mountain chain, is a true haven and refuge for life of all kinds. It represents warmth, protection and homeliness, the feminine yin, the place of shelter, fertility, strength, and well-being. And, because the valley is low, water naturally flows down to its depths, nurturing life in much the same way that the Dao essence flows fluidly downwards to the humblest and yielding of individuals.

This brings us to a significant point which needs further examination.

We are culturally conditioned to equate the 'greater good' with the highest aspirations of life, and we commonly use the appellation 'highest' in the most directly literal sense possible. Mountain tops are often our metaphorical goals, we 'ascend' to glory, we imagine 'success' is found on a 'pinnacle,' we speak of the 'peak' of achievement, and we often think of progress in ascension terms such as 'climbing the ladder,' or 'making our way to the top.'

The old boy is reminding us here that these perceptions, while perhaps useful and even sometimes valid in our contemporary material context of consumerism, career progression, and community influence, really need to be re-evaluated and reconciled with some very basic truths. He asks us to try to appreciate 'depths and great consequence,' and advises us, perhaps somewhat counter-intuitively at first glance, that when humility is advocated for the individual, it is because this brings one closer to the *lowliness* of the Dao essence.

The potential difficulty which Laozi is pointing to here is that these previously accepted and trusted modes of thought, based around the linked ideas of 'onwards and upward,' are linguistic associations, they have a contextual meaning that is misleading here and might easily promote perceptions that are facile and deceptive in the context of advancement along the way of the Dao as great journey.

We have encountered these entrenched metalinguistic notions before, and in common with previous examples, this notion of 'achievement' as associated with those not-so-subtle spatial indicators; topmost, highest, pinnacle, peak and etc., not only give us an essentially misleading and incorrect view of reality, but may sometimes even represent obstacles upon the real way and be a signal that we have not yet looked inwards enough.

It may be there is still some internal realization on this point that it would benefit us to find in self-reflection. The warning in short however, is that the semantic baggage of contemporary Western materialist culture can be a positive hindrance when applied to the amorphous concept of the unity in the Dao.

When speaking of, and working towards, the Dao as the 'spirit of the valley' as the old boy would have it, we necessarily take the global, big picture view - as opposed to the local, parochial, cultural view.

The language we must use in speaking of the Dao essence is always somewhat lacking - if it was fully capable, we would have no need to resort to the appellation 'unnamable.' In working with the language tools we have, the point to be made here is this; we do not need to ascend any steep path to reach any supposed zenith of enlightenment on some high plateau of being and accomplishment.

The Dao is not an 'upwards' progress - we could simply allow ourselves to fall, or slide effortlessly into it - right now.

Verse the sixty-seventh: On the three great strengths - Compassion, frugality, and humility.

It is known by all that the unity in the whole is vast and ill defined,
Resembling nothing, it can be overlooked or ignored,
But if you were to fix its limits - what then would be left as limitless?

I have three treasures to hold, to honor, and to lend strength:
The first of these is the strength of caring and compassion,
The second is the conserving strength of frugality,
The third is the yielding strength of humility,

Courage is born of the strength in compassion,
Generosity is born of the strength in frugality,
Leadership is born of the strength in humility.

Therefore, never forsake mercy for bravery,
Never forsake economy for embellishment,
And never forsake the people for your own power and status,
That is the way of destruction.

With compassion comes triumph in assault and security in defense,

This is heavenly protection.

The three great strengths of compassion, frugality, and humility the old boy speaks of here are the apparently simple prerequisites for an approach towards the essence that is the Dao.

'Compassion' is the caring and nurturing realization of one's place in the world, and the obligation of every individual on the way to take on the responsibility of doing 'the right thing' in every contingency. No exceptions are permitted or should ever need to be sought, no compromise of principles countenanced - wherever this characteristic is lacking, there is yet work-on-the-self to be done. Mistakes honestly made are allowed – we are only human – but the basic concern for others, and for nature, is essential. The focus must be on the common good.

'Frugality' here does not imply that the ownership of material possessions is always bad, but it does imply that there should be a lack of acquisitive desire for riches purely for the sake of flaunting wealth or for the building of grandiose status. The old boy might say that it is the desire for riches, and not the riches themselves, which block progress on the way, and that true frugality is the urge towards conservation and the wise use of the resources available rather than any special glorification of the ascetic life.

'Humility' we have discussed in some depth already, and here we are reminded by the old boy that this attribute is fundamental to proper leadership and good government. Once personal power and status takes precedence - the leader ceases to serve, and great injustice has occurred and will continue to occur. This advice is given to society's leaders and guiding bodies by the old boy with eyes glinting and bushy white beard twitching, and in the full knowledge that this precept is rarely heeded by career politicians in search of wealth, power, and glory.

This happy degree of harmony with the greater good is rarely found in the higher echelons of corporate affairs, and only very occasionally in the very best of national leaders.

The implication here, that the great leaders are generally not noted for their wisdom, point towards a conclusion the old boy sorrowfully supports; governments are remarkable both for their 'cleverness' in the restricted sense in which he defines it, and for their lack of any genuine wisdom at all.

The reasons for these common failures are quite clear, they are a foreseeable consequence of individuals neglecting their duty in taking proper responsibility for themselves and for the actions of their institutions - actions which must always be predicated on an honest assessment of what best furthers the common good. In allowing themselves to be primarily motivated by the potential for profit and influence without a corresponding consideration of any possible negative effects of their actions, the way is lost.

The old boy would reiterate once more that, wherever responsibility is diluted among groups, or is foisted onto nebulous legal entities, which are in fact, nothing but artificial constructs materialized onto pieces of paper, then the capacity for incorrect action - up to and including the horrors and atrocities of armed conflict - is created. Despite this advice, governmental leadership everywhere commonly evades accountability and continues to play the 'no blame game' – with leadership always first to claim credit for the happy chance and first to deny responsibility for miscalculation, disaster and misfortune.

Carl Jung is in absolute agreement on this point and speaks on several occasions in his work of the "dull brutality" of unregulated and improperly regulated organizations, and the lamentable fact that a dozen or so of the brightest people working together in committee constitute an entity with an effective IQ. of much less than any of its individual members. He writes in some depth on the failings of political and corporate organizations, and particularly of the ways in which they can go wrong, saying for example, "...it is notorious that a hundred intelligent heads massed together make one big fathead." Jung argues further that people in groups are not only less intelligent collectively than they are individually, but also that they are more prone to impulsive, emotional, and irrational acts of mindless cruelty. (Jung C. G., The Practice of Psychotherapy, 1981)

Given what we know about leadership and its failings throughout history, Laozi is reminding us that there is real pain and heartbreak behind these notions. Lapses by community leaders can, and do, have profoundly adverse effects on societies, by instigating and encouraging discrimination, bigotry, and vilification of minority groups, by supporting some sections of society at the expense of others, by normalizing xenophobia, nationalism, systemic inequalities, corporate predatory activities and a host of other negative and propaganda driven policy decisions - up to and including sending entire generations of young citizens off to die in pointless wars. In this respect, the old boy might also add that the state should no more sacrifice its citizens in self-aggrandizement, than parents should sacrifice their children to better their own positions.

Laozi would remind us here that organizations from the highest state ranking down to the smallest community grassroots level - all benefit greatly if at least some of their constituent members undertake proper work upon themselves. When decisions are influenced in this way and at least some are taken with the common good uppermost in mind, then the impasse described above may be avoided.

Great leaders are the faithful and compassionate servants of their people - and regrettably, they are also an extreme rarity in our corporate focused, economic rationalist times.

Verse the sixty eighth and sixty-ninth: On war, failure, and waste – The momentum of disaster.

The best of all soldiers is never the violent and belligerent, warrior
The best of all fighters is never driven by anger.
The greatest victors take no revenge on the defeated,
The greatest leaders are modest and unassuming.

This is the virtue of non-contention,
Advancement through harmony with nature and the efforts of others.
In this way, the ultimate unity is approached.

Strategists say:
Never be complacent about your advantages,
And know that the best advance may lie in retreat.
Not all forward progress requires movement,
And when rolling up the sleeves - the arm need not be shown.

Do not seek adversaries where there are none,
Being armed and ready is not about taking up weapons.
Do not go to war lightly - or underestimate the cost.

In advocating hasty confrontation - you risk the unity in the whole.

So, when battle is joined, know this -
Wars are won by those bringing most regret and sorrow to the conflict.

These short verses addressing the physicality of dispute and confrontation leading towards total war are best considered together as they provide comment upon what constitutes proper behavior when conflict has become inevitable.

It would be easy to label Laozi as strictly pacifist, since his message throughout the 'Dao De Jing' clearly indicates that he detests conflict of any kind. This judgment would, however, be inappropriate. Much though all forms of hostile confrontation are to be deplored and avoided, sometimes the battle is inescapable. So, when all negotiation has failed, and open warfare seems imminent and inevitable, the old boy has a message on the proper conduct of war that predates our own international conventions by more than two millennia.

The first thing to be noted, is that in averting strife, awareness of potential dangers itself constitutes a degree of preparedness, but the old boy would also warn leaders of state everywhere that this is often overdone - particularly when obsessively insecure leaders plunge their resources into ever-increasing military power. The formation of mighty armies and the creation of stockpiles of progressively more powerful, and more deadly weapons, may be less an indicator of overall wise preparedness, and more a clearly provocative signal of a pervasive sense of vulnerability, mistrust and fear.

At the level of individual personal conflict, the old boy is also here advocating an easy attentiveness and a harmonious acceptance of the environmental reality, rather than the adoption of an overly confrontational defensive posture which might indicate belligerent intention, and will at very least, raise suspicions of either some level of unnecessary paranoia or of hostile intent. He also advises that the willing anticipation of conflict where no adversary exists, substantially increases the likelihood that an adversary *will* eventually appear.

In this sense, a leadership that aggressively postures - regularly manufacture its own enemies, just as those individuals who look for trouble - find it.

Nonetheless, this wary tension between individuals, groups and nations, and the associated continuing expectation of hostility are prevalent enough conditions to be considered as almost standard positions in our mistrustful modern world. This raises the question; what causes our anger, our fear, and a widespread, fundamental distrust of others? A distrust which is so compelling that we are prepared to expend a sizable portion of our time, energy, and resources on self-protection? And all this (generally) to protect ourselves against an enemy we have either imagined or conjured from nothing by our own combative attitude.

The old boy has ideas upon this topic, and Carl Jung was in close agreement with these ideas when he observed that historically, wars are often fought between close neighbors (Jung C. G., Civilization in Transition, 1981), though the definition of 'neighbor' is often more flexible in our modern times when we are considering the intersecting spheres of influence of global powers. The principle however holds true today: Our neighbors are our natural enemies. Take any country in the world as example, and ask; historically, who did they fight against the most? The answer will always be - their near neighbors.

This is a point that the old boy has raised before. At every level of conflict, from individual and up to a state leadership level, whenever we are in times of trouble, whenever we find ourselves inadequate to some task, and whenever serious mistakes have been made, we look for some way to excuse ourselves. When there is a need to escape blame and exorcise the source of our inner doubts, uncertainties, and inadequacies, - we need a scapegoat.

In this instance, when someone really needs to be answerable - but hearth and home are to remain untainted - then the neighbors are there to fill the void and give representative substance to all that is negative in our lives.

In terms of answering the needs of state leadership in drumming up support for a job not very well done, neighboring states, with all their supposedly perfidious ideologies and meddling tactics are a godsend. Their iniquities can, and do, take the focus away from the leadership's own dismal performances. They also help stifle the mutterings of discontent within the population by creating common cause against the neighbor who is also now clearly the enemy.

Many an embattled government leader has escaped censure by pointing successfully towards the supposedly hostile plots and subversive activities of the neighbors, while exhorting the people to stand united to face this threat. When real harmony has failed, when the way has been lost to vision, then the unscrupulous, inferior, or plain uncomprehending, greedy or selfish leader may yet attain the illusion of unity and harmony by incitement of mob violence achieved entirely by invoking the threat posed by the neighbors.

Xenophobia, bigotry, prejudice, injustice, discrimination, lack of compassion, these are all essential items in the toolkit possessed by a leadership of poorly performing officials who have need to divert attention from their own failures and their own lack of vision. The usual tactic in the invocation of some massive external threat is to spread fear, uncertainty, and doubt throughout the population. If this tactic is then combined with tight control of information, and lots of nationalistic propaganda, the call to arms and invocation of patriotic duty, particularly for the lesser educated and more easily swayed populace, quickly becomes an almost irresistible tide with massive popular momentum.

The inferior leadership, sensing a groundswell of support, can now feel more secure and less fearful of being overthrown and quickly divert attention from their own incompetence by acting decisively to curtail civil liberties such as freedom of speech and association – all of which is done in the interests of 'the security of the state.' Then, as the leadership becomes more securely entrenched and backed by a solid, 'patriotic' base, and - since its ruling members are all self-serving individuals with a penchant for exercising control at every level, opportunities will soon arise for personal enrichment – and then the real corruption sets in.

This cycle represents a familiar historical pattern, and the old boy was fully aware of how this sequence can seize communities, even whole nations, and trigger the movements of mighty armies. At a single stroke, by conjuring up the threat of 'the neighbors,' a powerful popular movement is created, and even better, one which apparently offers unity and the prospect of personal fulfillment by uniting against a common enemy – because it mimics the harmony and unity of purpose of the genuine spiritual and altruistic journey towards the common good expressed as Dao...

As this impending disaster unfolds and gathers the force and momentum to shatter lives and potentially, deprive and weaken whole cultures and entire generations of people, the ambitions of the inferior leadership continue to be furthered. Their cravings for more power are nurtured by the prospect of conquest and meanwhile – ever more severe 'emergency' measures are introduced as the nation moves to 'war footing'...

The old boy would keep both his silence, and his distance, from the fray – but mourn that the way had, for now at least, been lost...

Verse the seventieth and seventy-first: On the way things fall apart – Fragmented reality.

My words are easy to understand, and simple in application,
Yet - the world neither understands nor applies them.

Even simple words may acquire intricate meaning over time,
And their application is for nothing if self-indulgence hides the goal.

Without proper understanding - words have no power,
Those people with true understanding are few,
But those who follow and emulate them gain honor,
Within the ordinary can hide real wisdom,
The poorest of homespun clothing can conceal a precious treasure.

To know that you may not know - is a strength,
Not knowing yet believing that you know - is a weakness.

Difficulties are avoided by remaining aware of all possibilities,
The wise are aware and meet with no difficulty.

It is a central tenet of the world's great religions and philosophies that a life of integrity, affirmation, compassion, and selflessness - is a good life - a life naturally attuned in some degree to a vital cosmic whole. To be in possession of these characteristics is also a universal hallmark of a person embarked upon the path of self-realization.

The old boy would say that to simply adopt the correct focus and attitude, and to take the first few steps in good faith – are all that is required to begin to experience some kind of direct communion with a universal whole. For Laozi, the cherished essence that is the Dao is always just a heartbeat away.

And yet things can always go wrong.

The various religions and philosophies of the world offer copious amounts of theological and metaphysical guidance on the topic of 'proper living.' The scope of advice on how to proceed on the 'way' - as the old boy would have it, are defined in contrasting ways that emphasize the enormous diversity of sectarian approaches to ultimate matters of the spirit. This is a perceived ultimate reality that is variously labeled as: the divine, the Godhead, the creator and destroyer, the all, the immortal, the supreme being, the higher power, the father, the lord, and the master - to mention just a few of a multitude of possible designations. Despite this apparent conceptual multiplicity of the object, and the very different ways of expressing belief and allegiance to it, what can be said - is that there are still many more similarities than there are differences between these superficially dissimilar beliefs.

Buddhism has its middle way, balanced in the moderate center between the radical poles of self-indulgent hedonism and 'purification' through self-mortification for example, and that same idea has its equivalents everywhere – in Christianity, Islam, Shinto, Hinduism, Judaism... The list goes on.

At the historical and contemporary cores of all genuine spiritual endeavor, the same message is to be seen repeatedly, albeit from the viewpoints of some vastly different perspectives on the cosmos. The essentials are these: There is always some conception of an ultimate unity, always some expressed need for self-reflection, and always some code of behavior that will help guide the soul-seeker towards some central mystery or revelation.

Given that the advice given in the 'Dao de Jing' has these universal characteristics, it is no wonder then, that the old boy tells us here, as he has told us before, "My words are easy to understand and simple in application."

As ever, he is speaking in the most literal and straight-forward way that he can, and at the same time acknowledging that despite this inclusive approach, for many, these words will never have real meaning or power - simply because the world is full of people who cannot see what is in front of their eyes, and who persist in living a life of home-spun illusion and self-denial.

Those last words are the key; denial of self is denial of all unity - and of the Dao essence itself. In the old boy's terms, this denial represents not just a failure of understanding, it is a loss of genuine potential, in essence, a commitment of the self to a second-best life, an ersatz existence in a bubble of manufactured reality. It is to miss out at some level, on the full beauty and abundance that is reality.

Carl Jung also recognizes this problem and sees this failure to connect as both a social and psychological phenomenon, describing it in similar terms to those we found earlier in the writings of Jean-Paul Sartre. Both agree with Laozi when they assert that it is our own inner fragmentation of consciousness, and our own inner lack of unity, that causes the difficulty. Jung remarks on the implication that the very fact of individual consciousness suggests isolation and disconnection, and that just as separation and alienation may lead to illness, the same fate can befall groups and even entire nations.

For Carl Jung, the actuality of mass psychosis of in both individuals and in entire populations was a fact of life. Historically, it has occurred numerous times and been seen in political and religious cult behavior in nations around the globe. Examples include the 'Supreme Truth' cult in Japan, the Ku Klux Klan in the US, Jim Jones and his murderous 'People's Temple,' The Manson family, 'Heaven's Gate,' and many others. In politics we have the cults of personality; Stalin, Pol Pot, and the rise of the Nazi party in the 1930's - not to mention even more recent developments in Western politics which periodically see a resurgence in fascist ideology within ostensibly democratic systems. Jung's view on this is that we are also currently experiencing a time of separation and ailment within society. (Jung C. G., Civilization in Transition, 1981; Jung C. G., The Symbolic Life, 1981)

For the old boy of course, this "separation and ailment," is simply the unresolved paradoxical nature of the Dao and an implied failure in self-reflection in those individuals involved. For those state institutions that have strayed from their purpose and are impacting negatively on communities - what is required is the responsible guiding hand of individuals who are also actively working towards the common good. The obvious inference here is that there are not yet quite enough of these good people to go around.

This fragmented consciousness which cannot achieve unity is essentially dishonest, or at least misled, since its actions are either selfish, driven by acceptance of something less than the truth, or formulated without proper regard, or awareness, of the greater good.

This may lead to any number of dire outcomes, including at worst, the rise of predatory, militant, and propagandizing organizations at every level of society up to and including the state itself. Failure to reconcile radical extremes in the moderate center, usually ends in a choice - one radical extreme is rejected - and demonized in the process - while another is accepted and promoted vigorously as 'true patriotic' action.

The unwholesome result of this lack of true understanding is the rise of innately aggressive ideologies in the form of political or religious extreme fundamentalist groups, and correspondingly oppressive doctrines which seek to radicalize whole populations. And in this manner begins the process leading to the horrors of civil unrest, blatant discrimination and racism, internecine strife, suicide bombers, terror attacks, starving refugees, mass graves, torture, beheadings, and the wretched misery of entire regions laid waste – sometimes for generations...

When Jung refers to this internal dissociation which transfers from individual to communities as "ailment," he means precisely that. This phenomenon is his 'mass psychosis' on a grand scale, as observed many times throughout history, from the medieval witch-hunts to political pogroms. This is the triumph of everything that is inferior within individuals and within societies - some 'ism' is exalted way above its station to become a rallying call for aggressive action - cruelty, death, and carnage – and as the great way is once again lost, the common good becomes a distant memory and all is selfishness, violence, and greed.

We might well wonder at how such perversions of human instinct can come about, but the rather simple and easy answer as the old boy would explain it, is that this can be, and historically has been, the result of entire cohorts of individuals failing in proper work-on-the-self.

In this sense the essential importance of the ideal of working towards the common good within society cannot be overemphasized. If this innate goodness and honesty is not the guiding principle of most people within a society, things begin to fall apart. As each of the cohorts of disassociated, self-indulgent, and aimless individuals advances through their societies and take their places within corporate and state organizations, their fundamental lack of integrity takes its toll and their legacy is systemic degeneration. The result is that decisions are poorly made and there is a general failure of responsible action with predictably negative results for all concerned.

All progressive advances in society - without exception - stem from the individual, and in this case at least some of those individuals have not heeded the messages of those who, like the old boy, have something profound to say about our lives and how we should live them. In the terms used in the 'Dao De Jing,' the way is abandoned and darkness, corruption, and the selfish urge towards individual power and enrichment are in the ascendancy.

At least for the time being...

Verse the seventy-second: On minimal control - The wise and distant leader.

When the people no feel awe and wonder - disaster looms.
Knowing this, the wise leader is unobtrusive,
The people live as they choose at home and at work,
And they never tire of their leader.

The wise leader is knowing, but not ostentatious,
And has a respect for self that is never arrogant,
The wise know when to choose and what to let go.

According to Laozi, keeping ordinary people happy is not that hard, in fact it is the most natural and easy thing to do - for the enlightened leader.

His advice to those in the community and to the great leaders of state in this respect is the same - that they will best maintain both the respect of the populace and their own status and mystique by cultivating a caring and compassionate, yet distant and unobtrusive, barely noticed, and non-threatening presence.

Resentment builds inevitably when restrictions are imposed on the people by their leaders, and the signs of this will inevitably appear whenever there is a proliferation of unnecessary rules and regulations. In these times, home and work life suffer undue interference and ordinary people feel themselves as imposed upon and devalued. This is also a time when the citizens feel their choices are limited, enjoyments curtailed, and their autonomy undermined.

To avoid this, the wise leader will know the value of inaction, remain aloof, circumspect, and tolerant, and imposes no unnecessary constraints on the people. As Laozi remarks in one of his more famous lines: "One should govern a country the way one cooks a fish – lightly."

Carl Jung, in his later writings, makes a similar point, (Jung C. G., Civilization in Transition, 1981) He is very much a proponent of individual growth and a critic of state pretensions of indisputable credentials to direct and organize every aspect of society. He speaks of leaders "who almost infallibly" develop inflated ideas of their own wisdom and ability, and of ordinary people as being dehumanized by overly intrusive leadership, which strips them of their essence and dignity - even to the extent sometimes of being compelled to abandon their own uniqueness of language, culture and identity and thereby becoming abstract statistics in the rationalist group context of ego-driven leadership.

For Jung as for the old boy, empowerment of the individual is the first prerequisite of the personal development that Jung calls 'individuation' and Laozi styles as work-on-the-self. Both are agreed that far too often, state leadership is predominantly heavy-handed with a tendency to isolate and suppress individuality in the interests of consolidation of power.

Since there is a sense of inevitability of trouble in the prospect of ordinary people dealing with sub-standard leadership, the old boys' usual caveats apply - we are advised to avoid confrontation, continue to act in accordance with the common good, take comfort in what we have, rather than nurture resentment for that we cannot have, and await the opportunity to further the change that will surely occur in time.

Verses the seventy-third: On arbitrary misfortune – Taking the valley road.

To have courage and boldness may bring early death,
To have courage and caution may preserve a life.

There is good here and there is harm - yet who can unravel this?
Some things are rewarded by heaven - while some are punished.
So, even the wisest must accept that chance may bring adversity.

The way of fulfillment in unity is overcoming without contention.
In responding without words - an answer may yet be found
In receiving without asking - attraction may yet be shown,
In being ordered, yet at rest - the wise may yet overcome.

Heaven's net is the coarsest mesh,
Yet nothing escapes it.

If I am a good person, will I be happy?

It can be a comfort to live with the knowledge that there exists a kind of natural justice that rewards the worthy and punishes the evil. If we just obey the rules, work always towards the common good, resist the distractions and the temptation to stray - all will eventually be well. Many people may console themselves throughout a lifetime of adversity with such comforting faith in their ultimate destiny.

So, what a pity it is that these beliefs are quite unfounded...

These lines on the chaotic nature of reality continue the theme of blind chance the old boy mentions in other parts of the 'Dao De Jing.'

"Even the wisest must accept that chance may bring adversity"

Is the way Laozi puts it, and what that means is, there are never any guarantees. The way to the Dao involves self-assessment, commitment, honesty - and an element of pure luck. There is no escaping the random and irrational aspects of the Dao as a cosmic whole. The swirls and eddies of a universe in constant and random flux, can bring disaster to some and good fortune to others. The reality of the Dao is that it is a vision of the all-encompassing totality - a reality that inevitably includes the wholly unreasonable and the completely illogical.

Carl Jung was one philosopher and observer of the human condition who also recognized that even the best laid plans are subject to the whim of fortune, remarking that in practice in human affairs, "Chance reigns everywhere." (Jung, 1981). Despite the firmness of our trust in the predictable nature of cause and effect, the ungovernable and irrational nature that is our reality ensures that all our intentions guided by reason are valid only up to a point.

The old boy is also reminding us here that we are not privileged, and that the universe is neither just nor unjust, it is simply the wholeness that includes all possibilities. It would be wrong to fight against this situation. We are empowered by self-knowledge, but may not productively impose our will towards reshaping reality, since acceptance of the innate uncertainty in the ebb and flow of life is key to a life of harmony.

As always, the individual overcomes by going with the flow, and if we try and fail - well, we can usually recover and try again.

There is an important message to be internalized in these verses. The whole world - all of life, and the universe itself - are genuinely chaotic places, and while it is proper to embrace the virtues of working towards the common good and to engage in honest work upon the self, there are occasions when diligent efforts, and correct action are not justly rewarded. The effort we make as individuals is for our own enlightenment, and no rewards, other than furthering a harmonious acceptance of our own situation, are offered. In every situation, there remains always this element of random chance – blind luck if you will – that can indiscriminately reach out of the chaos to help, hinder, enhance, or even destroy our lives.

Bravery, as the old boy pragmatically points out, may not help against this fickleness, and while perhaps admirable in all circumstances, it will also significantly increase mortality rates among those who possess it.

During a lifetime, any individual will witness, and probably also personally experience, both random good fortune and equally arbitrary misfortune. The reasons why one individual may prosper while a deserving other does not, are often not clear-cut, or capable of being rationally justified. The ever-changing essence that is the Dao encompasses all - the good, bad, wise, or capricious – and even right down to the utterly haphazard and senseless.

The old boy is relaxed about this, we are after all, grown-ups and should be able to make allowances to contend (at least usually) with the contrariness of nature. The great unity of the Dao is the sum of our self-realized actuality, it is not to be anthropomorphized as some kind of jolly, benevolent overseer, or a handy local deity whose aid an individual may usefully solicit in prayer or bribe with sacrifice when seeking to change or oppose the ebb and flow of the natural order.

In this sense we are truly alone and must learn to take absolute responsibility for ourselves, and, as we have seen before, for some - those who hope to put their faith in some external and benevolent deity, those who would prefer to act only on instructions received from some higher authority - this can be a truly frightening realization.

Jean-Paul Sartre was in full agreement with this position when he said we are accountable for ourselves, but uncertain about what it is we are, and:

> "Man is condemned to be free: because once thrown into the world, he is responsible for everything he does" (Sartre, Being and Nothingness, 1993).

Whereas Sartre characterizes 'freedom' as a kind of tragedy - the anguish and nausea of being totally bereft and yet wholly accountable, Carl Jung offers the flip side of this viewpoint, the idea of freedom as a redemptive process. He puts his views on the acceptance of personal responsibility another way:

> "The privilege of a lifetime is to become who you truly are." (Jung C. G., Jung on Christianity, 1999)

Any individual engaged in the self-reflective process may elect to be convinced by the tortured apprehensions of the existentialist mind-set as expressed by Sartre, or perhaps comforted by the more relaxed and inclusive approach of a humanitarian such as Jung - or again, guided by a philosophically practical mind like that of Laozi. Each choice remains popular, despite the immense burden of desolation and despondency inherent in adopting the Sartrean position.

It is possible that your ultimate choice will depend entirely on how much personal guilt you feel you need to assuage before you allow yourself to live a harmonious life.

As for the old boy, he might say on this point; do what you must do, but ask yourself, why choose a rocky and treacherous mountain path if there is a perfectly good road through the valley?

Verses the seventy-fourth and seventy-fifth: On oppression, fear, and liberation.

When the people are not afraid to die,
Threats of death are of little use.
Only when the people are afraid to die,
Can any control be exercised through intimidation.

Every state has some personage with the power of life and death,
But when this executioner's power is delegated to others,
As when the tradesman allows the novice the use of sharp tools,
Few escape without hurting their own hands.

Why are the people hungry?
Governments eat up more and more in taxes.
While the ordinary people are starving.

Why are the people rebelling?
Leaders interfere too much,
And the ordinary people revolt.

Why do the people treat death so lightly?
The leadership make life a misery and a torment,
And the ordinary people have little to live for.

But, in ceasing to value life, one may yet discover a wisdom and resolve,
That those who value their lives have not yet found.

There comes a time in any life of misery and oppression when the choice between living and dying is not so clear cut - the moment has arrived at which the subjugated individual feels there is now nothing left to lose. At this critical turning point, the choices are few; one may face extinction and die quietly and with resignation, or, perhaps choose to strike some final defiant blow in the name of freedom or justice. In addition, for some there may the option to run away from the trouble, while others might simply brace themselves and try to ride out the storm.

At the national and organizational levels of state, if this impasse has been reached, the leadership have only themselves to blame. They have long ago abandoned the integrity that would earn the respect of the population, and they have long since ceased to follow the old boy's advice on how the executive should behave in accord with the common good.

At this point, the leadership of the state has become a parasitic community of the elite, they are living the high life, embracing corruption and the opportunities for self-enrichment, while their privileged and extravagant lifestyles are subsidized by a dispossessed and mostly disenfranchised majority who are engaged in an increasingly helpless struggle for day-to-day survival.

At the personal and individual level, the old boy is describing to us here the calamity of those distracted people who have strayed from the path towards the greater good and lost themselves in some lesser pursuit - perhaps the acquisition of ever more material things, or commitment to an unworthy cause that influences the individual towards living a misguided and ultimately destructive life.

Sometimes the vision of the Dao recedes, the way is obscured, and life becomes bleak and meaningless in its lack of purpose. While any individual could choose to be resigned to failure here, the other option is to heed the old boy's advice and have the maturity to take on the full personal responsibility for your life and for yourself. You have one lifetime only, and if you are prepared to sit passively while others direct your affairs, in effect, you are surrendering your personal power and autonomy.

In the old boy's terms, if you hand over the use of the executioner's ax to an external force it might just be turned on you.

Work-on-the-self can, and should, continue through this time of trouble.

Laozi might also add that 'oppression' is often as much a feeling and attitude as it is a physical condition, if some of our materialistic desires remain unfulfilled, so what? Sufficient food, proximity to family and friends, and a refuge from the weather have sufficed for many a happy lifetime.

Patience is a primary virtue. There is also the fact of the enantiodromia implicit in the amorphous Dao, have we not already been advised that it is at that darkest time of night that the universal ebb and flow swings towards the dawning of the light?

That a new day will dawn is a reliable constant in the cycle of the Dao, it is up to us to have the patience to await it, and the good sense to make the most of it when it arrives.

At this extremity of distress, those who think themselves in unassailable positions of power and control should beware. At the community leadership level, an impoverished, starved, or mistreated populace is one most likely to rebel. Desperation means that fear is lost and what was once considered risky now becomes possible and even probable. The leadership loses its power to override objections as the people realize this new kind of freedom.

It is also at this time that archetypal and charismatic rebels often arise from within the citizenry to lead an insurgency, strike a blow for freedom, and to overthrow the oppressive rule. The revolutionary leader seen obviously working towards the common good at this time will inspire true loyalty and unselfish action even when that commitment risks the personal safety of the followers.

When translated to a more personal and individual level, the further message of these verses is very simple – you will complicate and probably alienate any relationships you attempt to dominate and otherwise meddle in - and whatever it is you try to force - will certainly meet resistance.

Verse the seventy-sixth: On life-force and identity – The world always turns.

A living body is soft and compliant,
While the dead are firm and unyielding.

Live plant growth is delicate, sap filled and pliable,
But in death - dry, shriveled and brittle.

Unyielding rigidity is the hallmark of death,
Gentle compliance the key to good and healthy life.

Force used without flexibility achieves little,
And what cannot bend under pressure - may break.

The great cycle of life fits the stronger for the lowest position,
While the submissive and compliant conquers all.

The old boy is giving us his views here on the healthy characteristics of life and living.

Think, for a moment on the respective characteristics of life and of death. Death is immovable, desiccated, a hard and withered, brittle and unyielding state of non-being. Life is dynamic, soft, flexible, and yielding, and capable of growth and creativity.

Even while considering ourselves as flexible and open-minded, we mostly still tend to also think of ourselves in quite rigidly defined terms. These are generally the familiar terms which define the categories of the groups we are a part of, for example, white Anglo-Saxon protestant, Irish Catholic, Italian American, Anglo-Indian, African American, Lebanese Australian, Malaysian Chinese - these are just a few of the myriad labels that might be employed in part explanation of who we are.

Each of these religious, ethnic, and social labels we adopt implies the existence of a whole subset of additional information that will help to determine, with differing degrees of accuracy, the individual's likely beliefs, educational level, social strata, economic position, and even quite probably their expected sporting affiliations, voting tendencies, social outlook, and interests and hobbies.

We are passionate about those things that give us identity, our religions, our countries of origin, our local traditions, our families and peer groups, our football teams, and the traditions of our way of life. And yet all these things, which so clearly define who and what we are - are entirely random attributes, chance occurrences, based on when, and more importantly, where we were born.

We are all of us accidents of time and geography.

We reside in a universe of blind chance and constant change and the old boy would advise us that absolutely nothing is as sure and constant as it might appear. Our consuming passion for affirmation of identity with our locale and our peer groups is thus a reflection of our desire for a more concrete sense of belonging, a device to solidify our most basic sense of connection with the world.

In moderation, the old boy tells us there is nothing wrong with this, the danger arises when a personal identity becomes rigid and inflexible in thought and deed.

In other words, when this highly localized self-image becomes fossilized and unbending, problems immediately arise. At this point we are effectively declaring that we will tolerate no further change, and in doing so, we step away from the path of the great way. This is the point at which we lose patience for foreigners and immigrants, fail to empathize with minority groups, and lack in acceptance for almost everyone who is not 'one of us.'

This tribal identification of self with place, peers, culture, religion, and traditions, is the source of much competitive rivalry, and is something commonly fostered between contestant sports teams and many other groups and communities - mostly in a harmless, non-hostile and team building way.

We do, however, need to remember that 'nationalism' and 'patriotism' (for example) are both influential 'isms' – and therefore potentially powerful substitutes for genuine work-on-the-self. They are ideals that can inspire a pseudo purpose in life with all the capacity for self-delusion and misapplication that is (as was discussed previously) attached to these terms.

The lines in the verse above warn us of the results of maintaining an unyielding and rigid attitude, "What cannot bend under pressure - may break." Patriotism and nationalism may be seen as virtues by many, and in moderation they are inoffensive enough, but both can be extreme positions resulting in intolerance, xenophobia, bigotry, racism, and at the radical extreme, a variety of murderous and suicidal behaviors escalating right up to, and including, emphasizing a political or ideological point through the killing and maiming of civilian populations.

The old boy might say that we should enjoy our affiliations but not take ourselves too seriously. At every level from national, through community down to the individual level, when we begin to oppose change, when we refuse to adapt, when we cease to be dynamic and supple, life has reached its peak and we are moving towards death and disintegration.

It then that the Dao is lost.

Yet the world will continue to turn - no matter how much of our energy is put into opposing it.

Verse the seventy-seventh: On correct balance and fine tuning.

The way to the greater good is as the tuning of a bow, or fine instrument,
What is too high is lowered, what is too low is raised,
Excess is removed, deficiencies augmented and corrected.
Until a final perfect balance is achieved.

The way of harmony through the common good -
is to take from excess and give to insufficiency,
Leaders lacking in wisdom - will take from those with need,
And give to those with plenty.

Who is it that can curb this excess and tend to the poor?
One who has achieved the harmony of the whole.

The best work is done by those with wisdom but no thought of recognition,
Success is attained more easily by those who do not prize it,
The very highest good arrives quietly and without fanfare.

There is nothing that is very difficult about these sentiments, a good life, as Laozi sees it, is about achieving balance and harmony, and yet, Carl Jung speaks repeatedly in his work about the inherent cultural difficulties Westerners face when attempting that equilibrium. This is a warning we should heed, and Jung borrows an ancient Chinese proverb when he advances this idea further and advises that, if the wrong person uses the right methods, the right methods will work in the wrong way. This is in contrast to the usual perception that the method is more important than the person using it. Laozi readily agrees that it is the individual who is important here, the method is the path taken, and only the individual can commit to the proper path of the greater good. (Jung C. G., Alchemical Studies, 1981)

It is not just that Western culture is different from Eastern culture, Jung sees it as actually deficient in lacking the natural symmetry that Eastern philosophy takes for granted from the very outset. In fact, as we saw earlier in his remarks on mass psychosis, Jung views our culture as, at its very heart, essentially sick and suffering an imbalance in its nature (Jung C. G., Psychology and Religion: West and East, 1981)

Surprisingly perhaps, but in terms the old boy would surely approve of, Jung goes on to argue that these deficiencies in Western culture, which he describes as being a loss of contact with nature and the real world around us, are also, paradoxically, the germinal source of a new and growing strength.

However, the most important ideas for our purposes here are these; firstly, that we should be aware that there exists a rational, spiritual dichotomy in our cultural traditions, and that this divide is far less confronting in Eastern traditions - such as that in which Laozi lived and wrote. Secondly, and again echoing Laozi in his ideas, Jung insists that we cannot just decide to 'become Eastern,' our European and Western cultures, and indeed everything which contributes to making us what we are needs – with all our faults and blemishes - needs to be accepted by us 'warts and all.'

Regardless of our consciousness of the flaws and imperfections in ourselves and in our own cultural traditions - these elements remain a part of us and count towards the sum of all the environmental factors which make us unique. The threads of our personal histories running through those traditions, are what make us what we are.

Ultimately our customs and history are, for better or worse, what Jung would describe as our "safe foundation," and in Jungian terms we must never try to wholly discard this reality and thereby to become lost in a confusion of words and ideas that are not native to European thinking and cannot be successfully integrated into it. (Jung C. G., Alchemical Studies, 1981)

Practically speaking, the implicit warning here is that we will not become better cooks by simply donning the old chef's hat. As the old boy has told us previously, flexibility is the key. Our primary imperative is to look within and be comfortable with the totality of who, and what we are. We are not free to engage in any dilettante cherry-picking of our own history and cultural practices (and our own reality of self) in a frantic race to embrace the precepts of the Eastern or any other mental attitude. Any such enterprise is bound to fail since it is in opposition to what is real and natural for us.

All proper work-on-the-self is honest endeavor, we are not pruning and grafting our essential selves, picking what is good and discarding the rest to achieve optimal results. Self-realization is acceptance, putting down deep roots and nurturing the whole. Only when we are comfortable with the integral depth of ourselves are we ready to build on this firm base and to continue to expand our horizons with the old boy's ideas.

At this point, the act of doing what is best for the common good should be a natural reflex.

This is important. We cannot just lightly agree this is true, and then expect that by simply nodding our assent, all the barriers will fall. We need to really feel that this is the truth - deep within our bones.

And then we need to act accordingly.

Verse the seventy-eighth: On effortless action – The water of life.

Nothing under heaven is softer, more amenable, than water.
And yet nothing surpasses its power,
It cuts through strength and solidity and all that will not yield,

In this same way - the weak overcome the strong,
In this same way - the submissive defeats the uncompromising,
This is knowledge readily acquired - although never readily practiced.

Heed these wise words:
One who takes on all the troubles of a people is a fit ruler,
One who takes on the misfortunes of the nation - is a great ruler.
The most straightforward of truths can seem paradoxical.

Any investigation of Laozi's timeless message in the 'Dao De Jing' begins with the knowledge that anything we may glean of the essential nature of the Dao is likely to stretch the descriptive abilities of language and to lead into sometimes strange territory. After all, the very first thing the old boy tells us in verse one is that, if we try to fix some kind of definition on that which is amorphous and ever-changing (i.e., to name the nameless) then any label we can apply is always going to be insufficient to our purpose.

The problem is one that has already been noted and discussed. The everyday linguistic baggage we all accumulate through our cultural association of concepts, highlights an inadequacy in our fixed definitions and labels. When our intention is to encapsulate an aspect of the Dao, language becomes slippery and unreliable, and like a magnetic compass at the pole – we get erroneous impressions from a previously reliable tool.

At this point, it is worth pausing to remember that in getting our occasional sideways glimpses of the essence that is Dao, we are only ever approximating - using whatever jargon and idiom of experience that appears most suited to offer some slight assistance to our overall comprehension. Many of the terms that appear to help us to navigate some of the perceived complexities of the old boy's thought might also (and quite incidentally) be giving us a quite flawed perception of how we might proceed on the great way that is the Dao.

We have for example, previously spoken of 'striving toward,' and 'grasping' the essentials of the Dao, whereas in fact 'striving' implies a concerted effort and 'grasping' implies some non-ethereal substance to be seized. It is unlikely the old boy would approve either of such exertion or such neediness. His way would be a very simple and effortless progression.

Similarly, we 'describe' the indescribable Dao, but do not always add the caveat that we are aware that we are illuminating only one of a possible myriad of ever-changing facets. We also speak of the Dao as an 'achievement,' or 'goal,' when such is not the case - it being in fact, as much a process as an end – and much more of a harmony of the inner self than something external we bring into ourselves...

Fundamentally then, none of these terms, or indeed any of our normal linguistic modes of expression, are really quite in tune with the old boy's principle of effortless action. Words are our tools and must be used as best we are able, but they are apt to become blunted with thoughtless use. Indeed, for many hundreds of years, exactly this happened to the philosophy espoused in the 'Dao De Jing' - the old boy's fresh and vital ideas became fossilized in dogma.

Much of the subsequent scholarship around the 'Dao De Jing' revered form over substance to such an extent that the old boy himself was raised to the status of a demigod in the eyes of many. This was a sad mistake, and something that he would have dismissed instantly as a triumph of mere 'cleverness' over true wisdom. It was also indicative of a serious mistake along the path of the greater good, but this kind of hijacking of substance is not uncommon, it has its parallels in many threads of the global history of spiritual development.

We need timely reminders to be wary of the power of words, they are as dynamic, and over time, as subject to change in meaning and association as the concept of the Dao itself. This should always be kept in mind when we are discussing the whole that is the Dao, the slippery concepts we are focused on seek to continually elude us – they are the eternal embodiment of constant change.

In this verse the old boy once more compares the Dao to water, with all its restless qualities of constant movement, its capacity to nurture and support life, its position, always flowing towards the low, its unstoppable weight, its dark mysterious oceanic depths, and its power to carve and shape even the lofty mountain chains. The imagery here is something absolutely universal, and both the existential writings of Jean Paul Sartre and the psychological and humanitarian writings of Carl Jung, employ this same weighty symbolism of water to stand for the depths of the unknown (or as yet unrealized) self.

Jung labels this unknown and innermost part of the unconscious self as the feminine yin principle 'anima,' in men, and the masculine yang principle 'animus' in women, and he frequently refers to them throughout his writings. Speaking of the life event the old boy would call "losing the path of the greater good," Jung emphasizes that we must continuously work to "consolidate our consciousness" but that we may eventually realize that this ongoing and necessary effort to combat the passing of time leads to a sense of unchanging dullness and spiritual dryness. Our deeply held beliefs become cliched, and the vitality that once fueled us begins to fade as we lose "the water of life." (Jung C. G., Symbols of Transformation, 1981)

Water is soft and weak, but overcomes all resistance, it envelops rather than opposes, and in its yielding, resilience, and its softness, it hides a mighty power. Water is the image for our inner being, unconscious, non-rational, intuitively feeling for the path of least resistance, creatively and artistically molding the landscape, and transcendent in its unrealized capacity for strength.

Here within the self, is everything that we need to fulfill our own true potential – if we dare to do so.

Verse the seventy-ninth: On being yourself, looking within – and letting it go.

When past enemies make their peace - resentments linger on.
What is there to do?

The wise keep to their side of the bargain,
And expect nothing of the other half.

The well-meaning keep to their side of the bargain,
And try not to concern themselves with the other half.

The unwise keep to their side of the bargain,
But then insist the other half discharge their responsibilities.

But the way of heaven has no favorites -
It is forever on the side of the common good.

'Forgive and forget.' 'No hard feelings.' These commonly repeated pieces of folk wisdom are easily said - but far more difficult to put into practice. Enmity between nation states, between communities, between individuals, and even between family members can be insidious and long lasting. Not unusually, parents, either by design or through indifference, pass on their prejudices to their children. In this way abhorrent, xenophobic, racist, misogynist, and bigoted viewpoints are unconsciously, or sometimes quite deliberately, fostered in a small child.

A personal memory will serve to illustrate this point. Around 2005, on a brief stopover in a large regional city in China, I was the only foreigner who entered a crowded lift in an office block in the business district. A small local boy of around four or five years old immediately shrank away from me in fear, telling his father anxiously; "I don't like Japanese people!" Since I am not Japanese, and certainly do not look Japanese, and since the boy was far too young to be aware of, or influenced by, knowledge of events such as the atrocities in Nanjing during the Sino-Japanese war in 1937, I quickly formed the impression that his father was a bigot and xenophobe – though he had not spoken a word. When I glanced at him, he simply gave me a tentative smile and was obviously hoping I had not understood a word of what his son had said.

This thought then crossed my mind; Why invest such time and energy in inculcating this abhorrent viewpoint in a small child, and what possible advantage could it give to either of them? The old boy would quickly advise that there is none. When resentment and bitterness are harbored, everyone loses. What this level of indoctrination did do in this case though, was to effectively perpetuate a deep and lasting hostility that was likely to be equally poisonous for both father and son.

Nevertheless, the coaching in this type of long-term resentment and active conditioning of children by parents and by peers is not so unusual, it happens all the time, and we are all products of our less than perfect environments in which such occurrences are commonplace.

Existential psychiatrist R.D. Laing, who was both personally and professionally strongly influenced by the philosophy of Jean-Paul Sartre, wrote extensively on the ways children are warped and twisted by the conditioning influences of parents and peers, describing the state of disconnected unawareness, and "being out of one's mind" as a fairly typical condition of an individual. Laing observes that society values individuals who conform to this normalcy and that it actively works to condition children to embrace it. He adds that unfortunately, this has led to a world where those considered "normal" individuals have caused the deaths of millions of others like them. (Laing, The Politics of Experience & the Bird of Paradise, 1984)

Regarding the spiritual impulse and the urge towards self-actualization that Laozi characterizes as work-on-the-self, Laing observes that in our society, not only are the natural instincts including sexuality, repressed, but that suppression is also applied to any form of spirituality or higher experience - and also to those individuals who insist on the validity of their experienced transcendence. (Laing, The Divided Self, 2010)

The old boy would tell us in no uncertain terms that unleashing all our own negative baggage and misplaced conclusions on our peers and our offspring is a less than ideal way to educate the next generation.

There is plenty of evidence to suggest that much of childhood experience falls well short of being totally idyllic, and the road to maturity is a rocky one. If we then compound these experiences with the trials and tribulations of early adulthood, we will not unusually reach a time when most of us harbor some 'skeleton in the closet' of our inmost being, and find ourselves with some painful or morbid aspect of the self we would just as soon forget.

So it is unsurprising that in the context of the old boy's injunction to accept the reality of our inner selves, some difficulties might arise.

While the old boy is asking for honest self-appraisal, Laing is telling us that:

"Human beings seem to have an almost unlimited capacity to deceive themselves." (Laing, The Politics of Experience & the Bird of Paradise, 1984)

Notwithstanding the often unpalatable and confronting nature of this self-examination the old boy insists upon, it remains an essential part of work-on-the-self. We are not looking for inner perfection, pragmatism is somewhere very near the core of the old boy's philosophy, right alongside the injunction to always work towards the greater good - what we are engaged in here is the acceptance of our whole being - reality as it is.

As Laozi sees it, there is little point in our rebelling against the fact that we have been force-fed negative impressions and repugnant viewpoints, or simply inherited them through exposure. Good or bad, these are the impressions that determined our characteristic responses to life experience. Similarly, we do ourselves a disservice in repressing, or even worse rejecting entirely, our past actions and experience. History is a reality that can never be wholly expunged.

Surprisingly, and contrary to the oft quoted aphorism of Heraclitus; 'Change is the only constant in life' The old boy will tell us that, barring genuine forgetfulness, the past is also something of a constant within each of us, and those things that happened, but now appear to damage or somehow negate the self-image we have fondly built for ourselves, will not be ignored or eradicated by rationalization and are unmoved by our shame and mortification. Ultimately, it is in our own interests that these truths are faced and reconciled. The path of the Dao requires that our reality is something that is accepted – the good, the bad and the ugly.

We must come to terms with ourselves.

For those trapped in the reality of long-term resentment, the old boy might argue; sure, it is possible to harbor grudges on a long term or even on an inter-generational basis if one is so inclined, and sure, anyone can start, or continue, a feud that will consume vital energies for years. The question is, how will that improve your life? There are no winners in this situation. Rather than waste energy on such unproductive and non-essential actions, would it not be better to simply move on? Accept the fact that some things happened that caused you pain, or caused you to inflict needless pain on others, and deal with it - once and for all.

Unlike the proponents of many creeds, Laozi does not require your penance, just your honest commitment to do your best to serve the greater good from this point on.

Although we may sometimes feel that we are disadvantaged by ignoring the peccadilloes of others and sticking to our own moral high ground, The old boy tells us in the lines above that this type of petty concern should be beneath us, and what is more, we will feel better when we really *feel* it is beneath us.

Why do we need to cheat if we have been cheated? Why do we want to retaliate if we are treated badly? These things: 'want' and 'need' beyond the basics of life's necessities, are obstacles on the great way, and while it may seem that if we simply stick to doing what is right, the unscrupulous may take advantage - does any of it really matter?

The old boy might say - let it go and have the last laugh. Somewhere along the way – it all becomes unimportant, unnecessary, then ridiculous, then funny – enjoy this change.

Verse the eightieth: On the ideal life – the bare necessities.

A state should not be burdened with too high a population,
Or, too heavy a bureaucracy.

The people should be prepared to fight for what is right,
But reluctant to enter into unnecessary conflict.

The people should be capable of traveling far when needs arise,
But happy enough to stay where they are.

The people should prize living enough to take death seriously.
Keeping the weapons of war hidden and unused,
And the nation's armor should be secured in its repository.

Meanwhile, the people find pleasure in the simple, ordinary things:
The goodness of plain home-cooking all can enjoy,
Good, homespun clothing, unadorned by fine brocade,
The security and comforts of home,
The company of family and the fellowship of friends.

And though they see and hear their next-door-neighbor,
And though their neighbor's dogs bark and their cock's crow,

They live in peace together to the end of their days.

In these lines from the old boy, he praises life in the serenity of a modest rustic utopia. Here are also echoes of the civic ideals developed more fully by both Plato and Aristotle - the virtues of a small city state or 'Polis' of around 5000 souls, the Greek word 'Polis' being, of course, the derivation of our modern words 'politics' and 'politician.'

The somewhat misleading reference here to the apparently miniature scale of the ideal municipal size is a reference to the number of actual citizens, that is, only the fully-fledged voting members of the community. These are the people who incidentally would also be the most well-educated, and also the wealthiest. Therefore, this is a figure which does not include the disenfranchised - minors, slaves, immigrants, criminals or females - which in turn implies that the real population figure may have been anything up to as high as 100,000 souls - but we get the idea, small is beautiful.

The Greek city-states founded on this model generally prospered and promoted the growth of democracy by virtue of being small enough for everyone to not only have their say, but also to become at some point in their lives at least, active participants in the executive decision-making and legislative process. (Plato, 1997)

A community like this has many similarities to the old boy's ideal, it is characterized by having a lightweight executive, excellent channels of communication, and little need for a dedicated, sprawling bureaucracy. It is small enough so that the people mostly know each other, there are few or no permanent members of the armed forces, and crime and delinquency are minimized.

With its strong sense of community and shared values thrashed out in public forums, the polis was, according to both Plato and Aristotle (Aristotle, 1996), more able and likely to adopt a government ethos based on the common good, and clearly in the lines above, the old boy agrees on this. Although there were tyrants and warlords aplenty in Laozi's China, there would also have been many small, relatively isolated communities operating along these or similar lines of mainly consensual support.

It seems there is a lesson here, a judgment that in our large and sprawling cities and mega-cities something is often lacking. Feelings of isolation and abandonment amid all this humanity are far more common than they are in small communities. This is because huge cities promote anonymity and are less conducive to fostering the communal egalitarian and participatory spirit than smaller, more unified, and cohesive communities. It seems that smaller societies can more easily bring a greater sense of belonging, and that in turn helps to develop that sense of self-worth and high regard for actions furthering the common good that the old boy describes as essential for healthy self-actualized living.

The alienation and lack of belonging that are commonplace in big, impersonal city life are no doubt much less of a problem if the individual has genuine roots and an established and available support network to rely upon. Notwithstanding the occasional revered hermit or ascetic recluse, people need good relationships and the care, assistance, and the sense of belonging, in family and community groups to live full and happy lives. In this sense the city may still nurture and provide a haven for personal development, providing we are comfortably engaged in one of the many sub-communities the city hosts.

If we have listened well to the old boy at this point, we now have some idea of who we are, and what we ought to do. We should appreciate the simple things in our lives, both personal and communal, but at the same time be mature enough to value our independence and be sufficient unto ourselves. What is of paramount importance in accomplishing this is that ability to look within, to feel good about ourselves but without conceit or any sense of inflated self-regard. In doing this we should also not worry too much about other people's choices or opinions, though if we listen with open mind and respect, we may yet learn something new.

In this endeavor, humor and a flexible attitude are our friends, and anger and resentment the enemies.

Although some commentators on the text have remarked that these lines seem to praise a rather dull and boring utopia, the old boy is not saying that a life of unnatural stasis is the ideal, in fact we have seen that the idea of change as a constant is a running thread throughout the 'Dao De Jing.' Everyone should feel free to indulge natural curiosities, enjoy new places, people, and experiences and appreciate the world at large, what Laozi is warning against is neediness, if we chafe against the restrictions of our lives and let impatience build into resentment and intolerance, then we fail to appreciate what is good and beautiful around us - and from there the path is lost.

The prime essentials for the 'good life,' as the old boy would have it, are few indeed, we need some personal space to be ourselves, the security of home and community, the comforts of family and friends, an ability to delight in ordinary things, and a friendly tolerance of differing viewpoints, our near neighbors, and the vagaries of life.

Verse the Eighty-First: Transcendence.

Truthful words are not always beautiful,
As beautiful words are not always true.

Persuasive words are not always wise,
As wise words are not always persuasive.

The greatest wisdom is often not heard from the most learned teachers,
But may come from those who say they do not know.

The wise hoard nothing to themselves,
But, in their unfailing generosity - never lack things to give.
Then having given all - they live in abundance.

The way of the common good is to benefit all in striving for wholeness.
In harmony, in refusal of contention -
And in bountiful generosity - is the way of unity and completion.

Almost 2,000 years ago, one of the world's acknowledged great leaders, Roman Emperor Marcus Aurelius (Aurelius, 2001), had some good advice which was entirely consonant with the views of the old boy:

> *"...fix your gaze on the matter in hand and see it for what it is, and then, keeping in mind your obligation to be a good man and the demands of your*

humanity, go right ahead and do it, in the way that seems to you to be most just. But do it with kindness and modesty, and without dissembling."

And:

"No more abstract discussions about what a good man is like: just be one!"

Every single day throughout the world vast numbers of people observe the rites and conform to the behaviors that their belief in their Gods prescribes. Almost since humanity took its first faltering bipedal steps on the dusty African plains, some form of religious, spiritual observance has been a core feature of the development of culture and civilization everywhere.

People express their individual spiritual natures in a myriad of ways, through organized religion, through mysticism or occult practice, through commitment to some vital cause, through dedication to meditation or in the pursuit of some other vital life goal.

Although we are each individually free to choose to renounce the reality of any, or of all, of our personified divinities, the transcendental aspiration - that search for a mysterious 'something or other' that might complete us – is something that, for many at least, always remains. And if this unfathomable impulse is ignored or denied on anything more than a temporary basis, it is at our peril. We simply fail to reach our full potential as human beings.

The Dao is a concept elemental to all spiritual enterprise and to all humanity. In this sense, the idea of a God in all things and all things in God sits as comfortably with Laozi as it does with any number of religious orders and certainly with all of those in the Mosaic tradition. As we have previously discussed, perceptions of the 'real' nature of that 'God' may vary, from an inner transcendent aspect of the self to some external deity perched on an unlikely golden throne. And if the idea of the deity itself is renounced, and the existence of God denied, the old boy is unperturbed - the 'Dao De Jing' remains what it always was, a practical treatise on unity, harmony, and personal integrity through commitment to always acting in total accord with the common good.

When all else fails, and the storm anchors of external belief will not hold, when adherence to ritual and form is not enough, then 'The Dao De Jing' is a collection of practical ideas on how to cope that remains wholly relevant to any personal, or community quest for the best possible life. And if the inner vision is to be pursued through some idealistic, social, or political form of commitment, to the old boy it matters little. That is, always providing that the acceptance and commitment to the common good is real and honest - then, each small advance is still a step along the way.

As Carl Jung observed, we should not be discouraged by the objection that ancient concepts such as free will, immortality, and God remain unproven. Their truth or otherwise is not relevant here. The important question to ask is whether these concepts are beneficial or not, and whether they improve the quality of life, and add meaning and satisfaction to existence. (Jung C. G., The Symbolic Life, 1981)

Psychologically, existentially, personally, philosophically; the transcendent impulse towards the formless unknown of our own latent possibility is a phenomenon as much a part of ourselves as is our physical body and as old as humanity itself. Ultimately, the search for life's meaning, the endeavor the old boy calls 'work-on-the-self,' the 'way 'or the 'path,' is not about applying a method, and it is also not about adopting a truth. It is about acquiring an attitude, a positive and harmonious orientation to reality.

The differences here are critically important. 'The way' embodies genuine substance – it is the uncompromising and honest expression of the totality of an individual nature, whereas a 'method' is only ever an adopted pretension – a form that will decay into empty ritual.

The path of the Dao is founded in a deep and sincere appreciation of a modest set of fundamental truths, and the application of the simple values those truths reveal - by contrast, even the best of methodical procedures is just the imitative mode of those adhering to the prescribed rules and policies.

At this point, the old boy might ask us to recall his previous cautions that it may not all be plain sailing. Sadness and joy are both a part of the flux of life, and we can never hope to experience one without ever knowing the other.

Aside from the various attitudes towards life that might impede advancement along the path, for example those discussed earlier in connection with Sartre and Maslow, there is some small but significant danger inherent in making a personal commitment to the principles of the Dao by someone with Western cultural values. This lies in the necessity for recognizing that an internal balance must be maintained.

The necessary acceptance and reconciliation of conflicts within the irrational inner self cannot be accompanied by any rash rejection of unpalatable fact. As the old boy has told us repeatedly, we cannot deny our own personality, nor can we reject the realms of science and empirical knowledge in thinking they may impede our progress. All these are part of our reality that must be faced, and they are modes of thought and expression that are as valid as they ever were - and still a part of the whole.

The old boy is never a mystic, his message is clear but needs to be thoroughly understood at every level, intuition, logic, emotion, and instinct are all a part of the mix. So, although this apparent partial abandonment of science and all that is rational the old boy advocates may seem at first to be a form of liberation in freeing the mind for the inward focus implied by the greater task, this is a delusion, nothing is discarded, the Dao is the whole, and nothing less - we are not denying one aspect while admitting the other.

Laozi has shown us that the ideal here is the integration and resolution of all opposing viewpoints - and most definitely not the exchange of one set of polarized viewpoints for another.

The old boy's final words in the final verse, relate to the commitment of self that the Dao as great journey implies; and our last question may well be; how difficult and strenuous is it really? How much exertion is required in working towards this amorphous and all-embracing greater good?

The old boy would gaze at you sardonically, white beard bristling...

'It doesn't have to be hard work - but you have to give it your all,' he might answer, 'Every fiber of your being. But perhaps before you start wondering if this is a high price to pay - think about who it is that you are giving this abundance to!'

Jack Parkinson 2023
Suzhou, Beijing, Fuzhou, Peoples Republic of China.
Barossa Valley, Gold Coast, Australia.

About the author.

Following an education in England and Australia, Jack Parkinson's early background was in various creative and managerial roles in electronic and print media. He has lived and worked on three different continents, and more recently, taught for thirteen years on (mostly) British university campuses around China. He was Deputy Director of the Language Centre at XJTLU (Xi'an Jiaotong-Liverpool University) in Suzhou for five years.

During his long career and on his many travels through more than forty countries, he also wrote a travel memoir (published by Lothian Books in Melbourne) on travelling overland from Australia to Europe using public transport and trekking the Himalayas and the jungles of Java.

He now lives a somewhat quieter life on Australia's Gold Coast and sometimes writes about it all.

WORKS CITED

Aristotle. (1996). The Complete Works of Aristotle. (J. Barnes, Ed.) Princeton: Princeton University Press.

Artaud, A. (1974). The Death of Satan and Other Mystical Writings. London: Calder and Boyars.

Aurelius, M. (2001). Meditations. Gutenberg.

Borges, J. L. (1999). Collected Fictions. London: Penguin Books.

Carroll, L. (1984). Alice's Adventures in Wonderland & Through the Looking-Glass. New York: Bantam Classics.

Dawkins, R. (1989). The Selfish Gene. Oxford: Oxford University Press.

Evans-Pritchard, E. (1990). Witchcraft, Oracles and Magic among the Azande. Oxford: Oxford University Press.

Hoff, B. (1983). The Tao of Pooh. London: Penguin.

Jung, C. G. (1981). Aion (2nd ed., Vol. 9 Part 2). (H. Reed, Ed., & R. Hull, Trans.) London: Routledge and Kegan Paul.

Jung, C. G. (1981). Alchemical Studies (Vol. 13 Collected works). (H. Reed, Ed., & R. Hull, Trans.) London: Routledge and Kegan Paul.

Jung, C. G. (1981). Archetypes and the Collective Unconscious (Vol. 9 Part 1 Collected Works). (H. Reed, Ed., & R. Hull, Trans.) London: Routledge and Kegan Paul.

Jung, C. G. (1981). Civilization in Transition (Vol. 10 The Collected Works). (R. F. Hull, Trans.) London: Routledge and Kegan Paul.

Jung, C. G. (1981). Freud and Psychoanalysis (Vol. 4). (H. Reed, Ed., & R. Hull, Trans.) London: Routledge and Kegan Paul.

Jung, C. G. (1981). Psychological Types (2nd ed., Vol. 6). (H. Reed, Ed., & R. Hull, Trans.) London: Routledge and Kegan Paul.

Jung, C. G. (1981). Psychology and Religion: West and East (2nd ed., Vols. 11, Collected Works). (R. F. Hull, Trans.) London: Routledge and Kegan Paul.

Jung, C. G. (1981). Psychology and Alchemy (2nd ed., Vol. 12 Collected Works). (H. Reed, Ed., & R. Hull, Trans.) London: Routledge and Kegan Paul.

Jung, C. G. (1981). Symbols of Transformation (Vol. 5). (H. Reed, Ed., & R. Hull, Trans.) London: Routledge and Kegan Paul.

Jung, C. G. (1981). The Development of Personality (Vol. 17). (H. Reed, Ed., & R. Hull, Trans.) London: Routledge and Kegan Paul.

Jung, C. G. (1981). The Practice of Psychotherapy (Vol. 16 Collected Works). (H. Read, Ed., & R. C. Hull, Trans.) London: Routledge and Kegan Paul.

Jung, C. G. (1981). The Spirit in Man, Art and Literature (Vol. 15). (H. Reed, Ed., & R. Hull, Trans.) London: Routledge and Kegan Paul.

Jung, C. G. (1981). The Structure and Dynamics of the Psyche (Vol. 8 Collected Works). (H. Reed, Ed., & R. Hull, Trans.) London: Routledge and Kegan Paul.

Jung, C. G. (1981). The Symbolic Life (Vol. 18 Collected Works). (H. Reed, Ed., & R. Hull, Trans.) London: Routledge and Kegan Paul.

Jung, C. G. (1981). Two Essays on Analytical Psychology (Vol. 7 Collected Works). (H. Reed, Ed., & R. Hull, Trans.) London: Routledge and Kegan Paul.

Jung, C. G. (1999). Jung on Christianity. (M. Stein, Ed.) Princeton: Princeton University press.

Jung, C. G. (1999). Man and his Symbols. New York: Bantam Dell.

Laing, R. D. (1984). The Politics of Experience & the Bird of Paradise. London: Penguin.

Laing, R. D. (2010). The Divided Self. London: Penguin Classics.

Lau, D. (1963). The Tao Te Ching. London: Penguin Books.

Lee, B. (2009). Wisdom for the Way. Burbank, Calif: Black belt Books.

Marwick, M. (1990). Witchcraft and Sorcery. London: Penguin Books.

Maslow, A. &. (1987). Maslow's hierarchy of needs. Salenger Incorporated, 14(17), 987-990.

Milne, A. A. (1944). Winnie The Pooh. London: Methuen.

Plato. (1997). The Complete Works. (J. M. Cooper, Ed., & Various, Trans.) Indianapolis: Hackett Publishing.

Pope, A. (1711). An Essay on Criticism. Gutenberg

Popper, K. (2002). The Logic of Scientific Discovery. London: Routledge Classics.

Sartre, J. P. (1982). Existentialism and Humanism. London: Methuen.

Sartre, J. P. (1993). Being and Nothingness. New York: Washington Square press.

Sartre, J. P. (2000). Nausea. London: Penguin.

Trujillo, L. T., Langlois, J. M., & Langlois, J. H. (2014). Beauty is in the ease of the beholding: A neurophysiological test of the averageness theory of facial attractiveness. Cogn Affect Behav Neurosci, 14, 1061–1076 . Retrieved 4 3, 2023, from https://doi.org/10.3758/s13415-013-0230-2

Watts, A. (2011). The Wisdom of Insecurity: A Message for an Age of Anxiety. New York: Vintage Books.

Wilhelm, R. (1977). The I Ching or Book of Changes. Princeton: Princeton University Press.

Wilhelm, R. (1979). The Secret of the Golden Flower. London: Routledge and Kegan Paul.